Reclaiming Indigenous Research in Higher Education

Reclaiming Indigenous Research in Higher Education

Edited by Robin Starr Minthorn and Heather J. Shotton

Foreword by
Bryan McKinley Jones Brayboy

RUTGERS UNIVERSITY PRESS
NEW BRUNSWICK, CAMDEN, AND NEWARK,
NEW JERSEY, AND LONDON

Library of Congress Cataloging-in-Publication Data

Names: Minthorn, Robin Starr, editor. | Shotton, Heather J., 1976– editor.
Title: Reclaiming indigenous research in higher education / edited by Robin Zape-tah-hol-ah Minthorn and Heather J. Shotton ; foreword by Bryan McKinley Jones Brayboy.
Description: New Brunswick : Rutgers University Press, [2018] | Includes bibliographical references and index.
Identifiers: LCCN 2017012268| ISBN 9780813588704 (hardcover : alk. paper) | ISBN 9780813588698 (pbk. : alk. paper) | ISBN 9780813588711 (epub) | ISBN 9780813588728 (web pdf)
Subjects: LCSH: Indians of North America—Education (Higher) | Indians of North America—Education (Higher)—Research—Methodology.
Classification: LCC E97 .R43 2018 | DDC 378.1/982997—dc23
LC record available at https://lccn.loc.gov/2017012268

A British Cataloging-in-Publication record for this book is available from the British Library.

Cover art by Jessica Rosemary Harjo (Otoe-Missouria, Osage, Pawnee, Sac & Fox). Graphic manipulation includes a painting courtesy of Ted Moore Jr. (Otoe-Missouria, Osage, Pawnee, Sac & Fox). The overall graphic depicts the past, present, and future of Indigenous research in higher education. The lines below represent the past, full of color, life, and richness. The red in the background above represents the current state in which Indigenous research lies—a glimpse of truth but not fully understood. The star in the middle represents a lens that Indigenous researchers are using to provide a view into the realms of truth, reclaiming identity in higher education while providing connections to the past and to the future.

∞ The paper used in this publication meets the requirements of the American National Standard for Information Sciences—Permanence of Paper for Printed Library Materials, ANSI Z39.48–1992.

www.rutgersuniversitypress.org

Manufactured in the United States of America

We dedicate this book to our grandmas and grandpas, whose lives and teachings continue on through our work. We write this to honor our ancestors, whose memory and wisdom live within each of us. As we humbly embark on this journey we acknowledge the Indigenous scholars who came before us and created a critical space for this discussion. We dedicate this book to the future generations of Indigenous scholars. We honor those who have shaped our past, who continue to break barriers in the present, and to those who will create new meanings and pathways for Indigenous research in higher education in the future. This book was formed in prayer, love, and wisdom. Ah-ho, day-ohn-day.

Contents

Foreword

Bryan McKinley Jones Brayboy (Lumbee)

In 1969, Lakota scholar Vine Deloria, Jr., writing about research in tribal communities, noted, "Academia, and its by-products, continues to become more irrelevant to the needs of people."[1] Deloria's frustration is one that has been shared by others, and continues to be relevant almost 50 years after being raised. This volume is a response to these frustrations. But, it is more than that. I would argue that the chapters in this volume point to what I call the four P's of Indigenous methodologies. Indigenous methodologies are: *Personal*; point to the concept of *Presence*; are rooted in *Place*; and construct *Positionality*. The four P's, taken together, reflect the *power* of Native scholars, thinkers, and authors.

For Indigenous scholars, conversations about methodologies—or the ways that we think about research and the research process—are rooted in relationships. These methodologies emerge from questions of identities; we may ask, can a Native person engage in research and still be Native? There is, in this way, a relationship regarding identity as it emerges through epistemological (how we think about, (re)produce *knowledge*) and ontological (how we engage larger questions of our *realities*). There are other points that are rooted in questions of method; we may ask, how do I interview and collect data from other Native peoples in the most ethical ways? There is a technical component here, but there is also an axiological one. That is, we are asking about the moral and ethical values that guide the work. And, there are large questions around how to engage in the research process in a way that is, in fact, "relevant to the needs of the people" and also *counts* for people in the Academy. As such, one way to think about relationships and methodologies is to agree that our methodologies are personal.

This volume offers views into the research of a cadre of Indigenous scholars whose work is focused on understanding different phenomena in and around institutions of higher education. The chapters engage the art and act of being Indigenous researchers, even when this is not the explicitly stated aim of the chapter. The descriptions in the chapters, however, when chewed on and savored, are wonderful examples of what it means to be both a Native person and a researcher. Of course, it bears noting that Native peoples have always been researchers. As such, we have always had ideas about the purposes and role of research. Early on, we observed the elements around us, the natural ebbs and flows of geographies and wildlife (that would later become part of how we nourished ourselves and families), and the factors that led to particular kinds of interactions between humans and their surrounding environs. We experimented with plants and other organisms to see how they interacted with our bodies. From these observations, we developed both theories about what might happen next and actions about how to best respond. We noticed when animal migration patterns changed, or what happened when we ingested a particular plant while experiencing a particular illness. This is what Native science looked—and continues to look—like. The relevance to people was that it allowed us to live happy, healthy lives. Survival (happily and healthily) was the purpose. The chapters in this volume have similar threads. They describe how Native peoples make sense of, and (happily and healthily) survive higher education. As is true for many of our ancestors, happiness and health were not always attained without a fair share of pain and harm. These chapters reflect this reality.

Indigenous methodologies are personal. The chapters in this volume also reflect the fact that our methodologies reflect presence. There are several ways to consider this point. First, the fact that such a talented, diverse group of Native scholars are engaging in addressing the ways that we make sense of research illuminates the presence of Native people in higher education. At the risk of demonstrating the fact that I grow older with every passing day and become increasingly reminiscent, this presence is different than when I emerged into writing about higher education. There is a robust, hearty presence in these chapters, which is joyous. The collection of scholars represented in this volume are leading the movement in Indigenous higher education. I am grateful for their presence. It is rooted in and produces a powerful collective.

And, presence emerges in other ways through their work. In several of the chapters in this volume, authors are engaging the challenges or triumphs of Native students as they navigate institutions of higher education. The studies point to the fact that there are, in fact, Native students, staff, and faculty on Native lands that now house institutions of higher education. The chapters make it clear that Native presence is part of the work. Ostensibly this is a book about Indigenous methodologies, and part of those methodologies is that there are Native people doing the research on, with, and for Native peoples in institutions of higher education. Methodologies generally point to theories of research; these chapters extend that notion to include the crucial point that Indigenous methodologies are ones of presence. In turn, presence is a form of resistance, resilience, resurgence, restoration, and repatriation. And, finally, these methodologies are an exercise of power.

That power lies in a connection to place. Indigenous methodologies happen in context, in a moment, and in a place. These chapters will help us understand that theories surrounding research are not abstract. Rather, they have real-life implications for the work that people do, and the lives they lead. My generation of scholars in the United States was taught in our academic preparation programs to use traditional methods, and their concomitant methodologies, to engage our work. We asked questions about a "new" population, even though Native peoples were enrolled at institutions such as William and Mary, Harvard University, and the University of Pennsylvania as far back as the 17th century. The newness of the population pointed not to the absence of Native peoples, but to the lack of awareness of our presence. Our presence was invisible, leading to the notion that there were not Native people in colleges.

These chapters change the conversation. The authors in this volume call for—they demand—that how scholars and practitioners engage in research be different. These demands are demonstrated in both the content of the chapters and the ways in which that content is produced. The use of metaphors is pronounced. So is the fact that research happens in a specific moment and place. We ask questions that are specific to a population, with the hopes that we can draw principles that may inform the work of others. Pushing this notion further, researchers come from a place. That place informs how we engage the world around us, what we value, and how we think about the research process. One powerful component of this volume is that it is filled with the work of self-determined, Native authors. They are powerful scholars.

Those authors engage the research process from a particular place of positionality. Indigenous research methodologies demand that individuals who seek answers to their questions are also clear about their place within a series of relationships. That is, they must be clear about how the personal connects with the professional. Positionality situates individuals within a constellation of relationships between people and place. It informs readers about who is behind the writing, by answering: who am I?; why am I doing this?; who do I serve?; how is my work relevant to the people and place? As it turns out, positionality, within an Indigenous methodologies framework, is not solely about an individual. Rather, it is connected to an individual in relation to others and to place.

The title of this book is *Reclaiming Indigenous Research in Higher Education*. I like the title, and it is fitting. The chapters not only reclaim, but they reassert, reiterate, repatriate/rematriate, and recognize the power of the personal, the presence, the place, and the positionality of Indigenous peoples as actors and doers in the research enterprise. Together, they offer hope of a future generation of Indigenous scholars, possibilities of how Indigenous peoples can assert power toward the relevant needs of the people, and the promise of a better future. This book is a gift.

NOTE

1. V. Deloria, Jr. (1969). *Custer Died for Your Sins: An Indian Manifesto.* Norman, OK: University of Oklahoma Press, p. 93.

Reclaiming Indigenous Research in Higher Education

INTRODUCTION

The Roots of Reclamation

Robin Starr Zape-tah-hol-ah Minthorn (Kiowa/Apache/Umatilla/Nez Perce/Assiniboine)

Heather J. Shotton (Wichita/Kiowa/Cheyenne)

The first thoughts of this book began to stir several years ago among a group of our fellow Indigenous scholars as part of our growing frustration with the continued gap in literature on Indigenous research in higher education. What was even more concerning was the fact that we knew that research was being conducted by Indigenous scholars in higher education; we knew because we were conducting such research, as were our colleagues and students. Yet, there remained a void in the scholarship. We all recognized and had been answering the calls sent out by previous scholars (Brayboy, 2005; Deloria, 2004; Mihesuah, 1998; Mihesuah & Wilson, 2004; Shotton, Lowe, & Waterman, 2013; Smith, 1999) to produce scholarship from an Indigenous perspective that was guided by our lived experiences, cultural values, and the embedded responsibility to address the needs of Indigenous people within research in higher education. There has been a small surge of emerging Native American, Native Hawaiian, and Alaskan Native scholars within the field of higher education, and within the last ten years we have witnessed a growing number of Indigenous scholars utilizing Indigenous methodologies and frameworks in their research. Empowered by the critical work of Linda Tuhiwai Smith (1999), Bryan McKinley Jones Brayboy (2005), Shawn Wilson (2008), and Margaret Kovach (2009), Indigenous scholars in higher education have begun to reclaim our own research spaces. Through the heartwork of our scholarship, we created a family of Indigenous scholars in higher education, a community of Indigenous brother and sister scholars engaged in this critical work. As a community of scholars, we began a push to create recognition of our presence within the larger community of higher education scholars. As scholars in higher education, much of this work was focused within the Association for the Study of Higher Education (ASHE). Out of this work an informal collective group was born, known as "Indigenize ASHE." The work of this collective has helped us to gain traction in our efforts to challenge exclusionary power structures that have served to silence our scholarship and render us invisible. Slowly, we have witnessed increased visibility of Indigenous scholars within the broader organization and a push for more inclusion of Indigenous centered scholarship. In 2014, we acknowledged the movement that had been created by our family of Indigenous scholars through a presentation at the World Indigenous Peoples Conference on Education (WIPCE) called "Igniting a Movement of International Indigenous Higher Education Scholars in the Academy." This presentation included several Indigenous professors and doctoral students in higher education, many of whom have contributed to this text.

All of this progress led to the fruition of this book. We were inspired to reclaim our space in academia, to reclaim Indigenous research in higher education. To reclaim means to start claiming or to take something back. Our intent is to utilize this book as a means to take back our academic space so that we may honor the good work of our Indigenous brother and sister scholars who are answering the call to Indigenize research in higher education.

Genealogy of Indigenous Methodologies and Frameworks

As Indigenous people it is important to acknowledge those who came before us. We recognize that we are not alone in our work and that none of us arrived at this place without the help of others. This involves the acknowledgment of our ancestors and the wisdom that has been passed on from them, the forethought and prayers of our families and elders that have sustained us, and the knowledge and space created by early Indigenous scholars; all of these elements make a way for us. Venturing into this work requires that we first acknowledge the genealogy of Indigenous methodologies. Doing so is like acknowledging our ancestors, without whom we would not be here. So, we respectfully provide an overview of Indigenous methodologies and frameworks by our "elder" scholars in the field.

In 1998, Devon Mihesuah pushed a critical discourse on the weakness of methodologies that had traditionally been used in the academy to research and write about Indigenous peoples. Her book, *Natives and Academics: Researching and Writing about American Indians* (1998), provided a critical space for Indigenous scholars to "write back to the academy" (Mihesuah & Wilson, 2004, p. 2), and to challenge the power structures and status quo within the academy. Mihesuah and Wilson (2004) followed up this work in *Indigenizing the Academy: Transforming Scholarship and Empowering Communities*, where they challenged the colonizing nature of the academy and its control of accepted knowledge. They urged us not only to resist the colonizing structures of the academy, but to utilize our research skills to decolonize the academy.

Linda Tuhiwai Smith's (1999) seminal work, *Decolonizing Methodologies: Research and Indigenous Peoples*, provided a space for us to begin to think about how to decolonize Indigenous research. She problematized the history of research in Indigenous communities in the context of European imperialism and colonialism, and pushed us to recognize our perspective as the colonized. Smith poignantly acknowledged the traumatic history of research among Indigenous people, stating, "The word itself, 'research,' is probably one of the dirtiest words in the Indigenous world's vocabulary" (Smith, 1999, p. 1). Her work moved us beyond a mere deconstruction of Western scholarship and approaches to research and explored various emerging methodological approaches from Indigenous scholars who were utilizing frameworks of self-determination and decolonization. Smith's work provided a critical tool for Indigenous scholars to begin to answer calls to decolonize our research and reclaim Indigenous spaces in the academy.

Bryan McKinley Jones Brayboy's (2005) development of Tribal Critical Race Theory (TribalCrit) marked an important turning point for Indigenous scholars in education. Through the nine tenets of TribalCrit, he provided an Indigenous based theoretical framework that allowed us as scholars to critically examine the issues of Indigenous people in educational institutions. More important, his work provided a theoretical framework that appropriately identified the issues of colonization for Indigenous people and acknowledged our unique position as both a racialized and political group. The development of TribalCrit created space for Indigenous theory in the academy, further stocking our Indigenous research tools.

In the last decade, two critical pieces of scholarship that focus specifically on Indigenous methodologies have emerged: Shawn Wilson's (2008) *Research Is Ceremony: Indigenous Research Methods*, and Margaret Kovach's (2009) *Indigenous Methodologies: Characteristics, Conversations, and Contexts*. Wilson and Kovach move us even further in our efforts to reclaim Indigenous research by providing methodological tools through Indigenous based research paradigms. Their work is grounded in Indigenous epistemologies and moves us beyond previous efforts that worked to incorporate Indigenous perspectives into Western research paradigms that privilege Western epistemologies (Wilson, 2001).

Kovach (2009) provides an example of an Indigenous methodological framework based in tribal knowledge; particularly she provides a framework centered in Plains Cree knowledge. She moves us beyond theoretical discussions into practical applications of Indigenous methodologies. In Wilson's book (2008), he centers his work within what he terms an Indigenous Research Paradigm in Indigenous epistemologies of relationality and relational accountability. He sets forth a research paradigm for Indigenous ways of "doing and being in the research process" (p. 19). Both Wilson and Kovach help us to answer the critical question, "What does an Indigenous methodology look like?"

Most recently, Oliveira and Wright (2016) introduced *Kanaka `Ōiwi Methodologies: Mo`olelo and Metaphor*, which provides a beautiful examination of Kanaka (Native Hawaiian) approaches to research. Their work explores ways that Native Hawaiian scholars are privileging ancestral knowledge and engaging research through their own lens as Kanaka `Ōiwi. More important, they further illustrate the development of Indigenous methodologies that allow Indigenous scholars to be responsive to their communities and create positive social change.

The genealogy we have provided is by no means extensive. It merely provides a brief introduction to the frameworks and methodologies that will appear in the following chapters. Of greater significance, it serves as a means for us to acknowledge the scholars who have done the critical work that has created space for this book and our efforts to reclaim Indigenous research.

Organization of the Book

There are some common threads throughout this book that will be highlighted. It is important to note that these threads are invisible and also interconnected to the topics and overall purpose of the book. Some of the chapters present a discussion of Indigenous approaches to research in higher education, while others present empirical research based in Indigenous approaches and methodologies; as a whole the chapters represent an effort to demonstrate, validate, and solidify Indigenous approaches to research in higher education.

One of the threads runs through the first part of the book and addresses Indigenous voice and identity in research. In chapter 1, you will find an overview of Indigenous methodologies and approaches to research. This is done from a broader level and then addresses the importance of Indigenous centered approaches in higher education research. The next two chapters address identity in Indigenous research. In chapter 2, Wright discusses the ties between culturally based, or what she has termed kuleana-centered, higher education and Kanaka ʻŌiwi identity. Through her Kanaka ʻŌiwi (or Native Hawaiian) centered approach to the chapter, Erin Kahunawaikaʻala Wright demonstrates the central place of her identity in the scholarship and embodiment of what it means to be a scholar. In chapter 3, Charlotte Davidson explores the use of Diné centered modalities and frameworks in the process and approaches to research. These are cornerstone chapters and set the tone for the book, as they address what it means to Indigenize and decolonize the research process in higher education through identity-centered work, as well as how to conceptualize and use it.

The next common thread woven encompasses chapters 4 through 10, which address the multitude of ways Native students make their own pathways for "success" in higher education. Success in this contest is defined as Native students persisting in higher education without losing their identity and culture in the process. In chapter 4, Adrienne Keene discusses the importance of relationships when negotiating the process of higher education and what that means in diverse contexts. In chapter 5, Amanda R. Tachine explores the higher education journey for Navajo students as they go through their freshman year of college. She presents her "story rug" as a Diné centered approach to understanding Navajo student experiences. Youngbull's chapter (chapter 9) discusses the critical role of relationships in Native student success in her presentation of her research with Native American Gates Scholars. In connection to this research, in chapter 10 Christine A. Nelson frames tribal financial aid for Native American students as an assertion of tribal sovereignty, as well as connection and responsibility to community. This ties in to Sweeney Windchief's presentation of his research on Indigenous student metaphors as it relates to persistence in graduate education in chapter 6. Windchief discusses the use and adaptation of relational connections as family connections for graduate students. Finally, Theresa Jean Stewart (chapter 7) and David Sanders and Matthew Van Alstine Makomenaw (chapter 8) highlight their approaches to quantitative research through the lens of Indigenous frameworks and interpretations. Stewart examines Indigenous student leadership development through existing data and interprets its use by identifying gaps and connecting meaning through an Indigenous lens in an attempt to better understand how Indigenous students develop student leadership skills. Sanders and Makomenaw provide an important contribution through the use of data on Tribal College and University (TCU) student transfer patterns. They explore the role of tribal identification and enrollment verification processes that honor TCUs and tribal nation relationships.

The last common thread within this book focuses on Indigenizing spaces in higher education. In chapter 11, Kaiwipunikauikawēkiu Lipe examines inequity and inequality in higher education as it relates to Indigenous people, particularly as it relates to Indigenous space and land, through her Hōʻālani Framework. Lipe calls for higher education institutions to examine their acknowledgment of Indigenous students and communities and to honor the agreements and rights of Indigenous students through the support, programming, academic course offerings, and various other levels across campuses. In chapter 12, Stephanie Waterman examines the role of Native student affairs units through an Indigenous feminist theory lens and discusses these units as a reclamation of space for supporting Native college students. Finally, in chapter 13, Pearl Brower introduces the narrative and history of Alaska's only TCU, Iḷisaġvik College, in her exploration of the process of Indigenizing leadership approaches and higher education.

This is a glimpse into the connective threads of the chapters within this book, but there are certainly intersecting chapter connections across the threads that are all tied to the concept of Indigenous centered research and the utilization of Indigenous frameworks. Indigenous approaches to higher education research are guided by a passion to contribute to a better understanding of Indigenous issues and the need to create systemic changes that create spaces for Indigenous people in higher education. More important, they allow us to reclaim our narratives. For many years, non-Indigenous scholars have studied Indigenous peoples without appropriately honoring our knowledge and cultures. Like Indigenous scholars before us, we continue efforts to push back against this by creating our own research spaces. This book builds on the work of previous Indigenous scholars and highlights the work of Indigenous scholars, both senior and emerging, and their approaches to Indigenizing higher education scholarship. Through this book we work to reclaim our research in higher education and to amplify our voices.

REFERENCES

Brayboy, B. M. J. (2005). Toward a Tribal Critical Race Theory in education. *The Urban Review: Issues and Ideas in Public Education, 37*(5), 425–446.

Deloria, Jr., V. (2004). Marginal and submarginal. In D. A. Mihesuah & A. C. Wilson (Eds.), *Indigenizing the academy: Transforming scholarship and empowering communities* (pp. 16–30). Lincoln, NE: University of Nebraska Press.

Kovach, M. (2009). *Indigenous methodologies: Characteristics, conversations, and contexts.* Toronto: University of Toronto Press.

Mihesuah, D. A. (Ed.) (1998). *Natives and academics: Research and writing about American Indians.* Lincoln, NE: University of Nebraska Press.

Mihesuah, D. A., & Wilson, A. C. (Eds.) (2004). *Indigenizing the academy: Transforming scholarship and empowering communities.* Lincoln, NE: University of Nebraska Press.

Oliveira, K. R. K. N., & Wright, E. K. (Eds.) (2016). *Kanaka `Ōiwi methodologies: Mo`olelo and metaphor.* Honolulu: University of Hawai'i Press.

Shotton, H. J., Lowe, S. C., & Waterman, S. J. (2013). *Beyond the asterisk: Understanding Native students in higher education.* Sterling, VA: Stylus.

Smith, L. T. (1999). *Decolonizing methodologies: Research and Indigenous peoples.* London: Zed Books Ltd.

Wilson, S. (2001). What is Indigenous research methodology? *Canadian Journal of Native Education, 25*(2), 175–179.

Wilson, S. (2008). *Research is ceremony: Indigenous research methods.* Winnipeg: Fernwood Publishing.

CHAPTER 1

The Need for Indigenizing Research in Higher Education Scholarship

Charlotte Davidson
(Diné/Three Affiliated Tribes: Mandan/Hidatsa/Arikara)

Heather J. Shotton (Wichita/Kiowa/Cheyenne)

Robin Starr Zape-tah-hol-ah Minthorn
(Kiowa/Apache/Umatilla/Nez Perce/Assiniboine)

Stephanie Waterman (Onondaga, Turtle Clan)

Well chronicled is the view of higher education, as a traditional structure of colonization, and its failure to maintain a cultural memory Indigenous to the earthen back upon which its buildings have been erected. Thus, the particular and contemporary impact this lack of remembrance has pedagogically prompted is the exclusion of Indigenized forms of research and its potential role to weave a new—and at the same time, layered—narrative into the academy. Writing on the dialectic of Indigenous and non-Indigenous knowing, Williams and Tanaka (2007) ardently point to how space-making, in the material and pedagogical sense, can impact the sensibilities belonging to the mainstream: "It is not a question of choosing one pedagogical perspective over the other. Rather, it is finding a way to make space for both—and to be enriched by both. This is a process that requires the dominant academic discourse to pause, listen, and make room for a discourse that may seem incongruous and dissonant at times" (p. 16). Thus, the concept of Indigenizing is not meant to express a destination, but a process that encourages Indigenous scholars to privilege what is within themselves as a starting point for scholarly and research inquiry. This is critical to understand, because Indigenous and non-Indigenous research approaches and practices are not coterminous. However, in circling back to Williams and Tanaka, the possibilities that exist from the willingness to expand research and scholarly perspectives depend precisely on the pedagogical positions of the scholar or researcher. What is further made clear by Tanaka and Williams is that it is often Indigenous scholars and researchers who make concerted efforts to gain a more balanced perspective.

To that end, we hope the ideas put forward in this book inspire readers to render a response to our clarion call for scholarship and research to increasingly become a site that holds positive regard for Indigenous perspectives and approaches. Along with this is the hope that those who read this book will acquire an appreciation of new definitions of what it means to Indigenize research in higher education. This chapter explores the landscape and foundation of what currently exists within the realm of Indigenous research in higher education, particularly focusing on research that is Indigenous authored and focused on Indigenous methodologies.

The Need for Indigenous Research in Higher Education

Much has been written about Native education, particularly the historical development of Native education in this country and Native students in K-12 systems. However, the research on Native people and issues in higher education remains limited (Brayboy, Fann, Castagno, & Solyom, 2012). Some scholars have pointed out the disturbing lack of attention paid to Native students in higher education research, despite the increasing enrollment of Native students over the years (Willmott, Sands, Raucci, & Waterman, 2015). In their analysis of 20 years (1991–2011) of scholarship in the leading higher education journals, Willmott et al. (2015) found that out of 2,683 articles, only 36 dealt with Indigenous people in higher education. Their findings assert that Indigenous experiences and voices have long been excluded from the broader higher education scholarship.

What is even more troubling is that much of the early research pertaining to Indigenous people in higher education was conducted by non-Indigenous scholars. The limitations and problematic nature of Western dominated scholarship about Indigenous people in academia has been well noted. Vine Deloria, Jr. (2004) was very critical of scholarship on Indigenous people written by non-Indigenous scholars, acknowledging the inherent challenges and issues:

> They were content to perpetuate the old stereotypes of Indians that they had learned in graduate school decades before. Academia has often been a hotbed of racism because scholars are taught to pretend that they can observe phenomena objectively. In fact they observe data through culturally prescribed categories that restrict the possible answers and understandings to a

predetermined few selections. With Western thought primarily a binary, yes/no method of determining truth, so much data is excluded. (p. 18)

At the heart of the problematic nature of this type of research is that it has allowed for the privileging of Western perspectives, ignoring critical Indigenous perspectives and silencing Indigenous voices.

Missing Perspectives and Voices of Indigenous People

Research in the academy often represents a continued form of oppression and colonization for Indigenous scholars, whose voices are marginalized and perspectives as Indigenous people are challenged. Gatekeepers within the academy maintain rules and methods that continue to colonize and oppress Indigenous scholars and populations (Mihesuah & Wilson, 2004). Scholars have long criticized the privileging of non-Indigenous scholars as "experts" on Native education. Swisher (1998) pointedly argued, "their authority is cited more often than the experts from whom their experience and information was gathered, and they have become the experts in Indian education recognized by their mainstream peers" (p. 193).

Indigenous scholars have noted issues with the invisibility of Indigenous people within the academy, particularly with regard to higher education scholarship, asserting that Indigenous people have been "virtually written out of the higher education story" (Shotton, Lowe, & Waterman, 2013, p. 2). This means that Indigenous perspectives are not represented in higher education scholarship, resulting in a large gap. A mere 1.3% representation in 20 years of scholarship (Willmott et al., 2015) is testament to the sheer invisibility of Indigenous people in higher education scholarship.

There has been a continued call for increased representation of Indigenous perspectives and voices in the scholarship. The need for Indigenous voices is critical, and the inclusion and centering of Indigenous epistemologies in scholarship provides for a richer understanding of Indigenous higher education (Shotton et al., 2013). Additionally, there continues to be a call for scholarship that includes not only our voices, but research methodologies that more appropriately address our unique positions and responsibilities as Indigenous people and scholars; or what Kovach (2009) more aptly acknowledges as our "collective responsibility to take back" research (p. 178).

Challenges to Indigenous Scholarship in Higher Education

Our experiences and stories as Indigenous scholars provide critical insight into some of the challenges to Indigenous scholarship in higher education. In this section we share some of the challenges we each encountered as emerging

Indigenous scholars. We each share stories from our early journeys and the challenges we faced throughout the dissertation processes with non-Indigenous faculty members, particularly with issues of asserting and including an Indigenous knowledge system and framework. These stories acknowledge the importance of understanding that we do not need permission to include ways of being as Indigenous people in the process of conducting research and writing.

In the first anecdote we hear Stephanie's story. Stephanie is one of the first Indigenous scholars in the United States in the field of higher education to be promoted to associate professor. Her story speaks to her challenges with the limited use of Indigenous methodologies, as well as the lack of acknowledgment of the need for Indigenous voices in higher education scholarship.

> When I completed my dissertation, Indigenous students in higher education, let alone Indigenous Knowledge Systems and methodologies, were not widely discussed or acknowledged in our field nor at my institution. When I first began submitting articles to journals I was asked to use a single term for Indigenous people. I also had an article returned from a journal in our field because they could not find someone "sufficiently qualified" to review my article. Another journal indicated that my article was too narrow as it focused on Haudenosaunee college students. A national conference proposal was rejected because "there was a lack of interest" in this population. Since the early 2000s the field of Indigenous higher education/student affairs has grown, and I no longer receive reviews such as those noted above. We have made great strides; yet, we have a long way to go.

The second anecdote provides Heather's description of her experience discovering critical theories, such as Tribal Critical Race Theory and Critical Race Theory, that were not taught in her doctoral courses. She also discusses her experience of using a decolonized lens in her research and having to justify and validate her own approach in her dissertation process with committee members.

> Throughout my dissertation work I struggled with locating a conceptual framework that really felt like it fit my work. At one point I came across Bryan Brayboy's (2005) Tribal Critical Race Theory. TribalCrit of course had not been discussed in any of my courses, nor had Critical Race Theory for that matter; so reading it was like an awakening for me in terms of my own research. It helped me to articulate what I had struggled to convey in terms of the unique issues of colonization for Indigenous people in higher education. During my dissertation defense one of my committee members argued with me at length about the use of the term colonization; they could not understand why I was not using the term assimilation and they incorrectly viewed the two terms as interchangeable. The argument represented a complete dismissal of my view as an Indigenous researcher, the use of Indigenous Knowledge Systems, and the

> experiences of Indigenous people. I was fortunate that I had a Native faculty member on my committee to step in and validate my use of TribalCrit and the term colonization. That was a salient moment for me. It solidified for me the need for more Indigenous scholars who could conduct appropriate and needed research, develop appropriate frameworks, and defend the value of our scholarship in higher education.

In the next anecdote, Robin shares her experience of including an Indigenous Research Paradigm in her dissertation research and how that led to further scholarship on how to assert an Indigenous voice in the writing styles for other, up and coming Indigenous scholars.

> I began my work in Indigenous research methodologies when I began my dissertation journey by beginning to use the Indigenous Research Paradigm and Relationality by Shawn Wilson (2008), who encourages the perspective of Research as Ceremony, also encouraging Indigenous peoples to view our own birthing and conceptualization of knowledge to be done through an Indigenous lens. In this effort, my dissertation was based on Indigenous thought and knowledge as seen through the eyes of the Native students in the research. Since then all of my work has included Indigenous research methodologies, especially, in the evolution and work of the book, Indigenous Leadership in Higher Education. This book used Indigenous methodologies and acknowledged the voice and writing styles of Indigenous leader authors, as well as the acknowledgment of capitalizing Indigenous and Elder throughout to connote the importance of who we are as Indigenous Peoples and the important role that Elders have in our communities. Lastly, when Indigenous leader/authors utilized their own Indigenous language we chose not to italicize it, because in APA standards they see italicizing for foreign language and we acknowledge our Indigenous and tribal language as original language, not foreign but a birthright. As Indigenous scholars we have the opportunity to use our voice and give power to the voice of those we work with and represent. We are the voice for current and future students and scholars to make an easier pathway for them.

In the last anecdote, Charlotte shares her experience of being able to insert her own tribal epistemology and knowledge systems in the academy and how she grappled with the validation of their use. This led to her own dissertation, which acknowledged the Indigenous/Diné tradition closely tied to her family that can be a lens to inform her research.

> An early challenge I grappled with was cultivating the capacity to question afresh matters long discussed in Diné creation narratives and to understand their significance to contemporary conditions of struggle within our

> life-worlds. More to the point, these stories chronicle a series of lessons for moral living and I wanted to arrive at an understanding of how to open a research process that remained in integrity with my identity as a Diné, Mandan, Hidatsa, and Arikara woman. After a short time and with counsel from family, I learned that an epistemological antecedent necessary in approaching the tradition of inquiry and knowledge making was to recover and enact practices inclusive of non-human relations (i.e., cedar, sweet grass, and sage)—practices customarily missing from linear, solitary, and disembodied academic training. Engaged meaningfully, non-human relatives improve our faculty of thinking by endowing us with maximum clarity. Engaged inappropriately or not at all, can result in the researcher exteriorizing themselves from their research. And so, what else does this involve and lead to when such exercises are influenced by cultural sensibilities? The answer is not simple. Like the processes associated with beading, sewing, carving, weaving, and painting, the manner in which knowing is made material is as diverse as the meaning of the patterns formed by their makers. That said, one thing remains clear; we must embrace the historical challenge to actively struggle against repressive forces that seek to rob us of our sense of humanity.

Within each of the anecdotes shared, one can see the progression of awareness in the ability to use Indigenous methodologies and frameworks in the dissertation and early scholarship for each of us. Over time, there has been a deepening awareness to be more Indigenous based and grounded in ancestral knowledge and ways of being in approaching research and scholarship. These anecdotes provide evidence of why this book is of utmost importance, so that current and future Indigenous higher education scholars see themselves being honored in what is accepted as scholarship in the academy.

Evolution of Indigenous Higher Education Scholarship

The evolution of higher education scholarship began in early works of non-Indigenous scholars writing about Native American students and often from the deficit perspective (Shotton et al., 2013). As referenced in the Introduction, in recent works completed since the turn of this century, Indigenous scholars have begun to transform scholarship to be Indigenous based and reflective of the conceptual frameworks and values of their own Indigenous roots and passion to give a strengths-based insight into Native student experiences. We are living at a time in which we have a growing number of Indigenous scholars in higher education to address critical issues facing Indigenous students, administrators, and campus contexts that affect the persistence and lived experiences of those who are Indigenous in higher education. In this section, we will address how spaces have begun to be created within the available literature surrounding Natives in higher education and then the need to plant seeds to grow and cultivate future generations of Indigenous scholars.

Creating Our Own Spaces Through Our Scholarship

Within the last 15 years we have witnessed an increase in the scholarship written by and with Indigenous practitioners and scholars in higher education. In 2003, the *Renaissance of American Indian Higher Education* (Ah Nee-Benham & Stein), which addressed issues and realities in Native higher education inclusive of a TCU perspective, was released. Following was the publication of *Serving Native American Students* (Fox, Lowe, & McClellan, 2005), which addressed the lived experiences of Native students, faculty, and administrators in higher education. This became a resource that many have cited and revered as a cornerstone publication. Subsequent to that, Warner and Gipp (2009) addressed the TCU perspective with their book *Tradition and Culture in the Millennium*. This book highlighted the specific issues and needs of TCUs, such as leadership and mentorship of future TCU presidents and the realities of retention and financial aid for TCU college students. A couple of recent pivotal books that address Native higher education realities include *Beyond the Asterisk: Understanding Native Students in Higher Education* (Shotton et al., 2013), which highlights practices in higher education from the first year college student, student affairs professionals, administrators, and faculty perspectives, and *Indigenous Leadership in Higher Education* (Minthorn & Chavez, 2015), which examines a specific topic in higher education that is often left out of the research and practice—Indigenous leadership. This book reframes how leadership is viewed in higher education from a Native American perspective, and more important, includes the voices of Native American students as authors. This is a cursory overview of books by Indigenous practitioners and scholars that have been released within the early part of this century; each has contributed an Indigenous voice and perspective to the broader scholarship. This book will add to those contributions by highlighting current research in higher education from an Indigenous scholar conceptual framework and methodological approach.

Planting Seeds and Cultivating Future Generations of Indigenous Scholars

With the growth of the numbers of Indigenous scholars in higher education there is an urgent need to mentor and ensure the growth of more Indigenous faculty in higher education. This growth should take place as well in other roles, such as non-profit organizations, statisticians, and public policy, where we are continuing to break the glass ceiling. This mentorship should begin early, prior to entering a doctoral program, at the undergraduate level and even as early as the high school level. The more that Native youth see other tribal members who have obtained a Ph.D. and can achieve a terminal degree, the better they can begin to see it as a possibility for themselves. A part of planting seeds is for those of us who have earned an advanced degree or who hold faculty positions to become the mentors, as well as system changers. With this book we are attempting to reconstruct the narrative and expectation that one who conducts research has to do so within a Western lens and approach. We are at a place and time in which we hope to change that narrative and expectation that allows authentic research and work that honors and allows for Indigenous perspectives that are not only accepted, but also expected within the publishing and tenure and promotion process. We hope to create a counternarrative that will become the new narrative of Indigenous scholarship in higher education. This narrative will enable the seeds planted for future Indigenous scholars to grow and have a system in place that can enable their transition into academia to be one of authenticity rather than assimilation.

The Need for Indigenous and Decolonizing Methodologies in Higher Education Research

Leigh Kuwanwisiwma of Bacavi, Arizona, recounted an event in *Beyond the Mesas*—a documentary film based on the boarding school experiences of Hopi people—that occurred in the early 1900s. This historical moment involved four Hopi chiefs who met with other village leaders to discuss the prospects of Western education for the Hopi. In the following vignette, Kuwanwisiwma shared Chief Looloma's pedagogical perspective on the issue of mainstream schooling and Hopi existence:

> Looloma said, "It is really futile to resist the white man's way. The way for the Hopi to survive as a culture, is like this: Learn how he thinks. Learn how he speaks. Learn his language. Leave the bad things alone. Take the best things of the White man's world, so that we can also survive with it." Looloma exemplified his words by binding two different colored strings around a ceremonial stick and said, "This is the good things of the white man and this is the good of Hopi. Twine them together and you're going to be twice as strong. That's how Hopi is going to survive." (Kuwanwisiwma, Koyiyumptewa, Gilbert, Eichner, & Holzman, 2006)

Looloma recognized very clearly that the Hopi had to re-pattern their thinking by cross-pollinating two traditions of thought to interpret and plot a path in an emergent bicultural world. Befitting the present time, Looloma's rendering is significant to the discussions in this book, for the prevailing distinction between the culture of higher education and that of Indigenous people is the manner in which we epistemologically encounter and understand one another. This view is readily supported by the fact that the settings of academe do not often allow for the thinking of knowledge as the hybridized bundling of cultural experiences, as mainstream methodological traditions often encourage us to marginalize ourselves (Davidson, 2015). To this end, academic training commonly involves the violent inversion of how the nature of knowledge is understood (i.e., using a Western lens to interrogate the Indigenous, as opposed to an unfettered study of the world through an Indigenous lens). Thus, what endures is the persistent and unapologetic need to make meaning of our existence, *on our own terms.*

A critical dimension of investigating phenomena, particularly within postsecondary contexts, is cultivating the research capacity to develop methodologies that harmonize with much older knowledge systems that have been genealogically passed on through eons of time. In practice, Indigenous research methodologies give greater salience to premodern sensitivities (i.e., praying, singing, dancing, beading, weaving, and other culture-centered faculties) that have been layered over with de-natured practices and approaches. Every research methodology has an umbilical origin. What cannot be overlooked is that Indigenous research methodologies include an ancestry that is embodied within the researcher. In this sense, Indigenous research methodologies have the propensity to become a site where local and familial knowledge are experienced as ways to re-see ourselves in relation to the world. That said, we must acquire the means to harvest a material collection of Indigenous and non-Indigenous cultural offerings that work in *cooperation* to promote a structure of accord—one that does not estrange us from our lived cultural experiences. To form the foundation of this approach, we need to critically assess the extent that a methodology can displace questions of relationality. These questions include, but are not limited to: Where do you originate your thinking process? Is it one that fosters a process of enfacement of Indigenous culture or nurtures an ancestral consciousness? When your methodology interfaces with your identity, does it obstruct how you indigenously function in the world?

As Indigenous scholars participating in the construction of knowing, many of us have come to embrace the idea that Looloma put forth generations ago: to remain phenomenally, and solidly, conscious within new social contexts by nurturing an ever-evolving understanding of who we are. And so, to begin this cycle anew, this book serves as a location of recovery as it endeavors to fill a pedagogical absence within academe.

Conclusion

In this chapter, we shared some of our challenges as Indigenous scholars as we navigate the field of higher education with integrity. For us, the process of Indigenizing our research, our re-claiming of these spaces, methodologies, and conceptual frameworks, is the only way we can do our research. To do otherwise would be to participate in the colonial project. We shared the lack of understanding and lack of support we experienced as Indigenous scholars. Re-claiming our

Indigenity in our work is an additional task many non-Native and dominant scholars do not have to undertake. This extra task, this tax if you will, can be exhausting. The non-Native academy, of settler colonial origin, does not readily make space for non-settler-colonial thought or anti-colonial thought (Patel, 2016). Not all of us had Indigenous faculty to validate our thinking. Giving back, mentoring those who follow, is one way we embody this work, humanize the academy, and express our Indigenity.

Indigenous scholars do not ignore or dismiss Western epistemologies. As is shared in this book, Indigenous scholars interpret Western methodologies and epistemologies through our own lenses. Non-Indigenous scholars do the same; however, being of the same settler colonial origin as institutions of higher education, they are not always aware, or encouraged to make visible, that lens. Reclaiming our relationship with Creation—our relationality (Wilson, 2008)—is a key difference in approach. We are making progress, however, as noted in recent publications, including this important book, through the increased numbers of Indigenous scholars, and through the international discussion of Indigenous knowledge systems and frameworks *on our own terms*. Our stories emphasize the need for Indigenous research. The following chapters are examples of how we reclaim our Indigeneity in research.

REFERENCES

Ah Nee-Benham, M. K. P., & Stein, W. J. (2003). *The renaissance of American Indian higher education: Capturing the dream* (Sociocultural, political, and historical studies in education; Sociocultural, political, and historical studies in education). Mahwah, NJ: Lawrence Erlbaum.

Brayboy, B. M. J. (2005). Toward a Tribal Critical Race Theory in education. *The Urban Review: Issues And Ideas In Public Education, 37*(5), 425–446.

Brayboy, B. M. J., Fann, A. J., Castagno, A. E., & Solyom, J. A. (2012). *Postsecondary education for American Indian and Alaska Natives: Higher education for nation building and self-determination* (ASHE higher education report, v. 37, no. 5). San Francisco, CA: Wiley Subscription Services.

Davidson, C. E. (2015). Indigenous dissidence: Cultivating a leadership politic of Hózhó. In R. S. Minthorn & A. F Chávez (Eds.), *Indigenous leadership in higher education* (pp. 100–110). New York, NY: Routledge.

Deloria Jr., V. (2004). Marginal and submarginal. In D. A. Mihesuah & A. C. Wilson (Eds.), *Indigenizing the academy: Transforming scholarship and empowering communities* (pp. 16–30). Lincoln, NE: University of Nebraska Press.

Fox, M. J. T., Lowe, S. C., & McClellan, G. S. (2005). *Serving Native American students* (New directions for student services, no. 109). San Francisco, CA: Jossey-Bass.

Kovach, M. (2009). *Indigenous methodologies: Characteristics, conversations and contexts.* Toronto: University of Toronto Press.

Kuwanwisiwma, L. J., Koyiyumptewa, S. B., Gilbert, M. S. & Eichner, G. (Producers), & Holzman, A. (Director). (2007). *Beyond the mesas.* [DVD]. Available from http://www.learningwhoweare.com/store

Mihesuah, D. A., & A. C. Wilson (Eds.). (2004). *Indigenizing the academy: Transforming scholarship and empowering communities.* Lincoln, NE: University of Nebraska Press.

Minthorn, R. S., & Chavez, A. F. (2015). *Indigenous leadership in higher education* (Routledge research in educational leadership series). New York, NY: Routledge, Taylor & Francis Group.

Patel, L. (2016). *Decolonizing educational research: From ownership to answerability*. New York, NY: Routledge.

Shotton, H. J., Lowe, S. C., & Waterman, S. J. (2013). *Beyond the asterisk: Understanding Native students in higher education*. Sterling, VA: Stylus.

Swisher, K. G. (1998). Why Indian people should be the ones to write about Indian education. In D. A. Mihesuah (Ed.), *Natives and academics: Researching and writing about American Indians*. Lincoln, NE: University of Nebraska Press.

Warner, L. S., & Gipp, G. E. (2009). *Tradition and culture in the millennium: Tribal colleges and universities* (Educational policy in the 21st century). Charlotte, NC: Information Age Pub.

Williams, L., & Tanaka, M. (2007). Schalay'nung Sxwey'ga: Emerging cross-cultural pedagogy in the academy. *Educational Insights, 11*(3). Retrieved from http://einsights.ogpr.educ.ubc.ca/v11n03/pdfs/williams.pdf

Willmott, K. E., Sands, T. L., Raucci, M., & Waterman, S. J. (2015). Native American college students: A group forgotten. *Journal of Critical Scholarship on Higher Education and Student Affairs*, 2(1), 79–104.

Wilson, S. (2008). *Research is ceremony: Indigenous research methods*. Winnipeg: Fernwood Publishing.

CHAPTER 2

"It Was a Process of Decolonization and That's about as Clear as I Can Put It"

KULEANA-CENTERED HIGHER EDUCATION AND THE MEANINGS OF HAWAIIANNESS

Erin Kahunawaika'ala Wright (Native Hawaiian)

A process of decolonization.
Helped me shift paradigms.
Looking for an answer to my questions.
You had been on this long, hot, dry hike or run.
Then all of a sudden someone gives you this ice-cold water.
It just quenched a thirst.
Made me understand why I was angry.
I need to know who I am and where I come from, learn for myself.
I was playing catch-up. I should have learned all this before.
Gave this language to things that I had seen or thought about
but didn't know how to speak about.
We could make this kīpuka.
Passionate professors. Influential. Inspiring.
Didn't imagine I would be part of a movement.
It's okay to make mistakes, it's okay to be scared, but just keep going.
Larger goal very clear, well-being and advancement of the lāhui.
Laser focused and unified.
Determined the entire course of my life.
Solidified my kuleana.
Where I found my voice.
Hawaiian Studies gave me values on improving myself to help the larger whole.

I felt really empowered.
Mindset always on nationhood.
What is our legacy?
Our kuleana is to advance and advocate.
Our kūpuna did impossible things, if they can do these crazy incredible things, we can do it too.
Other people believe in you . . . you better too.[1]

Author, poet, and Hawaiian nationalist Haunani-Kay Trask teaches us that colonialism diminishes Native[2] identity into "dispossessions of empire" like Native lands and resources (Trask, 2002, p. 35). Trask (1999) writes,

> Because of colonization, the question of who defines what is Native, and even who is defined as Native has been taken away from Native peoples by Western-trained scholars, government officials, and other technicians. The theft itself testifies to the pervasive power of colonialism and explains why self-identity by Natives of who and what they are elicits such strenuous and sometimes vicious denials by the dominant culture. (p. 43)

The very theft of the power to determine one's identity—that is, to define who and what is "Native"—speaks to the pervasiveness and insidiousness of U.S. colonialism. Osorio (2006) also connects the "confusion" over what it means "to be Hawaiian" to the consequences of colonialism. Osorio writes (2006), "It is huikau, confusion, over what our choices are and what they meant that is threatening our nation. How far are we willing to commit ourselves to be Hawaiian?" (p. 19). If identity is fundamental to political and psychological self-determination, how do we (re)cultivate Kanaka ʻŌiwi[3] identity and, instead, dispossess empire (wa Thiongo, 1986)?

The focus of this chapter is to understand the ways in which culturally based or what I've come to call "kuleana-centered" higher education influences the contours of Kanaka ʻŌiwi identity. "Kuleana" is often understood as "rights, responsibility, and authority" (Warner, 1999, p. 76), though I understand the kaona (hidden meaning) of kuleana also ties "responsibility" to feelings of privilege and burden through my own lived experience as an ʻŌiwi student, student affairs scholar-practitioner, and higher education teacher and scholar endeavoring to understand ʻŌiwi journeys to and through higher education. Additionally, I see this chapter as contributing another voice to the decades of important conversations Kanaka ʻŌiwi have had about the meaning and significance of identity through a diversity of scholarship (Goodyear-Kaʻōpua, 2016; Halualani, 2002; Holt, 1969/1995; Kikiloi, 2010; Kupo, 2017; Ledward, 2007; Osorio, 2001, 2006; Tengan, 2008).

As a way to highlight the centrality of kuleana throughout the chapter, I use words with the prefix "hiʻi" to open each section. "Hiʻi" means "to hold or carry in the arms, as a child" (Pukui & Elbert, 1971, p. 64). The ʻano (being) of hiʻi also implies deep caring for what is being carried. Therefore, hiʻi is also used to denote participants' contradictory and complementary feelings expressed in their narratives in which we can see them as college graduates with the cherished responsibility (and burden) to utilize their educational privilege to carry themselves, their ʻohana (extended family), and their lāhui Hawaiʻi (Hawaiian nation).

E hiʻipoi i nā ʻŌiwi: Tending ʻŌiwi through Culturally Based Education

Kanaka ʻŌiwi culturally based[4] educational contexts in Ko Hawaiʻi Pae ʻĀina (the Hawaiian archipelago) like Pūnana Leo Preschools, Ka Papahana Kaiapuni Hawaiʻi (Hawaiian language immersion program), and Hawaiian-focused public charter schools offer opportunities to nurture ʻŌiwi identities. These schools transform traditional K-12 deficits-oriented structures to environments of abundance that utilize ancestral knowledge, culturally relevant pedagogy, Hawaiian ways of being and knowing, and contemporary sociocultural, sociopolitical contexts to inspire ʻŌiwi youth to forge anti-colonial, success-based cultural identities (Goodyear-Kaʻōpua, 2013; Ladson-Billings, 1995, 2014; Meyer, 2003). The tools of culturally based K-12 education for ʻŌiwi youth integrate Hawaiian language, place-based, project-based approaches to teaching and learning and are fairly well-documented (Goodyear-Kaʻōpua, 2013; Kanaʻiaupuni & Kawaiʻaeʻa, 2008). The connection between culturally based education and its positive impacts on self-efficacy, self-esteem, and community engagement, especially in K-12 contexts, are also not new (Cajete, 1994; Castagno & Brayboy, 2008; Demmert & Towner, 2003; Ledward, Takayama, & Kahumoku, 2008). But the ways in which these connections are constructed continue to underscore the need for education to learn more about the broad/structural and particular ways cultural connectivity is carried between home, community, and school are established, strengthened, and used as best practices.

Previous studies in education that focused on understanding the relationship between conventional educational outcomes (e.g., standardized test scores) and culture-based education found improved academic performance for ʻŌiwi (Kanaʻiaupuni & Ishibashi, 2003; Kanaʻiaupuni, Malone, & Ishibashi, 2005; Luning & Yamauchi, 2010; Tibbetts, Kahakalau, & Johnson, 2007). More recently, Kanaʻiaupuni, Ledward, and Jensen (2010) conducted a large-scale quantitative study on the impact of culture-based education on conventional educational outcomes for ʻŌiwi. They found "a set of nested relationships linking the use of culture-based educational strategies by teachers to student educational outcomes" (p. 1), suggesting culture-based education supports positive socio-emotional development (i.e., identity) and in turn, increased performance on conventional measures of academic achievement such as standardized test scores for reading and math (Kamehameha Schools, 2014). While these findings are indeed valuable, as educational excellence is critical to the vibrancy of our lāhui, it also highlights the limited colonial ways in which we continue to think about "Hawaiian identity" (e.g., "I participate in Hawaiian cultural practices such as special food, music, or customs"[5]), how it informs ʻŌiwi student notions of Hawaiianness,[6] and educational (or academic) success. As Halualani (2002) writes, "we have retheorized identity as a formation greater than personal affirmation, self-recognition, natural essence, or mere invented rhetorical tradition" (p. xv). Therefore, we are compelled to (re)consider the complex ways identity is articulated[7] and rearticulated in relationship to larger social forces such as colonialism and broader social contexts such as public schooling and nation-building. Furthermore, we also must reflect on how these articulations, in turn, shape our interpretations of "educational success" for ʻŌiwi. What does Hawaiianness and student success look like through the lens of ʻŌiwi nation-building?

In Hawaiʻi public higher education, Kanaka ʻŌiwi culturally based higher education offers similar environments for nurturing ʻŌiwi identities immersed in Hawaiian notions of abundance and success. With the emergence of degree-granting programs like Hawaiian Studies, Hawaiian Language, and Hawaiʻi Lifestyles, courses utilizing ʻŌiwi epistemologies across disciplines, and ʻŌiwi-serving student affairs units throughout the University of Hawaiʻi System (UH), culturally based higher education continues to grow in interest and scope as illustrated in any UH campus's course catalog. Creating a "Hawaiian place of learning" has even gained institutional prominence by becoming a strategic direction for the University of Hawaiʻi at Mānoa (UHM), the system's largest campus and only research-intensive institution (University of Hawaiʻi at Mānoa, 2011). However, while many ʻŌiwi know from our lived experiences that a Hawaiian place of learning is a generative and challenging educational environment, research examining what a "Hawaiian place of learning" means for a Non-Native College and University[8] or for many ʻŌiwi is relatively absent.[9] Furthermore, research examining ʻŌiwi identity in higher education or culturally based higher education is also scarce.

Conventional student development theory, much of which informs the structures and operations of contemporary institutions of higher education, fails to adequately address the uniqueness of Indigenous (much less ʻŌiwi) students traversing the contested higher educational terrain (Benham, 2004; Pascarella & Terranzini, 2005; Freitas, Wright, Balutski, & Wu, 2012; Kupo, 2017). This is not to say there is an absence of scholarship on Indigeneity in higher education, because there is definitely a growing body of knowledge generated by many of our Indigenous colleagues (e.g., Brayboy, 2005; Brayboy, Fann, Castagno, & Solyom, 2012; Minthorn & Chávez, 2015; Salis Reyes, 2016; Shotton, Lowe, & Waterman,

2013; Wright & Balutski, 2013, 2016). But the extent to which we see this rich scholarship employed in "mainstream" texts like those used in student affairs preparation programs is limited.[10] So the impact of our collective scholarship on these social forces shaping higher education as a field is not as it should be. Furthermore, student development and identity literature focuses the inquiry solely at the individual level, which is conceptualized and discussed in terms of discreet and, usually, linear stages of development. Conventional thinking about higher education and, in turn, student development theory also assumes higher education impacts only the individual student, which scholarship on Indigenous students has found to be to the contrary (Brayboy et al., 2012; HeavyRunner & DeCelles, 2002; Huffman, 2001; Salis Reyes, 2016; Wright, 2003). In my exploratory studies of Native Hawaiian identity in higher education, meaning and practice of identity were often far more complex, contextualized, nonlinear, and relational (Wright, 2003; Wright & Balutski, 2016). Brayboy et al. (2012) most closely attend to the complexity of ʻŌiwi liminal identity, arguing that higher education for American Indians and Alaska Natives should be viewed and analyzed through the prism of nation-building, a critique similar to one I made in a previous study examining Native Hawaiian identity in higher education (Brayboy, 2005; Wright, 2003). "Nation-building" in this sense is more than addressing the contrivances of a Westphalian nation-state and the consequences this relationship has on Indigenous Peoples. Rather, it also speaks to Indigenous-led cultural (intellectual) sovereignty and self-determination—a movement toward Freirean (1993) notions of critical consciousness and liberation—as much as governance-related issues of citizenship and economic development. Salis Reyes (2013) underscores the significance of education in nation-building, "Education, as a space for knowledge production and perpetuation, is also an important site in the struggle for Hawaiian sovereignty" (p. 206). Consequently, examining the intersections of ʻŌiwi liminal identity (which is also different from other U.S.-colonized Indigenous Peoples) and education through the prism of nation-building has significant implications for the ways we conceptualize, structure, and realize higher education for ʻŌiwi students and, in turn, ʻŌiwi student success.

In this particular study, I focused on understanding the ways Kamakakūokalani Center for Hawaiian Studies (KCHS)[11] at UHM influenced the contours of Kanaka ʻŌiwi identity in higher education through what I call "kuleana-centered" higher education, the most significant thematic encapsulation of the culturally based educational experiences articulated by KCHS graduates in this study. Drawing upon Brayboy et al.'s (2012) and Goodyear-Kaʻōpua's (2009) utilization of sovereignty and self-determination as an analytical principle of Indigenous education coupled with the ʻŌiwi cultural moor of kuleana, this kuleana-centered approach emerged as an analytical tool to illuminate the meanings of Hawaiianness and its intersections with higher education after many hours of walaʻau (conversational approaches) with KCHS graduates. As such, assuming a kuleana-centered approach foregrounds the ways in which graduates understand Hawaiianness through kuleana. I begin this exploration by briefly outlining the study's context. I then move into discussing the ethos of kuleana-centered higher education at KCHS. Next, I explore the question of how kuleana-centered higher education has influenced graduates' meaning-making of Hawaiianness.[12] Finally, I end with a short discussion connecting these identity positions to shaping decolonial ideologies of educational success.

Hele ʻia i hiʻikua a hiʻialo: Social Movements and Shifting Contexts, 1990–2000

In 1893, our people also understood themselves to be Hawaiian, not American. I want us to consider the very interesting notion that we Hawaiians were better off in 1893 than in 1993.

—Jonathan Osorio (2006, p. 21)

As the subtitle infers, "gone far and gone near" (Pukui & Elbert, 1971, p. 64) best describes the multiple pathways used to draw a picture of the broader social forces influencing this decade at KCHS.[13] KCHS is the focus of this inquiry because of the tremendous impacts it had upon our contemporary lāhui (Hawaiian nation) through its scholarship, political activism, community engagement, and graduates. As such, I chose to examine the experiences of KCHS graduates to better understand the relationship between their educational and life journeys.

The 16 participants in this study are an intentionally demographically diverse representation of Kanaka ʻŌiwi. Not all graduates came to KCHS with a strong sense of Hawaiianness or even knew much at all about the major. However, the characteristic they do share (other than self-identifying as Hawaiian) is having matriculated through KCHS between 1990 and 2000. This decade was selected primarily because of the broad social and political forces influencing Hawaiʻi (and KCHS) at the time. Goodyear-Kaʻōpua (2014) writes, "The massive organization of the lāhui in the 1990s required popular education and consciousness-raising based on sound research. Not only academics but people of all vocations were striving to remedy a century of historical miseducation" (p. 16) exemplifying the tenor of the 1990s in the Hawaiian community.

In particular, 1993 marked the "centennial remembrance" of the U.S. military-supported coup d'état of the Hawaiian Nation energizing many ʻŌiwi to (re)engage in movements for sovereignty and self-determination (Goodyear-Kaʻōpua, 2014). Goodyear-Kaʻōpua identifies "several key events and texts [that] brought popular consciousness and politically engaged Hawaiian scholarship to new heights" (p. 16). Many of the texts and events during this time were created by KCHS faculty, affecting the broader Hawaiian movement and the KCHS ethos. Most prominently, Haunani-Kay Trask, the first KCHS director, generated two very influential works in 1993. In collaboration with activist filmmakers Puhipau and Joan Lander of Nā Maka o Ka ʻĀina, Trask helped to produce the award-winning documentary film chronicling the 1893 coup, titled *Act of War: The Overthrow of the Hawaiian Nation*. The film features KCHS faculty like Trask, Jonathan Osorio,[14] and Lilikalā Kameʻeleihiwa. Trask also published her foundational book on the contemporary Hawaiian movement, *From a Native Daughter: Colonialism and Sovereignty in Hawaiʻi*. A year earlier, Kameʻeleihiwa released *Native Lands and Foreign Desires: Pehea Lā e Pono Ai?* her groundbreaking culturally centered analysis of the 1848 Māhele.[15] Together, these texts played a significant role in attending to the historical miseducation about Hawaiʻi. KCHS faculty also were involved in numerous other public education projects locally and globally around nation-building, primarily focused on raising Hawaiian critical consciousness about sovereignty and self-determination, Hawaiian history, and community organizing.

This decade also witnessed KCHS's transition as an organizational unit. Established first as a permanent program in 1982 and then as the Center for Hawaiian Studies in 1986, KCHS moved toward a more formalized academic department as marked by its physical and programmatic expansion. In 1996, the Center for Hawaiian Studies opened its doors to the Hawaiian Studies building located at Kānewai across the street from the main campus (Omandam, 1996). KCHS also expanded its program's curriculum to include the growing range of expertise among its now four full-time faculty members,[16] as well as to address the diverse interests of its students. At the time, KCHS boasted more than 100 undergraduate majors and more than 1,000 students enrolled in its courses (Omandam, 1996). Also significant to this time of transition was the change in leadership from Trask to Kameʻeleihiwa. The third faculty member hired at KCHS, the late Kanalu Young (2005), alluded to the connection between leadership changes and changes in the KCHS ethos from political to spiritual as part of his personal reflection on the evolution of his own spirituality.

Finally, I decided to use this decade because of the time and experiential distance for the graduates, who had at least 10 years to settle into their post-KCHS lives and reflect on their experiences.

E hiʻipaka i nā ʻŌiwi: The KCHS Ethos of Engaging Kuleana-Centered Higher Education

> The struggle is not for a personal or group identity but for land, government, and international status as a recognized nation.
>
> —Haunani-Kay Trask (2002, p. 50, original emphasis)

As a KCHS graduate (1995) and Trask mentee, I clearly remember Trask's abhorrence of identity politics. It was individualistic and failed to integrate the "real" issues of Indigeneity, like land and sovereignty, she would say. So you can imagine her utter dismay when I shared that my dissertation research would focus on exploring intersections of identity and higher education! Ironically, my interest in these intersections arose from my own KCHS experience, a program considered by many to be an important legacy of Trask.

From a broader perspective, and in contrast to Trask's analysis, KCHS became a locus—a physical place and intellectual space—at UHM and within the Hawaiian community for ʻŌiwi to (re)engage in identity positioning as individuals and as a collective through Hawaiian Studies courses, faculty engagement scholarship, or hula practice. As noted, KCHS offered significant contributions to the Hawaiian movement through scholarship and activism, also shaping the KCHS ethos. Within the context of this study, I use "ethos" to mean "the prevalent or characteristic tone, spirit, or sentiment informing an identifiable entity involving human life and interaction. . . . seen in the shaping of human perceptions, attitudes, beliefs, and dispositions . . . in a distinctive way" (McLaughlin, 2005, pp. 311–312), which also attends to intentions and aspirations of an environment. Therefore, this section examines how graduates experienced KCHS and articulated its kuleana-centered ethos through the curriculum, pedagogy, and role modeling.[17]

Curriculum

The initial attraction of Hawaiian Studies to its graduates was the curriculum, much of which was rooted in history and politics. Several participants noted they were drawn to KCHS for the simple desire to learn, regardless of their previous knowledge/experience with Hawaiian culture. One participant said, "I just wanted to learn everything and anything about my ancestors." Another noted, "As I was growing up, I don't know if it [was] just being really interested in things Hawaiian, everything from fishing, the ocean, stories, genealogy, art, everything I was curious about . . . everything that had to do with Hawaiian stuff, I just flocked to it." The broader social forces also brought to the fore the relevance and significance of this knowledge. One participant shared as she reflected on her classes, "This [history] is something that may have happened in the past, but it's still very real for us and relevant now."

Another significant idea that emerged was the connection between the curriculum and its relevance to family. For the majority of the participants, the curriculum provided a greater understanding and compassion for their families. One participant noted plainly, "It made me realize, too, that a lot of that stuff I learned at Hawaiian Studies I could relate it back to my family. And that was the thing that blew my mind. So you realize you're trying to correct these problems within your own family on a really basic level."

The graduates also talked about the impact of the courses on their identity development, primarily articulated through the lens of decolonization. One participant shared, "every class is another push towards like breaking yourself free of these beliefs that structure your thinking that this is the only way the world can work and I think it was kind of liberating and I think it helped me in life." He went on, "I'm an independent and critical thinker and those are the skills that are important in life if you want to be successful." The curriculum also actualized decolonization by exposure to a range of knowledge by connecting participants to ʻike kūpuna (ancestral knowledge) as well as broader liberation movements. The participant went on to state, "I think it was genealogy [HWST 341] that made me realize it's more about the worldview, the perspective, the understanding." Another participant discussed the connection she made between Hawaiʻi and international liberation movements: "I'm almost going to my last years of college, but when you take her [Trask's] class [HWST 490] where she starts introducing you to Franz Fanon's 'Wretched of the Earth.' The way he describes it [decolonization], it's like you can connect it to where you are . . . and this guy has no concept of I'm assuming of Hawaiʻi or us or our issues." As such, KCHS curricula utilized ʻŌiwi epistemologies and non-ʻŌiwi epistemologies to shape participants' understandings of decolonization through relational understandings of colonialism.

Unlike contemporary higher education, graduates also made clear that they were not thinking about careers when they declared their major. A prevalent question among all participants from family members was, "What are you going to do with a Hawaiian Studies degree?" One participant shared, "It's not like anyone is looking for someone with a BA in political science! What does that even mean?" Their journeys through Hawaiian Studies signaled a delving into deeper questions of Hawaiianness. One participant connected this endeavor to her self-discovery, "So it wasn't about seeking a career. It was like this life journey . . . where you're discovering and rediscovering who you are as a Hawaiian, creating like what does that mean." Curriculum helped participants to carefully consider the consequences of colonialism on their families. Kuleana emerged for participants when they utilized this knowledge to address these consequences with their families. As one participant described, "It was a corrective process for my whole family."

Pedagogy

Pedagogy broadly refers to the strategies faculty used to engage participants in their higher educational journey. Particularly salient is the use of praxis by faculty to impart kuleana. The faculty helped the participants make sense of classroom knowledge through direct action. As one participant shared, "She'd [Trask] just find these little things to get us wrapped up about and then she'd say, 'Okay, now it's your guys' job to do something about it!' We felt really empowered." Another participant shared his analysis of praxis, "You're actually putting to physical use the theoretical things you're thinking about, learning about and from that practical deployment or through political engagement, you refine your theories, you redo them." Another participant captured this idea concisely, "Think then act . . . it wasn't just think. I mean, it had to have a purpose." So praxis can be viewed as a tool for encouraging deeper learning by doing, while also embedding the kuleana to "do something," be purposeful, and be imaginative. Most participants shared that KCHS faculty modeled praxis as well. Yet another said, "I really learned a lot about activism which wasn't any formal part of the curriculum but I learned so much whether it was directly from them or watching them or from the things I chose to get involved with as a result of being inspired by what I was learning at Hawaiian Studies." As such, praxis in this context was inspirational in nurturing more thoughtful action.

Participants also described KCHS as "rigorous." When examined more closely, "rigorous" meant the high expectations of KCHS faculty. These expectations were articulated in a number of ways, including class work, direct action (praxis), and post-KCHS aspirations. One participant described, "I always felt KCHS was academically rigorous in the classroom, like you were expected to excel." Several participants discussed the scholarly socialization by faculty as attention to critical questioning, "citing sources," working with primary documents, writing extensive term papers, and attending graduate or professional school. One participant shared a story about a faculty member writing, "See me" on her exam and when she did not, it was written on her next assignment. When she finally went to see the faculty member, the participant was told, "you really need to think about grad school" even though it was her first year at KCHS. Several others said they felt graduate or professional school was just "expected" by faculty. One participant shared a story about when he did not meet a faculty's expectations by skipping her class. The faculty member found him at his on-campus job and said his consequence for skipping class was leading the next class lecture on feudalism. He said, "[I learned] the importance of getting someplace, honoring each other's time and space." He explained further that even though she "went after [him]," he interpreted her actions as genuine concern about his educational success as a dropout of another institution of higher education.

All of the participants discussed the teaching expertise of the KCHS faculty. They specifically noted their skillful oratory and depth of knowledge. Their approach goes against conventional notions of effective teaching, especially for Indigenous students, as they primarily used direct instruction (i.e., lecture). Yet each participant noted their excitement with classes because of the faculty's skillful oratory as well as their ability to tie the material to each participant. One participant shared, "They had a way with their stories that they were telling [and] the materials they were exposing us to. Whether it was the written work or videos or whatnot just making the stories so real . . . like we were right there in the middle of it . . . they were somehow able to bring that out to the classroom so that you felt like they're not just lecturing to me about history." Another participant said simply, "She's [Kameʻeleihiwa] a master at her art." One participant expressed her thoughts on how their teaching informed her own, "She [Trask] had an emotional punch to what she was bringing that made a bigger impact because we could make it personal, our family, our lāhui, lives . . . it gave us permission to be emotional, too. So now as a teacher, I think like that's so much more powerful at learning when you can engage students at that affective level."

Faculty Role Modeling

Role Modeling offered personal insight into how KCHS faculty modeled kuleana. Most participants had specific stories about the impact these faculty relationships had on them in and out of the classroom, and beyond KCHS. KCHS faculty were characterized as "mentors," "dynamic," and "wise," and through role modeling, kuleana emerged as a desire to serve a similar role for others. As one participant reflected on her experience now as a professor, "seeing them being both in the classroom, [being] scholarly, and publishing and all that but also like right there engaging in lawsuits, and speaking, and leading marches and all that. That was really important." This role modeling helped her develop her own thinking about what it means to be an ʻŌiwi scholar.

The KCHS ethos at this time is often characterized as highly politicized. One participant said, "In the 90s, this place [KCHS] was going off! It was on fire!" But KCHS was far more complex, because while it was certainly political, there were many affective elements that were equally as impactful. Two stories in particular illuminate this complexity. The first participant shared his experience escorting Trask to an on-campus rally to support her in the face of institutional racism and death threats. He said, "We were walking down the mall . . . gathering plenty people [to march] and then we got to Sakamaki, you could see the whole Sakamaki just *full* with people. Haunani-Kay started crying. I was like, 'You okay or what?' [She said,] 'Yeah, yeah.' [I asked her,] 'You still wanna do this?' [She replied,] 'We gotta. We gotta.' So . . . she cleaned up then 'BOOM!' She just turned. You know, like how everybody sees her." Witnessing her vulnerability, he said, offered him keen insight into her leadership. Despite her immense fear and the enormous pressure, she fulfilled her kuleana. Another participant shared her thoughts about how a faculty member helped her process her spiritual conflicts, "He [Young] opened that space where we saw not just the connection between what we were learning and what was going on in the world, but like that inner life. He let us into his inner life. Like what he was thinking when he was feeling what he was going through and how that connected with what he was teaching."

Several participants also shared how role modeling continued after they left KCHS. One participant shared, "Even after I was in graduate school, Lilikalā [Kameʻeleihiwa] was still trying to figure out how to give us opportunities." Other participants shared this sentiment, saying KCHS faculty members continue to serve as role models through their scholarly work, teaching, and visible advocacy for Hawaiian liberation.

Hiʻilei aloha no ka Lāhui: Kanaka ʻŌiwi Kuleana Consciousness

As reflected in the chapter title, participants in this study utilize "decolonization" to characterize their experience with KCHS. In turn, participants emerged with a very conscious (and conscientious) sense of kuleana instilled through the curriculum, pedagogy, and role modeling. One participant said, "there's so much emphasis on kuleana and obligation and that idea of leadership is threaded throughout everything we do." Each participant spoke about kuleana in relationship to self, family, and lāhui, particularly focused on connecting their KCHS education to identifying their specific kuleana to "advancing the lāhui." As a result, these participants are in fields such as education, law, information studies, and planning, contributing to the lāhui in ways they have identified for themselves. So when I pose this idea of Kanaka ʻŌiwi Kuleana Consciousness, it's obviously a take on Freire's (1993) "conscientizacao," or critical consciousness, but specifically expressing Hawaiian identity in terms of "critical kuleana" which attends to understanding self in relationship to sovereignty, self-determination, and nation-building.

On a fundamental level, the experiences of participants resonated with much of the culturally based literature confirming the positive socioemotional impacts. One participant shared, "I think it helped me to be able to speak with more confidence . . . and more proud to be Hawaiian and represent." Similarly, another participant said her experience was "finding my voice as a Hawaiian, as a woman, as a student, as a person even." She went on to state, "I don't think I expected to be . . . transformed as a human being."

A concept connecting these kuleana articulations is recognition of the lāhui and the personal responsibility to it. One participant said, "I was involved with KCHS and I had those values developed through my time there and that my education was going to involve improving myself for the purpose of helping the community, the larger whole." Similarly, another participant shared, "To me when I went to Kamehameha we heard it too like how many . . . didn't get into Kamehameha. [But] when you got to KCHS it was more about now you have kuleana, now you have a responsibility to give back because you were one of the ones who made it here."

For several participants, this recognition of lāhui also meant nation-building. As one participant explained, "I'm always looking at it from the mindset of nationhood and if we had our own government . . . the missing link is government and the land base, again, being able to make decisions for your own people." Hawaiianness, as articulated by kuleana, is clearly connected to the well-being of the lāhui, as ʻŌiwi and nation.

One participant discussed his "culminating moment" in truly understanding the weight and enormity of kuleana. He was left on his own in a place unfamiliar to him and very dangerous to conduct his groundbreaking research. He said, "So I remember thinking, 'You just get through this because that's what responsibility is about that they [KCHS] teach you about. You gotta just suck it up. You can do this. We can do this. Our kūpuna did. If they did it, we must be able to do it, too.'" He continued, "It was those key moments of critical decision making where it was, you know, all those lessons of responsibility and the bigger picture of what they are trying to achieve that weighed in and make you think, okay I don't have a choice. I have to do this. That helps you to break through in the end . . . if it's about your family, your nation, your kids, your future kids, your grandfather . . . you fully expect to come through." As exemplified by this participant, kuleana is a complex aspect of Hawaiianness. In one sense, there is a heavy feeling of responsibility to the collective well-being of the lāhui, but it also serves as a guide for ʻŌiwi to move past their fears and anxiety for the well-being of the lāhui.

Kūmaka ka ʻikena iā Hiʻilawe: Lifting Kuleana to Assess ʻŌiwi Educational Success

They tell us all kinds of things, but what do we think of ourselves?

—John Dominis Holt (1969/1995, p. 19)

Hiʻilawe is a majestic and storied waterfall (and river) in Waipiʻo Valley on Hawaiʻi Island, dropping 1,450 feet from the heavens.[18] I had the opportunity to see Hiʻilawe myself when some friends and I were invited to visit the loʻi project site for Kanu o ka ʻĀina New Century Public Charter School (Kanu), the kuaʻana of our Hawaiian culture-based charter schools. Our gracious hosts were the school's founders and culture-based education champions, Kū and Nālei Kahakalau. I remember thinking how fortunate it is for Kanu students to be surrounded by this unparalleled beauty, learning about themselves through our kūpuna, their knowledge systems, and the ways we can utilize and/or adapt that ʻike (knowledge, understanding, clarity) to our contemporary society. I also remember thinking, how do we understand, capture, and articulate the depth and complexities of this learning?

Parts of the answers to these questions became even clearer when I served two terms on the governing board for Hālau Kū Māna (HKM), a Hawaiian culture-based charter located in Maunalaha, Oʻahu. My service not only reified the critical need for us to retheorize our sense of Hawaiianness but also to connect it to these ideas of educational success. I had the distinct honor of serving as a judge for two HKM senior capstones. Each student presented her year's worth of work connecting their HKM learning to community-based projects. Like KCHS, HKM grounded these students in their Hawaiianness that in turn helped them to understand and identify community needs in ways they were uniquely able to contribute. Throughout the presentations, I was filled with a sense of amazement and pride but also worry because I know the wealth of knowledge these young women expressed so beautifully will not be cultivated in the same way outside of HKM unless we can provide the frameworks and opportunities to do so.

So, what do we 'Ōiwi think of ourselves? How do we better understand ourselves and other Indigenous peoples, especially in relationship to education? By utilizing a kuleana-centered approach to understanding the intersectionalities of identity, education, and environment for 'Ōiwi, I learned the KCHS ethos challenged its students to consider their identity as both meaning and action beyond individual benefit. Twenty years after graduating from KCHS, this small group of graduates maintains very close personal and professional ties to strengthening the broader 'Ōiwi community as attorneys, teachers (K through higher education), social entrepreneurs, planners, and farmers. This study has also reinforced my belief that a significant piece to holistically answering questions of identity and, in turn, providing an educational journey that is intentionally designed for 'Ōiwi success is developing appropriate research frameworks (and methodologies) resonant with the cultural/political context of our 'Ōiwi students and lāhui Hawai'i.

NOTES

1. Mahalo a nui to my dear friend and colleague, Nālani Balutski, for authoring this remarkable poetic transcription. In her composition, she included at least one quote from each of the participants for this study to weave together an overall story. Note: A slightly modified version appears in our coauthored piece (Wright & Balutski, 2013). Glesne (1997) defines a poetic transcription as "a creative analytic practice in which the researcher fashions poem-like pieces from the interviewees" reflecting the author's analysis (p. 282). I'd also like to acknowledge her invaluable contributions to this study, as she conducted many of the interviews and provided a critical sounding board for the emerging ideas presented in this piece. All shortcomings, though, are mine alone.
2. "Native," "Indigenous," and "Indigenous Peoples" will be used interchangeably in the way Smith (1999) problematizes "Indigenous," "[to] internationalize the experiences, the issues and the struggles of some of the world's colonized peoples" (p. 7) while also acknowledging the specific histories of Indigenous Peoples with colonialism.
3. Kanaka 'Ōiwi, 'Ōiwi, Hawaiian, and Native Hawaiian are used interchangeably to refer to the autochthonous peoples of Ko Hawai'i Pae 'Āina.
4. "Culturally based," "culture-based," and "culturally responsive" are primarily defined as educational initiatives grounded or centered on Hawaiian people, culture, and society. To be clear, I am not a scholar of culture-based education but find some of its framing, especially as articulated by Ladson-Billings (1995, 2014) and Castagno and Brayboy (2008), very helpful in examining the higher educational context for Kanaka 'Ōiwi, especially as it includes issues of inequality, racism, sovereignty, and self-determination, and valuing student/Native epistemologies into its analysis.

5. Taken from the "Student Hawaiian Cultural Affiliation Scale" used in their study. There are several different identity measures used to understand how culturally based education impacts educational outcomes and Hawaiian identity, but I believe this approach continues to essentialize identity in ways that reinforce the "check list." This check list ascribes Hawaiianness to our ʻŌiwi rather than ʻŌiwi engaging in a critical dialectical process of identity positioning.

6. I borrow "Hawaiianness" from Halualani (2002), in which she explores "different identity positions created *in the name of Hawaiians* by larger structural interests . . . and Hawaiians themselves" (pp. xviii–xix, original emphasis). Similarly, I investigate Hawaiianness as an "identity position" or Hawaiian subjectivities within KCHS—how Hawaiianness is constructed by KCHS as well as the meaning made of Hawaiianness by its graduates.

7. "Articulation" is used in my interpretation of Hall's theory of articulation expressed by Slack (1996). She says, "Theoretically, articulation can be understood as a way of characterizing social formation without falling into the twin traps of reductionism and essentialism" (p. 112).

8. Shotton, Lowe, and Waterman (2013) use the term "Non-Native College and University" to describe Predominantly White Institutions (PWIs), or "mainstream" institutions of higher education. At the University of Hawaiʻi at Mānoa, people of color constitute the majority of students (though Caucasians constitute 24%) while 50% of the faculty is Caucasian. Hawaiians and Part-Hawaiians compose about 15% of the student body and 6% of the faculty.

9. See Kaiwipuni Lipe's chapter 11 in this collection. Dr. Lipe insightfully and thoughtfully guides us through these significant queries illuminated by the voices of trailblazing Native Hawaiian women.

10. I have not done a formal study but in my experience as a scholar-practitioner developing student support programs or courses preparing student affairs professionals, one is hard-pressed to find research on Indigenous student development theory, students, scholar-practitioners, or faculty in higher education publications or handbooks.

11. In 1997, the Center for Hawaiian Studies was renamed Kamakakūokalani Center for Hawaiian Studies in honor of Gladys Kamakakūokalani ʻAinoa Brandt, a prominent Native Hawaiian educator and advocate. Brandt was appointed to the University of Hawaiʻi Board of Regents from 1983 to 1989, serving as chair for four of those years.

12. I borrow "Hawaiianness" from Halualani (2002) in her exploration of "different identity positions created *in the name of Hawaiians* by larger structural interests . . . and Hawaiians themselves" (pp. xviii–xix, original emphasis). Similarly, I investigate Hawaiianness as an "identity position" within KCHS—how Hawaiianness is constructed by KCHS as well as the meaning made of Hawaiianness by its graduates.

13. A brief history of KCHS can be found at: http://manoa.hawaii.edu/hshk/kamakakuokalani/history-op/ as well as in Goodyear-Kaʻōpua (2016).

14. At the time of filming, Dr. Osorio was not part of the KCHS faculty but was hired shortly thereafter.

15. On a very simplistic level, the 1848 Māhele was incredibly significant for Hawaiians as it shifted land tenure from communal to private ownership, playing a direct role in disconnecting Hawaiians from their ancestral lands and natural resources.

16. KCHS faculty have grown in number from four in the 1990s to 12 in 2016 as well as in disciplinary representation, having been initially dominated by historians (three of the four faculty earned doctorates in history).

17. Due to considerations of space, I focused in this chapter only on the most significant themes.

18. The first part of the subhead above translates as "All eyes are on Hiʻilawe," which is the opening line to a very famous Hawaiian song "Hiʻilawe" written by Sam Liʻa Kalainaina, Sr. "Hiʻilawe" also means "to lift or carry."

REFERENCES

Benham, M. K. P. (2004). Where can we collectively be that is greater than we are now? *Hūlili: Multidisciplinary Research on Hawaiian Well-being, 1*(1), 35–49.

Brayboy, B. M. J. (2005). Toward a tribal critical race theory in education. *The Urban Review, 37*(5), 425–442.

Brayboy, B. M. J., Fann, A. J., Castagno, A. E., & Solyom, J. A. (2012). Postsecondary education for American Indians and Alaska Natives: Higher education for nation building and self-determination. *ASHE Higher Education Report*, 37(5).

Cajete, G. (1994). *Look to the Mountain: An Ecology of Indigenous Education*. Durango, CO: Kivati Press.

Castagno, A. E., & Brayboy, B. M. J. (2008). Culturally responsive schooling for Indigenous youth: A review of the literature. *Review of Educational Research, 78*(4), 941–993.

Demmert, W. G. Jr., & Towner, J. C. (2003). *A Review of the research literature on the influences of culturally based education on the academic performance of Native American students. Final Paper*. Retrieved from ERIC. (ED483013)

Freire, P. (1993). *Pedagogy of the Oppressed* (new revised 20th anniversary edition). New York: Continuum.

Freitas, A., Wright, E. K., Balutski, B. J. N., & Wu, P. (2012). Development of the "Indigenous self" in Indigenous-centered student services: An examination of Kokua a Puni Summer Enrichment Program. *Educational Perspectives, 45*(1 & 2), 82–94.

Glesne, C. (1997). That rare feeling: Re-presenting research through poetic transcription. *Qualitative Inquiry, 3*(2), 202–221.

Goodyear-Ka'ōpua, N. (2009). Rebuilding the 'auwai: Connecting ecology, economy, and education in Hawaiian Schools. *AlterNative, 5*(2), 46–77.

Goodyear-Ka'ōpua, N. (2011). Kuleana lāhui: Collective responsibilities for Hawaiian nationhood in activists' praxis. *Affinities: A Journal of Radical Theory, Culture, and Action, 5*(1), 130–162.

Goodyear-Ka'ōpua, N. (2013). *The Seeds We Planted: Portraits of a Native Hawaiian Charter School*. Minneapolis, MN: University of Minnesota Press.

Goodyear-Ka'ōpua, N. (2014). Introduction. In N. Goodyear-Ka'ōpua, I. Hussey, & E. K. Wright (Eds.), *Nation Rising: Hawaiian Movements for Life, Land, and Sovereignty*. Durham, NC: Duke University Press.

Goodyear-Ka'ōpua, N. (2016). Reproducing the ropes of resistance: Hawaiian studies methodologies. In K. Oliveira & E. K. Wright, *Kanaka 'Ōiwi Methodologies: Mo'olelo and Metaphor*. Honolulu, HI: University of Hawai'i Press.

Halualani, R. T. (2002). *In the Name of Hawaiians: Native Identities and Cultural Politics*. Minneapolis, MN: University of Minnesota Press.

HeavyRunner, I., & DeCelles, R. (2002). Family Education Model: Meeting the student retention challenge. *Journal of American Indian Education, 41*(2), 29–37.

Holt, J. D. (1969/1995). *On Being Hawaiian*. Honolulu, HI: Ku Pa'a Publishing.

Huffman, T. (2001). Resistance theory and the transculturation hypothesis as explanations of college attrition and persistence among culturally traditionally American Indian students. *Journal of American Indian Education, 40*(3), 1–23.

Kamakakūokalani Center for Hawaiian Studies (n.d.). "Mission." Retrieved from: http://manoa.hawaii.edu/hshk/kamakakuokalani/mission-op

Kame'eleihiwa, L. K. (1992). *Native Lands and Foreign Desires: How Shall We Live in Harmony: Ko Hawai'i 'Āina me na koi puumake a ka po'e Haole: Pehea lā e pono ai*. Honolulu, HI: Bishop Museum Press.

Kamehameha Schools. (2014). *Ka Huaka'i: 2014 Native Hawaiian Educational Assessment*. Honolulu, HI: Kamehameha Schools Publishing.

Kana'iaupuni, S., & Ishibashi, K. (February 2003). *Hawai'i charter schools: Initial trends and select outcomes for Native Hawaiian students*. Honolulu, HI: Kamehameha Schools, PASE 4–5:22.

Kanaʻiaupuni, S., & Kawaiʻaeʻa, K. K. C. (2008). E Lauhoe mai nā waʻa: Toward a Hawaiian Indigenous education teaching framework. *Hūlili: Multidisciplinary Research on Hawaiian Well-being*, 5, 67–90.

Kanaʻiaupuni, S., Ledward, B., & Jensen, U. (2010). *Culture-based Education and Its Relationship to Student Outcomes*. Honolulu, HI: Kamehameha Schools Research & Evaluation.

Kanaʻiaupuni, S., Malone, N., & Ishibashi, K. (2005). *Ka Huakaʻi: 2005 Native Hawaiian Educational Assessment*. Honolulu, HI: Kamehameha Schools, Pauahi Publications.

Kaomea, J. (2009). Contemplating kuleana: Reflections on the rights and responsibilities on the non-Indigenous participants. *AlterNative*, 5(2), 78–99.

Kikiloi, K. (2010). Rebirth of an archipelago: Sustaining a Hawaiian cultural identity for people and homeland. *Hūlili: Multidisciplinary Research on Hawaiian Well-being*, 6, 73–115.

Kupo, L. (2017). Questions of legitimacy and right to claim Hawaiian identity: Moving Native Hawaiian identity conversations from margin to center. In S. D. Museus, A. Agbayani, and D. M. Ching, *Focusing on the Underserved: Immigrant, Refugee, and Indigenous Asian American and Pacific Islanders in Higher Education*. Charlotte, NC: Information Age Publishing.

Labrador, R. L., & Wright, E. K. (2011). Engaging the indigenous in Pacific Islander Asian American studies. *AmerAsia Journal*, 37(3), 135–147.

Ladson-Billings, G. (Autumn 1995). Toward a theory of culturally relevant pedagogy. *American Educational Research Journal*, 32(3), 465–491

Ladson-Billings, G. (Spring 2014). Culturally relevant pedagogy 2.0: a.k.a. the remix. *Harvard Educational Review*, 84(1), 74–84.

Ledward, B. C. (2007). On being Hawaiian enough: Contesting American racialization with native hybridity. *Hūlili: Multidisciplinary Research on Hawaiian Well-being*, 4(1), 107–143.

Ledward, B., Takayama, B., & Kahumoku, W. (June 2008). *Hawaiian Cultural Influences in Education (HCIE) ʻOhana and Community Integration in Culture-Based Education*. Honolulu, HI: Kamehameha Schools Research & Evaluation.

Luning, R. J. I., & Yamauchi, L. A. (Fall 2010). The influences of Indigenous heritage language education on students and families in a Hawaiian language immersion program. *Heritage Language Journal*, 7(2), 46–75.

McLaughlin, T. (September 2005). The educative importance of ethos. *British Journal of Educational Studies*, 53(3), 306–325.

Meyer, M. (2003). *Hoʻoulu: Our Time of Becoming: Collected Early Writings of Manulani Meyer*. Honolulu, HI: ʻAi Pōhaku Press.

Minthorn, R. S., & Chavez, A. F. (2015). *Indigenous Leadership in Higher Education*. New York, NY: Routledge.

Omandam, P. (1996). Hawaiian style: The University of Hawaii's new Center for Hawaiian Studies is a showcase of the island's cultural heritage. Retrieved from: http://archives.starbulletin.com/96/08/13/news/story1.html

Osorio, J. (2001). "What kine Hawaiian you?" A Moʻolelo about Nationhood, race, history, and the contemporary sovereignty movement in Hawaiʻi. *The Contemporary Pacific*, 13(2), 359–379.

Osorio, J. (2006). On being Hawaiian. *Hūlili: Multidisciplinary Research on Hawaiian Well-being*, 3(1), 19–26.

Pascarella, E. T., & Terranzini, P. T. (2005). *How College Affects Students: A Third Decade of Research*, Volume 2. San Francisco, CA: Jossey-Bass.

Pukui, M. K., & Elbert, S. H. (1971). *Hawaiian Dictionary*. Honolulu, HI: University of Hawaiʻi Press.

Salis Reyes, N. A. (2013). ʻIke kūʻokoʻa: Indigenous critical pedagogy and the connections between education and sovereignty for ka lāhui. *Hūlili: Multidisciplinary Research on Hawaiian Well-being*, 9, 205–227.

Salis Reyes, N. A. (2016). *"What am I doing to be a good ancestor?": An Indigenized phenomenology of giving back by Native college graduates* (Unpublished doctoral dissertation). The University of Texas at San Antonio.
Shotton, H. J., Lowe, S. C., & Waterman, S. J. (2013). *Beyond the Asterisk: Understanding Native Students in Higher Education*. Sterling, VA: Stylus Publishing.
Slack, J. D. (1996). The theory and method of articulation in cultural studies. In D. Morley & K. Chen (Eds.), *Stuart Hall: Critical Dialogues in Cultural Studies*. London and New York: Routledge.
Smith, L. T. (1999). *Decolonising Methodologies: Research and Indigenous Peoples*. New York: Zed Books.
Tengan, T. K. (2008). *Native Men Remade: Gender and Nation in Contemporary Hawai'i*. Durham, NC: Duke University Press.
Tibbetts, K. A., Kahakalau, K., & Johnson, Z. (2007). Education with aloha and student assets. *Hūlili: Multidisciplinary Research on Hawaiian Well-being*, *4*, 147–182.
Trask, H. K. (1993). *From a Native Daughter: Colonialism and Sovereignty in Hawai'i*. Monroe, MA: Common Courage Press.
Trask, H. K. (1999). *From a Native Daughter: Colonialism and Sovereignty in Hawai'i* (2nd ed.). Honolulu, HI: University of Hawai'i Press.
Trask, H. K. (2002). *Night Is a Sharkskin Drum*. Honolulu, HI: University of Hawai'i Press.
Trask, H. K. (2008). Settlers of color and "immigrant" hegemony: "Locals" in Hawai'i. In C. Fujikane & J. Y. Okamura (Eds.), *Asian Settler Colonialism: From Local Governance to the Habits of Everyday Life in Hawai'i*. Honolulu, HI: University of Hawai'i Press.
University of Hawai'i at Mānoa (2011). *Achieving Our Destiny; The University of Hawai'i at Mānoa Strategic Plan 2011–2015*. Retrieved from: https://manoa.hawaii.edu/strategicplan/vision-2011-2015/pdf/achieving-our-destiny.pdf
Warner, S. L. N. (1999). Kuleana: The right, responsibility, and authority of indigenous peoples to speak and make decisions for themselves in language and cultural revitalization. *Anthropology & Education Quarterly*, *30*(1), 68–93.
wa Thiong'o, N. (1986). *Decolonising the Mind: The Politics of Language in African Literature*. London: J. Currey Heinemann Educational Books.
Wright, E. K. (2003). *Education for the nation: Forging Indigenous Hawaiian identity in higher education* (Doctoral dissertation). Retrieved from ProQuest. (UMI #3121160)
Wright, E. K., & Balutski, B. J. N. (2013). The role of context, critical theory, and counter-narratives in understanding Pacific Islander Indigeneity. In S. D. Museus, D. C. Maramba, & R. T. Teranishi (Eds.), *The Misrepresented Minority: New Insights on Asian Americans and Pacific Islanders and Their Implications for Higher Education*. Sterling, VA: Stylus Publishing.
Wright, E. K., & Balutski, B. J. N. (2016). Ka 'Ikena a ka Hawai'i: Toward a Kanaka 'Ōiwi Critical Race Theory. In K.A.R.K.N. Oliveira & E. K. Wright (Guest Eds.), *Kanaka 'Ōiwi Methodologies: Mo'olelo and Metaphor*. Honolulu HI: University of Hawai'i Press.
Young, K. G. T. (2005). Education through one lens: Sources of spiritual influences at Kamakakūokalani. *Hūlili: Multidisciplinary Research on Hawaiian Well-being*, 2, 135–169.

CHAPTER 3

A Methodology of Beauty

Charlotte Davidson
(Diné/Three Affiliated Tribes: Mandan/Hidatsa/Arikara)

> *The Indigenous mind is the tribal mind and the feminine mind; it is the mind that has been suppressed, oppressed, colonized, shamed, and killed out of framework of thinking and knowing.*
>
> —Paula Noel Hibbard (2001)

This chapter attempts to contribute to the search for an Indigenous research methodology upon which to reclaim a beauty-centered politic of research inquiry, and by so doing, to reassert the political vision to "walk in beauty." To a deeper extent, walk in beauty, known in Diné Bizaad (The People's Language) as Hózhóogo Naasháa Doo, is a form of existence that compels Diné to be conscious of our historical and contemporary capacity as human beings to harm or heal, and to be mindful of the aftereffect that occurs by our pursuit of either possibility. Thus, what ensues is a careful discussion concerning an embodied lens-making practice centered in Hózhó. The terms Hózhó and beauty will be used interchangeably throughout this chapter.

> As a philosophical idea, Hózhó has been described by Navajo scholars as being central to Navajo life and integral to the philosophy of Sa'ah Naagháí Bik'eh Hózhóón (SNBH) and the Hózhoojí (Blessing Way) and Naayee'jí (Protection Way) teachings. SNBH is our life that we strive to live, yet it is also part of our thoughts, language, prayers, and songs and is integral to our inherent human quality for making sense of our lives and striving for harmony, peace, and justice. (Werito, 2014, p. 27)

In concert with the above, "Scholars including myself should not go beyond that realization. SNBH can only be clearly understood in the Diné language with a Diné chanter providing the necessary explanations and understandings" (Lee,

2004, p. 137). At the same time, none of the above is possible without the ongoing reframing of Diné thought.

My knowledge, experience, and once simple understanding of Hózhó matured through my quest for a methodological space that would protect the sanctity of Diné knowledge associated with the pedagogy of weaving—a familial legacy central to the lived experiences of my matrilineal line that also served as the focus of my doctoral dissertation.

Organized into four parts, the first two sections of this chapter will explain the genealogy of a methodology of beauty. Next, Beauty Way principles for research will be discussed. Since the creation of this methodology, new material practices have come to view. I will highlight these emergent patterns of understanding in the last portions of the chapter.

Understanding Beauty

Over ten years ago, Harry Walters testified that Diné people are in the process of reconstructing our cultural practices and, in so doing, are "altering [our] technology to maintain [our] epistemology" (Walters, as cited by Hedlund, 1996, p. 63). Toward this end, an array of new songs, prayers, and traditions are emerging as a means to render new readings of the world; this is especially true in higher education settings as Diné-centered research paradigms have gradually come into view (Begay & Maryboy, 1998; Benally, 2008; Clark, 2009; Emerson, 2003; McAlpin, 2008; Secatero, 2009). It follows then that many Diné scholars, like myself, seek to link Diné thought processes with the creation of material scholarship.

Kodóó Hózhó'dooleeł (it begins with beauty) is often uttered at the start of Diné prayers and Hózhó Náhasdlìì (it is done in beauty) is said at the end, conveying that the nature of our intentions begins and ends in a manner of beauty (Werito, 2014). Simple and complex expressions of beauty as a moral beingness of Diné include, but are not limited to: balance, Beauty Way, Blessing Way, corn pollen pathway, good, harmony, ideal, kinship, order, positive, Protection Way, well-being, Hózhó, and SNBH (Haskie, 2002). Shimá (my mother) further explains, "Regardless of the degree of dysfunction in your environment, make consistent efforts to refresh your thinking process by eliminating negative words, thoughts and actions throughout your path in life. When your beingness is centered in this way of thinking, you experience inner contentment and serenity knowing you are not adding harm to the world" (N. Wilkinson, personal communication, March 23, 2016). Thus, this manner of thinking strongly affected the course of creating a powerful lens in which to closely study the pedagogy of weaving. However, this methodological embarking could not begin without understanding the sociohistorical context that influenced its development. While the following provides a very brief and general introduction to the primacy of Diné thought, some may contend that additional concepts should have been included, or that some constructs have not been given the emphasis they deserve.

In the privation of Hózhó, Diné often look to episodes of Diné Bahané (Diné Creation Stories) to recalibrate ourselves in an effort to emerge from discord (L. Emerson, personal communication, April 22, 2010). Within these narrations, the formation of Diné Bizaad (the People's Language); the birth of Asdzáá Nádleehé (Changing Woman); the creation of the four original clans known as Kinya'áąnii (Towering House), Honágháhnii (One Who Walks Around), Hashtłishnii (Mud People), and Tódích'íi'nii (Bitter Water); the making of day and night and the four seasons; the construction of the first Hoghaan (home place) and sweat lodge; as well as the origination of animals and ceremonies are some of the many special events that occurred within these stories (Lee, 2004). Naturally embedded within a methodology of beauty, Clark (2009) offers a cursory view of our ancestors' upward travel through a series of underworlds (Ni'Hodiłhił, also known as First World, Black World, and Black Air; Ni'Hoodootłiizh, referred to as Second World, Blue World, and Blue Air; Ni' Haltsoh recognized as Third World or Yellow Air), into the current world we call Ni'Halgai (also known as the Fourth World, White and Glittering World):

> Diné origin stories of Hajiinei (the emergence), told through oral accounts, describe an evolution through four worlds and Diné believe that origin stories can only be absorbed through one's life time and not through books or tapes (Glenabah Hardy, Personal Communication, December 26, 2008) . . . The Diné people emerged upward through those four worlds with no particular date attached, but only as four ancient events, which endure as lessons and teachings for the Diné people to know. (Irene H. Clark, Personal Communication, October 25, 2008, p. 92)

Clark goes on to define the prevailing thesis of this historical migration:

> The teachings from these stories implant appropriate respect for the clan system and regulate proper relationships, or "K'e" among the Diné people. During the time of creation, various ceremonies emerged to correct the disharmony that would confront the Diné people. These ceremonies were conducted to preserve and restore order among the elements and with the Diné people for all time. In keeping with these narratives and through the use of Blessing and Protection Way ceremonies, order and balance were restored whenever disharmony occurred. In most, if not all the stories, the improper action of animals as well as of individual Diné was corrected so that harmony, "Hozho," could be restored through ceremonies and oral teachings . . . Those stories serve as a reminder to the Diné of historical events, and they bestow wisdom, knowledge, and guidance about proper ethical and moral character and behavior.

(Irene H. Clark, Personal Communication, December 25, 2008; Glenabah Hardy, Personal Communication, December 26, 2008; Tommy Singer, Personal Communication, January 1, 2009; Yazzie, 1971; Roessel, 1971; Aronilth, 1980; Zolbrod, 1984; Mitchell, 2001). (Clark, pp. 102–103)

Extending this awareness is Shicheii (maternal grandfather, by way of the Diné clan system), Larry Emerson (2003), who explains that Hózhǫ́ǫji (Beauty Way) is not only foundational to all other major ceremonies, but is a pre-existing ceremony that promotes a myriad of blessings prayerfully linked to restoration, happiness, and protection: "The Hózhǫ́ǫji (Beauty Way) ceremony is considered the central stalk ceremony. The Beauty Way provides the central meaning, purpose, and lifeway for other Diné ceremonies, making Hózhó, as a truth, belief, and value occupies a central location in all Diné ceremonial thinking" (p. 59). Beauty Way emphasizes all that is good about Diné people and speaks to the best ways in which to live our lives. Given this history, Diné Bahané historicizes the role of the Beauty Way researcher that endures to the present.

Higher Education Encounters the Beauty Way Researcher

Undiscussed in much of the literary landscape concerning research methodologies was the encouragement to have insight into my own power as a Diné, Mandan, Hidatsa, and Arikara woman. Power, here, is meant to describe a political primacy spurred from material, ideological, and subjective struggles and using my increased consciousness to indigenously conceive a new vision of the world. Like many non-Indigenous colleges and universities, methodological spaces may be experienced as locations where Beauty Way researchers-in-the-making, like myself, may lose heart and hope that produces a feeling of estrangement from their cultural, political, and intellectual agency. In this vein, I felt overwhelmed by the myriad of methodological processes that showed signs of serving as a disembodied task to conduct institutional research.

Adding to this painful sensation, I neither possessed the language nor the tools to forge a new moccasined manner in which to "walk in beauty." Living this out in a non-Diné context—specifically, a higher education setting—meant cultivating research approaches, practices, and conclusions of beatitude and not recreating harm. Here, let me say quickly that preparing methodological ground in this manner was not an inherent capacity I believed I possessed. Over time, what became clearer to me was that, like the confluence of water where my mother's clan group, Tó'aheedlíinii (Water Flows Together), originated, I, too, served as a historic point of origin for the flowing together of knowledge tributaries. It is to the emergence of a methodology of beauty that I will now turn.

Indigenous Learning Modalities

Clearing a path to better understand my experiences within higher education (a phenomenon of our fourth world) was an American Indian Studies graduate seminar at the University of Illinois at Urbana-Champaign titled "Indigenous Learning and Decolonizing Methodologies." The class consisted of a cadre of educational policy doctoral students, who belonged to historically colonized populations. Together, we experienced teaching and learning through a course design that was pedagogically based on the Diné worldview: "Facilitated by Diné artist, activist, and scholar, Dr. Larry Emerson, student participants were required to produce a class project in the form of an [Indigenous] learning modality which we understood to be 'a non-modern way of creative expression that follows familiar, age-old procedures and material typically found in the natural world'" (L. Emerson, personal communication, April 12, 2008; Davidson, 2015, p. 104). In possessing the capacity to think, feel, smell, taste, hear, and see, Indigenous learning modalities (for example, cedar bag, ceremonial basket, corn pollen bag, cradleboard, fire poker, hoghaan, shawls, moccasins, and drums) or "beings" impart endless teachings regarding the manner of human existence. What a Beauty Way researcher-in-the-making often discovers is that these "beings" incite a deeply felt engagement with the dimensions of learning, because our human faculties are invited into an intrinsically communal learning process (Davidson, 2015; McAlpin, 2008). To that extent, Indigenous learning modalities contain pre-modern truths and have the longest history of any research methodologies discussed in methodologies literature—Diné creation narratives well illustrate this point.

At this juncture, it is vitally important to share that it is impossible to discuss all the significant moments that came into view through Diné-centered teaching and learning. And so, rather than grappling with fully expressing an embodied inquiry process inextricably grounded in the collective memory, story, and journey of Beauty Way researchers-in-the-making, I will focus on how my gendered subjectivity served as a material site to re-matriate the process of research inquiry. My intentions are not to treat the group efforts as separate, but to give voice to the reunion between myself and a manner of beauty.

Womb-based Knowing

Signifying where life begins, the doorway of a Hoghaan always faces east (see figure 3.1). The Hoghaan "is a place of conception, birth, growth, [and] development" (Cannella & Manuelito, 2008, p. 53). Thus, the Hoghaan is regarded as a mother, because this is where Diné garner strength and knowledge (Clark, 2009). Appropriate to this description, the majority of student members from the graduate seminar gathered at Tsedaak'aan, Diné Bikeyah, New Mexico, for the expressed purpose of participating in a series of Hoghaan dialogues, so aptly named by our

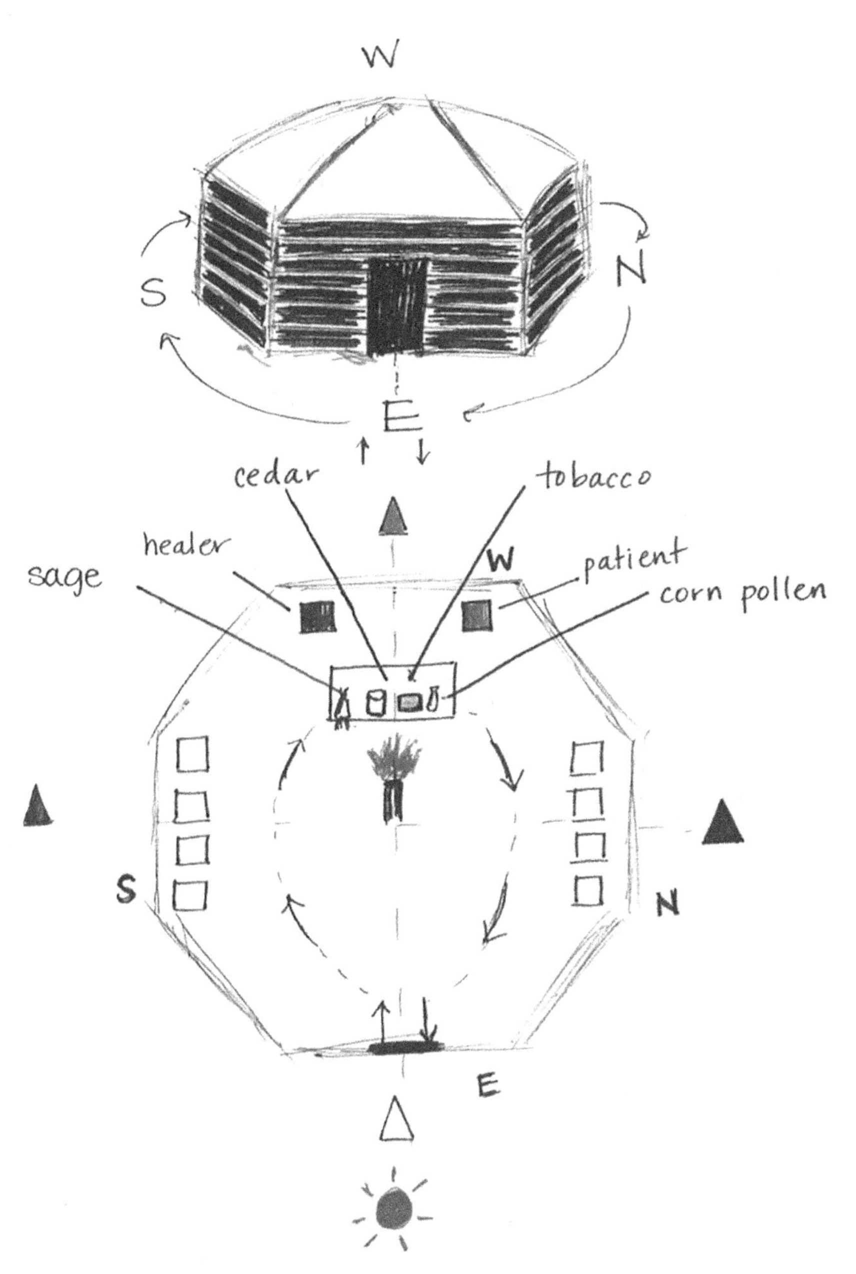

Figure 3.1. Hoghaan (Tsosie-Mahieu, 2009)

facilitator, Shicheii, Larry Emerson, "Na'abidikid: Nitsahakees doo Nahat'a" (To Inquire: Mindfulness and Self-Directed Knowing). The hand-drawn graphic in figure 3.1 illustrates the presence of fluidity in the Hoghaan interior throughout this gathering, by showing the internal movement as clockwise and cyclical. Also represented is the purposeful arrangement of people, the precise placement of Diné learning modalities, and a burning fire that occupied the center.

Five consecutive days of meditative contemplation, replete with ceremony, prayers, and songs, resulted in an increased decolonized Diné sensibility. On a more personal level, I began to re-see my maternal strivings—as a mother of two sons—as an inconspicuous power source within the academy. And, more forcefully than ever, I recognized that the maternal spirit moves in ways unimagined by hegemonic structures, as it resists being diminished, oppressed, and shamed out of existence. Given this reality, a methodology of beauty was rooted up.

Beauty Way Research Principles

Beauty Way researchers struggle to keep alive the cultural and political dimensions linked to beauty-based research. Exposing this effort are Begay and Maryboy (1998), who developed a Diné rendition of qualitative assumptions that describes the relationship between Diné thought and research:

- [My] research is process-oriented, meaning, it is an emerging design primarily concerned with relationship and process.
- [I] am the primary instrument for data collection and analysis. Results are mediated through [my] knowledge of Diné epistemology.
- Ontological assumptions: Navajo spiritual language and ways of knowing are highly subjective in the sense of relating the human experience to the totality of the cosmos. The oneness of all things subjects the human to this holistic relationship.
- Epistemological assumptions: [My] methodology is participative and collaborative. I live within the culture being researched.
- Axiological assumptions: [I] rely on Indigenous ways of knowing, including intuition, spiritual direction, and holistic thinking.
- Methodological assumptions: Culturally correct research is provided through verification by Navajo knowledge holders as well as through community-acknowledged principles of indigenous ways of knowing. (pp. 124–129)

To matrifocally root a methodology of beauty in the same assumptions, I narratively expressed how four Diné learning modalities—Tádidíín Bijish (corn pollen bag), Hoghaan (Home place), Awéétsáál (cradleboard), and Ts'aa' (ceremonial basket)—shaped a principled sense of beauty. There is no question that while spoken about individually, I recognize Diné learning modalities as being fundamentally bundled together, working in cooperation to inform a methodology of beauty:

- An incarnate of the Hoghaan, a methodology of beauty is a balancing construct pregnant with feminine interpretations of how to live, engage, and experience the world. As our mother, a methodology of beauty reminds us of the fragility of our genealogical intent. What is more, a methodology of beauty returns us back to our children—a restorative return that renders us to reawaken and be more fully intact.
- Pedagogically identical to the Ts'aa'—and the pattern that dwells within it—a methodology of beauty contains a storied design that reminds us to exist in healing cooperation with the world around us. And like the central whorl of the Ts'aa', Hózhó serves as the umbilical nexus of inquiry and decision making. Owing to this origin, the Beauty Way researchers and their methodology share the same navel connection.
- Having the same restorative capacity as the Tádidíín Bijish, a methodology of beauty awakens us to the regenerative power of thoughts and words; particularly when they are used to give form to a material body. Said another way, a language of fertility is central to a methodology of beauty.
- Epistemologically commensurate with the Awéétsáál, a methodology of beauty is lovingly grounded in a principled obligation to maternally experience the world. Thus, a methodology of beauty is a space that nurtures a female by recognizing her as a life source. That is to say, to exclude this consciousness from the textual province of scholarship and research is to rob the capacity of Beauty Way researchers to honor, in another way, the reproductive capacity of women.

Conceived this way, it is futile to surmise that a methodology of beauty can ever be complete. Given the changing dimensions of life spaces and how we experience them, a Beauty Way researcher understands that his or her interpretation is always partial and unfinished, and can take on a life of its own. At the heart of this methodology is the critical understanding that Diné learning modalities are not simply heuristic and methodological tools: We, in fact, attend to *their* work, for we are *their* tools to restore order to the world.

Bundling Beauty with Practice

Webbed in deep moral commitment, a methodology of beauty is a way of life. And as such, an indefatigable spirit is required to hold steady a vision of beauty. This manner of understanding occurred as a consequence of my professional rise as a senior diversity administrator at a public institution. Egregious and sexist behaviors became a difficult and persistent thread in the very fabric of my labor within the university. To my great disappointment, this insidious and destructive comportment—among other hostilities and interferences—was minimized and ignored. Yet, while this work experience was largely saturated with relational aggression, it has served as one of the more powerful examples of how the anguish I underwent evoked a wiser sense of the difficulties that are inherent to the climate of the institution. In short, it inspired an aim to bundle beauty with practice.

To do this, I mapped my lived understanding of beauty—as experienced within the inner constitution of Hoghaan and non-Hoghaan structures (an organizational chart is used to represent a university context)—as a means to provoke a deeply reflective critique of my function and purpose within these respective settings. The result of this interface was the creation of a set of cultural introspective inquiries that reminded me of my role as Beauty Way researcher to foster learning environments centered in womb-based knowing (see figure 3.2). This active questioning, thus, re-seeds a consciousness systematically pushed to the fringes by hegemonic practices and structures. What remains clear is that the manner in which I enact relational ways of existence goes unchanged, despite the prevalent differences in these contexts.

To the Beauty Way Researchers and Scholars-in-the-Making

During an interview for a student affairs position I was asked, "If you had to choose one tool to perform your job, what would that be?" Without pause, I resoundingly replied: "Story!" The concept of story, varied though it may be, can reveal itself as a cultural, biological, and symbolic "being," as was the case with Diné learning modalities. Story, in this form, is often unfinished owing to its natural tendency to be inherited and carried forward. As a consequence of this unfinishedness, ontological, axiological, and epistemological sensibilities can be reimagined. In light of this, I deeply believe that once you cultivate the capacity to speak in response with your story, you reclaim a profound sense of where your umbilical cord is buried—an umbilical connection that lovingly nurtures and validates your human story, as it struggles against being systematically and narratively removed from the ground of academe. Through striving to develop this capacity, I, like so many Beauty Way researchers, have come to understand through private and public trips and falls that even the darkest narrative crevices are fertile with storied teachings waiting to be harvested—as this is often where beauty lives.

And so, to the Beauty Way researchers and scholars-in-the-making, I offer you this political counsel: Learn how to answer with your story. As a timeless practice, it continues to serve us well.

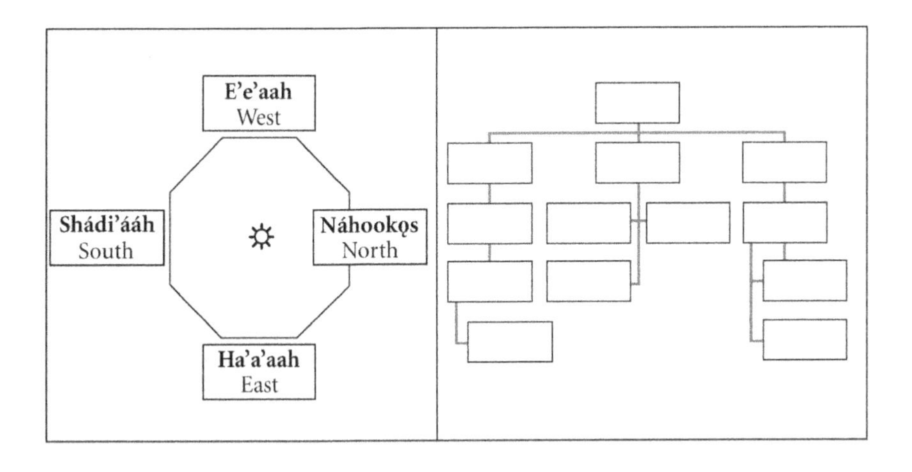

A place to:	Womb-based Inquiry
Uniquely inquire using my story and journey	What do I know so far and still need to learn about myself in non-hoghaan contexts?
Apply Diné thought as a lense to re-see conditions belonging to the present time	What is important to me about upholding Hózhó and K'é and why do I care?
Recognize natural law and its relevancy to our foundation as human beings	What has the possibility of taking shape when institutions reconcile with land historically stewarded by tribes indigenous to the area?
Encourage beatitude and not recreate harm	What's the next level of thinking I need to do, if resotration, kinship, harmony and balance is the language from which my efforts must be derived?
Nurture growth and mediate understanding	What challenges may come my way-and how might I meet them-as I work toward the campus-wide creation of a womb-based space?
Develop a practice of showing up with good intentions	What would it take to create an institutional practice of diversity and inclusion, if a premium was placed on Indigenous concepts of being a good relative?

Figure 3.2. Hoghaan and non-Hoghaan structures (Tsosie-Mahieu, 2009)

REFERENCES

Begay, D. H., & Maryboy, N. C. (1998). Nanit'á Sa'ah Naagháí Bik'eh Hózhóón living the order: Dynamic cosmic process of Diné cosmology (Doctoral dissertation). Retrieved from Proquest Dissertations and Theses database. (UMI No. 9930321).

Benally, H. J. (2008). HÓZHǪǪGO NAASHÁ DOO: Toward a construct in Navajo cosmology (Doctoral dissertation). Retrieved from Proquest Dissertations and Theses database. (UMI No. 3348324).

Cannella,G. S., & Manuelito, K. D. (2008). Feminisms from unthought locations: Indigenous worldviews, marginalized feminisms, and revisioning an anitcolonial social science. In N. K. Denzin, Y. S. Lincoln, & L. T. Smith (Eds.), *Handbook of Critical and Indigenous Methodologies* (pp. 45–59). Los Angeles, CA: Sage.

Clark, F. (2009). In becoming SA'AH NAAGHAI BIK'EH HOZHOON: The historical challenges and triumphs of DINÉ college (Doctoral dissertation). Retrieved from ProQuest Dissertations and Theses database. (UMI No. 3360201).

Davidson, C. E. (2015). Indigenous dissidence: Cultivating a leadership politic of Hózhó. In R. S. Minthorn & A. F Chávez (Eds.), *Indigenous Leadership in Higher Education* (pp. 100–110). New York, NY: Routledge.

Emerson, L. (2003). *HÓZHÓ NÁHÁZDLÍÍ: Towards a Practice of Decolonization*. Unpublished Ph.D. dissertation, Claremont Graduate University and San Diego State University.

Haskie, M. (2002). Preserving a culture: Practicing the navajo principles of hózhó dóó k'é (Doctoral dissertation). Retrieved from ProQuest Dissertations and Theses database. (UMI No. 3077247).

Hedlund, A. L. (1996). More of survival than an art: Comparing late nineteenth- and late twentieth-century lifeways and weaving. In E. H. Bonar (Ed.), *Woven by the Grandmothers: Nineteenth Century Navajo Textiles from the National Museum of the American Indian* (pp. 33–42). Washington, DC: Smithsonian Institution Press.

Hibbard, P. N. (2001). Remembering our ancestors: Recovery of Indigenous mind as a healing process for the decolonization of the Western MIND (Doctoral dissertation). Retrieved from ProQuest Dissertations and Theses database. (UMI No. 300469).

Lee, L. (2004). 21st century diné cultural identity: Defining and practicing sa'ah naagháí bik'eh hózhóón (Doctoral dissertation). Retrieved from ProQuest Dissertations and Theses database. (UMI No. 3144036).

McAlpin, J. D. (2008). Place and being: Higher education as a site for creating Biskabii—Geographies of indigenous academic identity (Doctoral dissertation). Retrieved from ProQuest Dissertations and Theses database. (UMI No. 3314841).

Secatero, S. L. (2009). Beneath our sacred minds, hands, and hearts: Stories of persistence and success among American Indian graduate and professional students (Doctoral dissertation). Retrieved from ProQuest Dissertations and Theses database (UMI No. 3368075).

Werito, V. (2014). Understanding Hózhó to achieve critical consciousness: A contemporary Diné interpretation of the philosophical principles of Hózhó. In L. L. Lee (Ed.), *Diné Perspectives: Revitalizing and Reclaiming Navajo Thought* (pp. 25–38). Tucson, AZ: University of Arizona Press.

Wilson, S. (2008). *Research Is Ceremony: Indigenous Research Methods*. Winnipeg, MB: Fernwood Publishing.

CHAPTER 4

Understanding Relationships in the College Process

INDIGENOUS METHODOLOGIES, RECIPROCITY, AND COLLEGE HORIZONS STUDENTS

Adrienne Keene (Cherokee Nation)

Fourteen years ago, I was a student in a pre-college access program called College Horizons (CH). I was a rising senior in college, ready to tackle the college application process, but unsure about where I would end up, or how my family would pay for it. At the program, a weeklong crash course in applying to college, I met a group of adults who would become my mentors, friends, and family throughout college, my life, and my career. It was at CH that I met the Native recruiter for Stanford, who read through the application materials I had worked so hard on throughout the week, offering kind feedback and strong encouragement. Once on campus, knowing that he was in the admission office offered a sense of connection, and seeing him at orientation events, knowing he knew my story and that my admission wasn't a mistake, made all the difference. He introduced me to the staff of the Native American cultural center on campus, which became my home away from home, and the staff members became my aunties and uncles who always watched out for me.

When I think back to this path and this story, the relationships are what truly stand out. The ways that the small interactions grew into meaningful, reciprocal, long-lasting friendships, mentorships, and support, and the ways that those relationships allowed me to push on and navigate the difficult and oftentimes contentious spaces of a Non-Native College/University (NNCU) (Shotton, Lowe, & Waterman, 2013).

It was these experiences as a student, and later faculty member, at College Horizons that led me to my research with alumni of the program. When I was imagining, building, and planning my research with these alumni navigating their freshman year of college, I wanted to mirror these relationships, extend the foundations we had built together at CH, and complicate the relationship of "researcher" and "subject."

In this chapter, I will explore how relationships—to home, to campus, and to their nations—remain a central part of navigating the freshman year transition for Native students, while weaving in my own journey as a Native researcher coming to understand Indigenous research methods, researcher/"subject" relationships, and the implications for both as we seek to support and understand Native students in college.

Background

College Horizons is a pre-college access nonprofit founded in 1998 by Whitney Laughlin. The program is an eight-day residential program hosted at various college campuses throughout the United States, and serves approximately 100 students from American Indian, Alaska Native, and Native Hawaiian communities at each of the two to three sites per summer. The program curriculum mirrors the motto of the program, "College Pride, Native Pride," offering concrete skills students will need to successfully apply and be admitted to colleges of their choice ("college pride"), but also unique identity-based programming that assists students in beginning to understand what it means not just to be a college student, but a *Native* college student ("Native pride"). The current director, Carmen Lopez, who is Navajo, centers Native cultures and identities throughout the program, with the schedule including opening prayers, resident elders, and constant reinforcement of the centrality and importance of Native beliefs and worldviews.

Throughout the College Horizons curriculum, relationships are key (Keene, 2016). Students are divided into "small groups" of 10–12 students, headed by 4–6 faculty members. The faculty members for the program come from three groups: admission officers from CH "partner schools" (colleges and universities throughout the United States), college counselors from highly resourced private high schools, and counselors from Native community schools and organizations. The faculty members are assigned to mentees within the small groups, with whom they build strong and lasting relationships throughout the week and beyond the program. Part of de-mystifying the college application process for the students comes from breaking down barriers between admission officers and students—making the students realize that the faculty members are real people who can assist with their college application process, but will also be their allies and friends once they arrive on their college campus. This "letting your hair down" process is new for many admission officers, who are used to wearing a suit and standing behind tables at college fairs.

This spirit comes through in interviews with faculty members of the program. To Josh, a first time CH faculty member, who also organized early-morning basketball games between the students and faculty, the space of College Horizons creates a new kind of relationship between admission officers and applicants: "Now that is the crazy thing, no other applicant that I will get from [my school] can ever say, 'We played basketball together.' You know what I am saying? Not like he is going to write his essay about that or it really means that much in the whole thing . . . [but] no one sees me in shorts. You know what I mean? It's like suited up all the time. So, I mean this is great." Josh, who is non-Native, most likely didn't realize the power of basketball to bring together Native folks, or the importance placed on the game in rural reservation communities. But for many of the students, his actions may have transformed him from a distant college representative in a suit to a friend who could be trusted and relied on—for his wicked jump shot *and* his knowledge of financial aid.

Carmen Lopez agrees that relationship-building is one of the crucial parts of the program, that the students really "open up" to the faculty, and that "they're developing a different kind of adult relationship, so quickly. And, they're really seeing these adults as allies, as people in the future that they can connect with."

The goal is for these relationships to carry on after College Horizons. Carmen often stresses to the admissions officers that this process is not just about recruiting students, it is about assisting them through the college process, no matter where they end up. Students can, and do, utilize these relationships to access college representatives during the college application process in ways that other students may not.

Once these students transition to college, the research on Native students in college demonstrates that relationships can often be the piece that makes or breaks their experience, especially in the first year (HeavyRunner & DeCelles, 2002; Jackson, Smith, & Hill, 2003; Pavel & Padilla, 1993; Shotton, Oosahwe, & Cintrón, 2007; Springer, Davidson, & Waterman, 2013; Waterman, 2012). Understanding the critical role of relationships in Native student success, I now ask, how do these relationships extend to the research process itself? How can a research relationship provide reciprocity and respect between the student and researcher, and lead to positive outcomes for both parties?

Centering Relationships: Building a Study Utilizing Indigenous Methods

Understanding the foundations in relationships in College Horizons, and interested in the ways that CH alumni were and are navigating their freshman year of college utilizing the skills from the program, I sought to build a study that would allow deep insight into the lived experiences of students, while also subverting "traditional" research relationships that always felt inherently exploitative to me.

I was also cognizant of the politics and legacy of "research" in Native communities. Research has often been a tool of colonialism, offering justifications for policies of assimilation and cultural eradication (Smith, 2012). Well-meaning anthropologists went into communities to record and document what they thought were "dying" cultures, only to publicly share, and in many cases grossly misinterpret and misrepresent, stories and ceremonies that were not meant for public consumption (Deloria, 1969). These stories have not faded with time. However, many other Indigenous scholars have laid the groundwork for research that is respectful of Indigenous ways of knowing, in service to community, and allows for communities to have a say in the ways their voices and stories are shared in academia and beyond.

In my research I used the "Four R's of Indigenous educational research": Respect, Relevancy, Reciprocity, and Responsibility (Kirkness & Barnhardt, 1991) as a foundation, but also explored the role of a fifth "R," that of *relationships* in Indigenous methodologies. As I read more and more about Indigenous research methods and approaches, I found validation in the words of other Indigenous scholars. The feelings I had about my research—that it was deeply personal and important not only to me, but to my community, and that importance needed to be reflected in respect and even ceremony, were validated and reified through these scholarly works. There is power and importance in relationships in an Indigenous research agenda, where Western value judgments such as validity and statistical significance come secondary to fulfilling obligations in a research relationship, "that is, being accountable to your relations" (Wilson, 2008, p. 77).

I drew upon Wilson's (2008) notion of research as ceremony and the importance of an Indigenous research paradigm that is "relational and maintains relational accountability" (71). He says: "Research is a ceremony . . . the purpose of any ceremony is to *build stronger relationships* or bridge the distance between the cosmos and us. The research that we do as Indigenous People is a ceremony that allows us a raised level of consciousness and insight into our world" (Wilson, 2008, p. 137; emphasis mine). With this frame in mind, I entered into the ceremony of my research, keeping relationships and reciprocity at the center.

My understanding of reciprocity and relationships in the research process began at the micro level, with the individual relationships with each of my students, but also carried through to broader ideas about the use of my research to Indian Country as a whole. With the students in my study, I thought about reciprocity in the small things, such as buying meals and bringing small gifts, volunteering to edit essays for school or transfer applications, providing advice about summer opportunities and helping with resumes, and other small but tangible ways. I did this in an effort to honor values of reciprocity and to ensure that I wasn't only taking from my students and not providing anything in return. On a broader level, I thought about reciprocity in the overall goals of my research. From the first days of graduate school, I knew that my project needed to serve

Native peoples and Indian Country as a whole. I desired to move our communities forward, and advance ideas of self-determination, sovereignty, and nation-building—an endeavor that meant uprooting many colonial notions of research.

It is with these experiences and theoretical grounding that I embarked upon this project. My story of becoming a Native researcher is a continuing journey, and one that includes constant transformation, learning, and growth. One of my classmates once asked me, after hearing about Indigenous methodologies, "How is that different than just good qualitative research?" In many ways, Indigenous methods are "just good research," but they also constitute a level of responsibility, accountability, and commitment that many non-Native researchers may not be able to understand (Smith, 2012; Kovach, 2010; Wilson, 2008). Additionally, if history is any indication, many "good researchers" have not properly engaged in these practices. I have learned, and continue to learn, that in order to perform research grounded in the service of self-determination, sovereignty, and community empowerment, I must acknowledge and be in relationship not only with my subjects, but also with our communities, our lands, and our ancestors. I also must balance those relationships with reciprocity. Native college students use ideas of "giving back" as motivation to complete their college degrees, and this can be seen as an act of transformational resistance to oppressive, white, patriarchal institutions of higher education (Brayboy, 2005). I see this framework extended to my own research—I am acquiring "credentials and skills for the empowerment and liberation of American Indian communities" (p. 196). It is through the lens of my own past experiences and the support of Indigenous and decolonizing methodologies that I created this study.

Methods

The data for this chapter come from a larger portraiture study (Lawrence-Lightfoot & Davis, 1998). Portraiture, in many ways, is a natural fit with Indigenous and decolonizing methodologies, for its focus on voice, agency, and researcher positionality. It is a methodology designed to "capture the richness, complexity and dimensionality of human experience in social and cultural context, conveying the perspectives of the people who are negotiating those experiences" (Lawrence-Lightfoot & Davis, 1997, p. 3), which combines rigorous empirical inquiry with aesthetics and the art of writing to create research that is accessible to a wide range of audiences in the academy and beyond. The method concerns itself with a search for "goodness," though realizing that goodness is inherently "laced with imperfection" (9).

The search for goodness allowed my research to move away from the narratives of failure that dominate the research on Native students in higher education and instead to focus on stories of strength and success. However, the aim is not to romanticize or idealize. The path to success is paved with challenges, setbacks, and contradictions, and in performing this research I sought to maintain a standard of authenticity—wishing to highlight true and authentic portrayals, not a romantic ideal. Second, situating my own voice and perspective in the research project was extremely important because of my many roles and relationships with College Horizons—as participant, alumna, faculty member, and researcher. Portraiture contains an "explicit recognition of the use of self as the primary research instrument for documenting and interpreting the perspectives and experiences of the people and the cultures being studied" (Lawrence-Lightfoot & Davis, 1997, p. 14). Instead of viewing this as a deficit or bias, my personal perspectives offer strength to the study and analysis.

Portraiture is written in a narrative form, full of thick description of place and context, use of metaphor, and with the researcher voice providing the analytic insight that moves the research story forward, offering questions, theoretical interventions, and possible alternate explanations. This deep relationship of the researcher to the physical place and space of the interactions, attention to participant voice and perspective, and researcher voice bring together many of the values of Indigenous methodologies.

Student Perspectives

After a summer of research attending two College Horizons programs and navigating the space as both a researcher and a small group leader, I chose four of my incredible students to follow through their freshman year of college—Duca, Bryan, Noelani, and Megan. I selected these particular students in an attempt to represent various demographics that make up Indian Country and a range of college experiences. Within my sample, I have a student at a public flagship university (Bryan), two at elite private colleges (Megan and Noelani), and a student at a prestigious music school, who is now a transfer student (Duca). I have reservation perspectives, mixed-race perspectives, urban Native perspectives, first-generation college bound, private high schools, public high schools, single-parent households, male and female, and more—including the intersections between these varying dimensions of identity. While the students are in the study because of their identity as "Native," I also believe that these other pieces of their identity equally contribute to their experiences as marginalized students, and we cannot separate these various dimensions (Crenshaw, 1991).

On the basic mechanics level, this study consisted of more than a year of work with the students, with monthly or bimonthly conversations either over Skype, phone, or in person, a two- to three-day visit with them on their college campuses, and a home visit with each. In addition, there were the materials and documents from our time at CH, as well as from the students' courses and classes in their first year of college. They also graciously allowed me access to their social media profiles—Twitter, Facebook, and Instagram, to gain insight into their day-to-day college lives. While this chapter is not written in traditional portraiture form, the broader study and methods underlie my approach and findings.

I will now offer short introductions to each student to provide individual context and voice before exploring their experiences through their freshman year in a more collective manner.

Noelani. Noelani identifies as a first-generation, low-income college student. She is Native Hawaiian and Black, Jamaican specifically. She grew up in Southern California, raised by a single mom who worked her hardest to get her daughters all of the educational opportunities she could. As a result of her mom's advocacy, Noelani attended a wealthy, high-powered private high school on a scholarship. She attends Stanford University, where she has taken time to explore her Black roots, living in the African American theme dorm on campus, and working closely with the Black Community Services Center. She is an explorer, a risk taker, and a confident student.

Bryan. Bryan is Navajo, and was born off the reservation to a college-enrolled single mom, who then graduated and moved her son back the reservation. He attended a private parochial school on the Navajo Nation for high school, and then enrolled in the competitive BA/MD program at University of New Mexico. His motivation for getting his MD is to come back to the reservation and be a doctor for his people, while being able to combine traditional Navajo beliefs with Western medicine. He is a hard worker, a keen navigator, and strives to embody the Navajo concept of "hozho"—walking in balance and beauty.

Duca. Duca is Aquinnah Wampanog and Black, from the Boston area. He comes from a highly educated family, with both parents having PhDs, though they divorced when he was a child. For his freshman year, Duca attended Berklee College of Music, a highly selective professional music school, but found the experience isolating, expensive, and not living up to his college expectations, so he transferred at the end of his sophomore year, to Wake Forest University. Duca is charismatic, a deep thinker, a brilliant musician and producer, and dedicated to social and racial justice.

Megan. Megan is Eastern Cherokee, and was raised off the reservation throughout the southern United States. In high school, after her parents' divorce, she moved to the reservation with her mother and siblings. Through this transition, she developed a strong dedication to serving her Cherokee people, and is a pre-med student at Duke University, with the goal of returning home as an obstetrician/gynecologist. Megan is kind, thoughtful, committed to her family, and a strong leader in her campus and home communities.

Indigenous Relationships

Vine Deloria described the concept of *place* as "the relationship of things to each other" (Deloria & Wildcat, 2001, p. 22), a striking idea in the context of Native students and college. Place is not just the physical location of their campus, or their homelands; it is the relationship between themselves and that location, as well as the relationship to the others in the environment, and the natural lands their campus or home inhabits. This relational way of thinking about place helps contextualize what it means to be a Native person—it is the importance of place, and therefore the importance of relationships. Wildcat affirms this, saying, "stated simply, indigenous means 'to be of a place'" (Deloria & Wildcat, 2001, p. 31).

My work with these students showed me that relationships can be expanded and re-interpreted, looking at relationships to campus communities, to place and home, and to tribal communities, as well as my own relationships to the students, to college horizons, and to research more broadly. This research is additionally about place—physical locations of home, school, dorm, classroom, and the intersections contained within. It is also about power. It is about the power of education to create and transform students, communities, and nations; it is about the power contained in individual students; and it is also about the power of research to be a tool for positive change, social justice, and giving back.

In each of these students' experiences, we can see the complications and challenges of entering a college environment as a Native student and navigating these complex relationships. Noelani, Megan, Duca, and Bryan have found success on their college campuses, though that success did not come without challenge and struggle. In the following section, I will examine the relationships the students have engaged in, and where their ideas and experiences intersect, as well as where they diverge. I will end by offering lessons and implications for universities, communities, and research that come out of this work.

In beginning this process of synthesis, I offer Lawrence-Lightfoot and Davis's (1998) assertion that "in the particular lies the general"—I do not wish to draw upon the students' experiences as a means to generalize the entire population of Native college-enrolled students. I in fact hope for the opposite. I hope to highlight the particularities and importance of each individual student experience, with the hope of illuminating broader themes and thoughts that may resonate with a larger population. This is an idea with which Deloria agrees, saying, "The key to understanding Indian knowledge of the world is to remember that the emphasis was on the particular, not on general laws and explanations of how things worked" (Deloria & Wildcat, 2001, p. 22).

Relationships to Campus Communities

While much of the research on Native students in college emphasizes the academic aspects of the college experience, interestingly the majority of the actions and interactions that I observed were not those in the classroom, or those that occurred in the classroom were not necessarily about the academic content of the course. The moments, spaces, and interactions that shaped and defined the relationships of the students to their college environments were the outside-the-classroom interactions, relationships, and spaces. This was a phenomenon that Brayboy (1999) observed in his study of Ivy League Native students as well—the social spaces and navigational strategies emerged as the salient above and beyond the academics. Brayboy also demonstrated, as did my students, that the lines between academic and social spaces and strategies are often made unnecessarily distinct in the literature on students in college. The reality is that the boundaries between the two are far more permeable. Guillory (2009) identified tension between these two spheres as well in examining academic versus social supports as a means for persistence—administrators on campus identified academic supports as a key factor in getting Native students to graduation, whereas Native students themselves identified the social supports (such as Native American programs and spaces) as much more important.

I think about an interaction I observed in Megan's chemistry course—her fellow group-mates actively questioned us about our Native backgrounds, our relationships to our communities, and broader questions about Native peoples in the United States. This experience occurred while Megan and her group were simultaneously working on their problem set for class. While Megan and her group may have been working to complete the academic task at hand, it also was necessary for her to engage and navigate the questions about her Native identity—even while physically in the classroom space. Additionally, for the other students, conversations about classes and classroom interactions took a backseat to conversations about relationships, interactions with fellow students and faculty, and where they were finding support.

As a student at Stanford, I relied heavily on the Native American Cultural Center on campus as a source of support—using my work-study hours at the center, doing my schoolwork there, working with the writing tutor on site, and as a social space, connecting with other students. When I began this research, I fully assumed that the students would utilize these support networks on their campuses, if they were available. But I was surprised to find that none of the students engaged with the Native communities on their campuses during their first year, beyond a scattering of largely social events. When I began to think about my own experiences more deeply, I realized that I, too, didn't become actively involved in the community until my sophomore year. Researchers have found that these affinity groups and spaces are important for Native students, though Jackson et al. (2003) did find that students might be initially reluctant to join the organizations. This reluctance may have been the students' resistance to the institution—viewing the student services as a part of the institution, and not wishing to feed into a system that served to keep them marginalized (Brayboy, 1999).

It was interesting to me that these support systems weren't something the students naturally gravitated toward. Native community centers can serve as a "switchboard" of sorts, providing a one-stop location for students to get connected quickly with resources on campus (Guillory, 2009; Martin, 2005), and though the students didn't engage with the Native communities on campus—Bryan didn't even know his campus *had* a Native community service center—they did all (with the exception of Duca) have a structured system of support that provided the connections and resources they needed to find success.

For Noelani, that support was the Leland Scholars Program (LSP), which provided aid in the transition to Stanford over the summer, but also had ongoing programming, social spaces, advisors checking in, and other support through the year. Megan had Cardea, a pre-med program which offered a similar structure and support, especially on the academic side of things, helping her navigate the challenges of a pre-med program—from planning her weekly schedule to providing mandatory study sessions. Bryan's BA/MD program provided academic and social networks throughout his first year, which carried over to his living space as well, as he lived with his cohort-mates. For Noelani, Bryan, and Megan, not only did they have resources and support on campus, they also had a network of adults and advisors who cared about their progress, checking in often, knowing their names and their stories, and who became a familiar face and name on a large campus. As Megan told me during my visit to Duke, when you "just die" from the stress and challenges, having faculty and adults who know your name and check in with you can be what she needs to get through. The community aspects of these programs seem to be critical as well, creating built-in friend networks and social spaces that can help the students maintain balance in their hectic lives.

The commonalities that emerged out of these structured programs were a network of caring adults, which is a success factor identified in the literature (HeavyRunner & DeCelles, 2002; Jackson et al., 2003), as well as a peer community that assisted with social integration into the campus community. The academic support is not to be discounted—though many of the interactions that emerged as salient in the portraits occurred outside of the classroom, for Megan, Bryan, and Noelani, all interested in being pre-med, having resources to guide them through the challenging core science classes allowed them to be successful.

Duca, on the other hand, had no such program or structure on his campus. He had a group of friends, and his family off-campus, but in our interactions, I never heard him mention a network on campus that helped him to find community or support, and that was evident in our interviews. He felt disconnected and a bit lost on his campus, which ultimately contributed to his decision to transfer. He criticized the institution and the way they set up events to encourage interaction, like his early orientation events, but had no plan in place to assist students in connecting with each other or resources on campus. Duca wanted and needed community and support, but without a structure for that support on his campus, he was left to negotiate on his own.

While I was initially surprised that the students didn't immediately become involved in their Native communities on campus, it makes sense—they didn't necessarily need the support that the community could provide. All of their programs (LSP, Cardea, BA/MD) had other Native students involved, as well as students of color, so there was affirmation of their backgrounds in those spaces as well. Now in their sophomore years, Megan, for example, has become the secretary for the Native student group on campus and Noelani is involved in the big sib/little sib program at the Native center—they are reaching out now that they've established their roots and community on campus. In my own experiences, it was during my second year on campus that I began to realize the constant microaggressions (Solórzano, Ceja, & Yosso, 2000) and affronts to my Native background were not going away. I knew I needed a space where I could be around other Native peoples who could reflect and affirm my experiences—though this work cannot illuminate whether that was the case for Megan, Noelani, and Bryan.

The theories on integration to and navigation of campus communities look closely at the role of culture in the process—and these students each approached their college environments in different ways in regard to their Native backgrounds. Both Bryan and Megan utilized their community and cultural connections as motivation to get them through school and as a source of strength and guidance. Bryan saw his Navajo culture as something he had to *do* everyday—to him his culture was a verb rather than a noun. I also see resonances with Brayboy's (2004) study of Ivy League students and maintenance of cultural integrity. Like the culturally traditional students in Brayboy's study, Bryan didn't often speak up in class—and when he did, he remarked that he "thinks differently" than his classmates. He relayed a story of a professor asking if anyone knew how long sheep lived, and Bryan telling the class that he didn't know because they butchered them before they died naturally. His decision to speak up about the sheep, which subsequently in his words "scared away the white people," demonstrated that, while he felt he could reconcile the differences between his Navajo ways of knowing and the university ways of knowing internally, speaking out only served to otherize and marginalize him in the classroom. He was able to preserve his cultural integrity by remaining, in his words, "a typical introverted Navajo."

The students built and negotiated relationships with their campus communities, outside the classroom, inside the classroom, and through structured systems of support. The literature identified many success factors that occur in the relationships between Native students and their campus communities, and my students affirmed many of these findings—and were able to access and build many of these relationships in one location through their structured support programs. Duca's relationship with his campus community was strained, ultimately leading to his decision to transfer—demonstrating the importance of finding a way to belong on campus.

Relationships with Their Nations

For Native peoples, the idea of "home" is complex—home is where you were raised, where you currently live, where your community is based, and also where your homelands are, as well as your relationship to your tribal nation. So when I attempt to think through what "home" means for each of these students, I realize there are layers, and constant tensions and balances between them. For Noelani, home is in San Pedro, California, but it is also with her family and ancestors in Hawaii. At Stanford, her home is Ujamaa, the Black ethnic theme dorm, and with the Black community on campus. For Duca, home is Cambridge, Medford, and Boston, Massachusetts, but also Martha's Vineyard, where his tribe is based. For him, it was a challenge to find his home in the Berklee environment, so instead he remained rooted in his home and family in Boston, where he felt comfortable and supported. He wants to continue to build his connection to his homelands and community on the Vineyard, and make that a place and space that can be a home for him as well. Bryan is lucky in that his home is also his homelands, where his people come from and have always been, and he knows that he wants to return home to his people. But his home also pulls him away from campus, having to decide if he'll travel back to the reservation on weekends to assist his stepfather in ceremonies and dances, or remain at UNM. Megan seeks to find home wherever she is, and sees herself "at home" in many environments—with her family in Georgia and Mississippi, on the reservation, and on Duke's campus. But to her, there is an additional layer of importance to her "home" in Cherokee, knowing that her people and culture are grounded in that place and those lands.

For Megan and Bryan, giving back to their homes and nations is their entire motivation for moving through college. They see the challenges and problems in their communities and see it as their role to return home and make changes in those areas. Megan clearly feels that her community and family have given her so much, so it only seems fair for her to give them something in return. She also has a keen understanding of her role as a citizen of her tribe, seeing it as a responsibility that can give her strength. Bryan wants to be able to be a doctor in the community that understands and sees the importance of traditional Navajo culture and methods of healing, as well as Western ways of knowing. He wants to be able to tell a patient to "see the medicine man" on a prescription pad alongside Western medicine. For these two students, giving back to their communities is not just the outcome of their education; it is the *reason* for their education.

However much motivation and power the students are able to draw from their desires to return to their communities, there are also deep personal sacrifices and costs that they must balance to do this work. This is reflected in Brayboy's (2005) work on transformational resistance and social justice, studying the experiences of Native students with degrees returning to their communities. Brayboy addresses the problem of "reintegration"—while communities push for their students to go to college and "come back," often neither the infrastructure nor the jobs are available to support them in that process. Additionally, students can feel separated from their community, as if college has "marked" them as apart. For the students in my study, these are challenges they may encounter in the future, but for right now, so early in their college careers, the desire (and expectation) of "giving back" creates an immense amount of pressure. While other non-Native students may be applauded and rewarded for heading off to Wall Street to make money and gain power, it is unclear if this would always be the case for Native students. Native students have the weight of their tribe on their shoulders, and this is a huge burden for a teenager to carry.

In addition, the path to giving back is clear for Megan and Bryan, the pre-med students in the study. They have a clear path laid out for them, knowing that after undergraduate success and medical school, they can return to their communities and work for Indian Health Services (IHS)—thereby accomplishing their goal to give back to their community. They know the path is long and hard, but at least it is clear. For Noelani and Duca, who are still figuring out what route their journey will take, the path to giving back is less clear. I feel that we have a disconnect in these areas in our communities. We press rhetoric and ideals of nation-building, sovereignty, and self-determination, and see education as the means to accomplish that goal—yet we have not set up the structures to show students the multitude of forms that can take, or provide the support to bring the students back home and reintegrate them into the community.

Is Duca becoming a music producer and creating socially conscious music giving back? Is Noelani becoming a doctor and focusing on tropical infectious diseases giving back? I would argue that the mere existence of Noelani and Duca is a giving back to their communities. They are strong, soon-to-be-college-educated Native students who will bring their culture and heritage with them wherever they go. While we have desperate and pressing needs in our communities, Native peoples are also completely invisible in mainstream society. We are not well represented in areas of business, science, arts, or media. As a result, Native peoples continue to be represented by and associated with stereotypes of historic or cartoon images, wild Indians with tomahawks and braids. I often argue that in order for mainstream society to recognize our "real" problems, we need to challenge these representations. Having Native peoples in all sectors of society is a part of that process, and in an indirect way, then can contribute to the nation-building of our communities. In order for our communities to assert our rights of sovereignty, we need allies outside of our tribes. We need businesses that will work with tribes directly, we need congressmen and -women who will support sovereignty in the U.S. government, we need teachers to educate non-Native students about the history and power of Native communities.

In thinking about relationships with nations, there is also a thread of authenticity that came up in all of the students' experiences—what makes them a "real" or "authentic" Native person? What does it mean to be a tribal citizen? This is a theme examined by other scholars working with Native college students (Garrod and Larimore, 1997; Brayboy, 1999, 2004, 2005), with Brayboy referring to students navigating their "Indianness," or what I would call "Nativeness." For Bryan, connection to traditional culture and community was how he determined authenticity, especially cultural markers from his own Navajo community, noting how interacting with other Navajo students who "knew their clans" was important to him, and in our interviews pausing to question what I meant by "Native student"—did they know their language and their traditions? Noelani made a distinction between herself and the other Native students at CH, saying that it was powerful to see students who had such a deep spiritual connection to their cultures. She is still negotiating what her Hawaiian identity means to her experience as a young woman of color.

Megan and I had long discussions about identity and belonging, talking about our own experiences as young Cherokee women. She has a sophisticated understanding of her own tribal citizenship, thanks to her mother "really working with her" to understand how she fits into the community and what rights and responsibilities her citizenship confers. She and I also talked about "young Native identity" and, since Native students are enrolling in college at rates unprecedented in any previous generation, what it will mean for there now to be a generation of highly educated Native young people. For Megan, citizenship does have some level of responsibility to give back. And for Duca, his connection to his nation was about ownership and knowledge. He asked, "who owns me and my identity?" and tied his authenticity back to his own knowledge of his family and tribal history. Being about to "shoot back" with knowledge was what made him feel secure in who he is as an Aquinnah Wampanoag person.

The relationships between students and their nations was at the heart of my interest in the study—since the language of nation-building is a part of the curriculum of CH, Noelani, Megan, Duca, and Bryan were exposed directly to these ideas. While the literature is clear that "giving back" is a success factor and motivation that many Native students have relied on for decades, the framework of nation-building and education's role in that process is relatively new. What the experiences of my students demonstrate is that giving back is still a motivation, but being able to conceptualize your role as a tribal citizen and community member at this early stage of college is dependent on your relationship with your nation prior to enrollment. For Bryan and Megan, who already had strong commitments and connections to their tribal communities, thinking about their degrees as a way to build up their nations felt natural. For Duca and Noelani, on the other hand, they and I struggled to see where they fit into the process. While realizing that the students still have three more years to learn, grow, and change, it also demonstrates the need to think more deeply about the ways we can discuss how tribal citizens can still be engaged in the nation-building process more broadly, or think about the ways to engage tribal citizens and community members who are still growing their connections.

Implications for Universities

From the students' stories and experiences, several implications for universities emerge. The first is the importance of person-to-person connections and interactions for students, whether that comes from an administrator, a structured support system, a Native community center, or a caring faculty member, in each of the students' journeys these ties (or lack thereof) to individuals on campus were the make-or-break for their first-year experiences. In large campuses where Native students may be one of only a few, these personal relationships can be critical. From their experiences, it also becomes clear that the supporters don't necessarily have to be Native themselves—just have a willingness to support and learn.

The second implication would be in the realm of reintegration and relationships to "home" and tribal nations. NNCUs at this point rarely think about the journey back home to Indian Country for Native students, and this is a process that can and should begin much earlier in the college journey. NNCUs can begin by building strong connections with the local tribal communities, and creating opportunities for students (Native and non-Native) to engage with these communities through their coursework, volunteer opportunities, or events. These ongoing relationships can help Native students see the relevancy of their degrees for Native communities more broadly, and provide tangible skills that may make their transition back to their home community easier, if that is their ultimate goal. The connections with tribal nations can be continued through funding for summer internships on tribal lands, or even loan repayment programs that would allow students to have university debt forgiven if they engage in public service work (including tribal work). While there is still much to do to facilitate the "giving back" that students aspire to, NNCUs have existing structures that can be re-applied in new and creative ways.

Implications for Research in Higher Education

This study and approach to Indigenous research methods can offer lessons for future research in higher education with Native students. In order to fully understand the experiences of Native students navigating the college process, we need to understand the relationships that they hold and negotiate, and see these as central to their experiences. Much of the research today on Native students still operates from a deficit perspective, reporting results that delineate what students are lacking, the reasons for their failures, or the barriers they need to overcome. An Indigenous research approach asks the researcher to build and acknowledge relationships through the research, and search for ways to make the research respectful, relevant, reciprocal, and responsible (Kirkness & Barnhardt, 1991). If we think about our research in higher education as a ceremony meant to build stronger relationships (Wilson, 2008), it means the results of our research will not be a laundry list of the ways Native students are failing, but rather an exploration that showcases their complexities, their complications, their desires, their thoughts, and their strengths. If our goals in research are to see our students succeed, beginning with relationships is the heart of that work.

When I began this research I wanted to explore what it would mean to build a study that grounded my own experiences and centered the relationships that were crucial to my success as a student but also to my identity as a Native woman—and found that balance through Indigenous methodologies and portraiture. In this research process, I saw that Megan, Duca, Noelani, and Bryan, as diverse, multifaceted Native students, each engaged in their own relationships in different ways, but at the center was the desire to more fully understand their place in their universities, homes, Native nations, and the world at large. It is my hope that Native communities, universities, and students can take these student experiences and begin to think about what it means to engage indigenous relationships in the college process.

References

Brayboy, B. M. (1999). Climbing the ivy: Examining the experiences of academically successful Native American Indian undergraduate students at two Ivy League universities (Unpublished doctoral dissertation). University of Pennsylvania, Philadelphia, PA.

Brayboy, B. M., & Deyhle, D. (2000). Insider-outsider: researchers in American Indian communities. *Theory into Practice*, *39*(3), 163–169.

Brayboy, B. M. J. (2004). Hiding in the ivy: American Indian students and visibility in elite educational settings. *Harvard Educational Review*, *74*(2), 125–152.

Brayboy, B. M. J. (2005). Transformational resistance and social justice: American Indians in Ivy League universities. *Anthropology and Education Quarterly*, *36*(3), 193–211.

Carmen, A. Z. (2006). Recruiting Native American college students: "Why don't they just show up from their high schools like other students do?." Unpublished doctoral dissertation, University of Oregon.

Crenshaw, K. (1991). Mapping the margins: Intersectionality, identity politics, and violence against women of color. *Stanford Law Review*, 1241–1299.
Deloria, V. (1969). *Custer Died for Your Sins: An Indian Manifesto*. Norman, OK: University of Oklahoma Press.
Deloria, V., & Wildcat, D. (2001). *Power and Place: Indian Education in America*. Golden, CO: Fulcrum Publishing.
Garrod, A., & Larimore, C. (1997). *First Person, First Peoples*. Ithaca, NY: Cornell University Press.
Guillory, R. M. (2009). American Indian/Alaska Native college student retention strategies. *Journal of Developmental Education*, *33*(2), 14.
Guillory, R. M., & Wolverton, M. (2008). It's about family: Native American student persistence in higher education. *The Journal of Higher Education*, *79*(1), 58–87.
HeavyRunner, I., & DeCelles, R. (2002). Family education model: Meeting the student retention challenge. *Journal of American Indian Education*, *41*(2), 29–37.
Jackson, A., Smith, S., & Hill, C. (2003). Academic persistence among Native American college students. *Journal of College Student Development*, *44*(4), 548–565.
Keene, A. J. (2016). College pride, Native pride: A portrait of a culturally grounded precollege access program for American Indian, Alaska Native, and Native Hawaiian students. *Harvard Educational Review*, *86*(1), 72–97.
Kirkness, V. J., & Barnhardt, R. (1991). First nations and higher education: the four R's—respect, relevance, reciprocity, responsibility. *Journal of American Indian Education*, *30*(3), 1–15.
Kovach, M. E. (2010). *Indigenous Methodologies: Characteristics, Conversations, and Contexts*. Toronto: University of Toronto Press.
Lawrence-Lightfoot, S., & Davis, J. H. (1998). *The Art and Science of Portraiture*. San Francisco, CA: Jossey-Bass.
Martin, R. (2005). Serving American Indian students in tribal colleges: lessons for mainstream colleges. *New Directions for Student Services* (109), 79–86.
Pavel, D. M., & Padilla, R. V. (1993). American Indian and Alaska native postsecondary departure: an example of assessing a mainstream model using national longitudinal data. *Journal of American Indian Education*, *32*(2), 1–23.
Shotton, H. J., Oosahwe, S. L., & Cintrón, R. (2007). Stories of success: Experiences of American Indian students in a peer-mentoring retention program. *The Review of Higher Education*, *31*(1), 81–107.
Shotton, H. J., Yellowfish, S., & Cintrón, R. (2010). Island of sanctuary: The role of an American Indian culture center. In L. D. Patton (Ed.), *Culture Centers in Higher Education: Perspectives on Identity, Theory, and Practice*, Sterling, VA: Stylus, 49–62.
Shotton, H. S., Lowe, S. C., & Waterman, S. J. (Eds.). (2013). *Beyond the Asterisk: Understanding Native American College Students*. Sterling, VA: Stylus.
Smith, L. T. (2012). *Decolonizing Methodologies: Research and Indigenous Peoples*. London: Zed Books.
Solórzano, D., Ceja, M., & Yosso, T. (2000). Critical race theory, racial microaggressions and campus racial climate: the experiences of African-American college students. *Journal of Negro Education*, 69(1/2), 60–73.
Springer, M., Davidson, C., & Waterman, S. J. (2013). "Native American Student Affairs Units," in *Beyond the Asterisk: Understanding Native American College Students*. Sterling, VA: Stylus.
Waterman, S. J. (2012). Home-going as a strategy for success among Haudenosaunee college and university students. *Journal of Student Affairs Research and Practice*, 49(2), 193–209.
Wilson, S. (2008). *Research Is Ceremony: Indigenous Research Methods*. Winnipeg: Fernwood.

CHAPTER 5

Story Rug

WEAVING STORIES INTO RESEARCH

Amanda R. Tachine (Navajo)

During my dissertation journey, I began to see research as a weaving process. I am neither an expert nor an avid rug weaver; only at this point in time an interested, curious learner. Growing up on the Navajo reservation, much of my knowledge of rug weaving has been from formal schooling, observing Navajo weavers, listening to stories from family, and from embarking on my own novice attempts at weaving. In this chapter, I explain how the formation of what I term *story rug* evolved. I begin with sharing the powerful effect Indigenous methodology and stories had on me as a Navajo woman, which ultimately helped me to find the courage to begin weaving my story rug. I then briefly explain my research with Navajo first-year college students' stories as they journeyed into college. I provide a condensed overview of the research to help contextualize the story rug development. Using story rug as an Indigenous methodological structure, I next describe and elaborate on my progression in weaving the story rug throughout the dissertation. I conclude with final thoughts on how story rug and Indigenous metaphorical frameworks can deepen methodological approaches in research.

Indigenous Methodology, Stories, and My Awakening

As Manulani Aluli Meyer asserts, "We must develop new theories from ancient agency so we can accurately respond to what is right before our very eyes" (2008, p. 217), meaning that Indigenous methodology has been a part of our life since time immemorial to help us answer many of the questions of today. Indigenous peoples have skillfully passed on methodology through storytelling. Storytelling and stories within Native societies encompass symbolism and philosophical formations (Cook-Lynn, 2008) that remain profoundly critical to understanding and navigating through the multifaceted dimensions of life (Archibald, 2008; Denetdale, 2014; Kovach, 2009; Smith, 1999; Wilson, 2008).

Cajete (1994) asserts that experiential stories are essential for learning and in forming positive transformation for Indigenous communities. Stories provide a space to learn from and unite with others, as listening to or reading a story privileges us to be connected to or belong to that story world. Story and knowing, or method and meaning, is an inseparable relationship such that "stories are vessels for passing along teachings, medicines, and practices that can assist members of the collective" (Kovach, 2009, p. 95). And a collective, "*we*" concept is what centers Indigenous methodology as stories are often conveyed with someone or with others for the betterment of those listening (Meyer, 2001; Archibald, 2008). For Native peoples, stories are a legitimate tool for relating with others, sharing knowledge across generations, analyzing life circumstances, and seeking solutions for the future.

During the dissertation journey, I immersed myself in Indigenous methodological scholarship as a way to grasp what it means to utilize Indigenous methods in research. But as I read, I struggled with how to make the connection between Navajo teachings and research. Allow me to explain what awakened within me to understand that intricate relationship. I recall feeling a sense of relief and excitement when I submitted a draft of my findings chapter to my dissertation advisor. I felt confident that the chapter was well written, and I naively believed that I would only need to make a few edits. Days later, I received a thoughtful and critical email from my advisor in which she encouraged me that I could do a better job and suggested that I dig deeper in my analysis. I was crushed. My confidence plummeted. In my mind I was thinking, "I can't do better. This is the best I could do. Maybe the doctoral degree is not for me? Maybe writing is indeed my weakness?" Insecurities resurfaced as I questioned my ability to dig deeper and complete the dissertation.

I took a few days to gather myself. Then, early one morning, I prayed and sought guidance from the Creator about how to dig deeper in research. While praying, I heard a quiet voice that delicately told me, "Write like you are weaving a rug." At that moment, I recognized that weaving a rug was like weaving stories. Meyer eloquently states, "The spirituality of knowledge . . . [is] the light of fundamental empirical knowing" (2008, p. 218). I understood what Meyer meant in acknowledging that *spirit* and *knowing* are intricately connected just as story and knowing are linked together. Immediately, I started writing. I surrendered my ego and wrote from the light of fundamental empirical knowing. And in that writing process, the story rug emerged.

Indigenous Storywork and Narrative Analysis: Interpretative Strategies

Before I share the components of the story rug framework, I provide a brief overview of Indigenous Storywork (Archibald, 2008) and narrative analysis (Riessman, 2008), which were the interpretative strategies that guided my process. To be clear, my dissertation research focused on ten Navajo college freshmen students' experiential stories as they navigated into college. By placing Navajo students' stories at the center of analysis, I de-centered the dominant discourse that too often generalizes Native student experiences and individualizes Natives as deficits.

In gathering stories this way, I employed a combination of qualitative methodologies. Indigenous Storywork (Archibald, 2008) and Narrative Inquiry (Riessman, 2008) both feature stories as an influential mode of inquiry. Indigenous Storywork was developed by Jo-Ann Archibald (from the Sto:lo Nation) in her work with Sto:lo and Coast Salish elders and storytellers as a way to bridge Indigenous storytelling into formal educational contexts. Seven theoretical principles guide Indigenous Storywork, including adhering to respect, responsibility, reciprocity, reverence, holism, interrelatedness, and synergy. Overall Indigenous Storywork acknowledges and claims Indigenous ways of knowing into research.

Narrative analysis complements Indigenous ways of knowing such that narrative analysis acknowledges that "Individuals must now construct who they are and how they want to be known" (Riessman, 2008, p. 7). Reclaiming the research space by asserting "who they are and how they want to be known" is a promising step toward decolonizing methodologies (Smith, 1999). Narrative analysis provides a space where people can make sense of the past, engage others in the experiences of the storyteller, and mobilize others into action for progressive change. A distinction of narrative analysis from other forms of qualitative methodology is that, "narrative study relies on extended accounts that are preserved and treated analytically as units, rather than fragmented into thematic categories as is customary in other forms of qualitative analysis" (Riessman, 2008, p. 12). Therefore, individual stories are honored in the gathering stage and throughout the analytical process. However, narrative analysis also acknowledges that individual stories can be moved to generalize theoretical propositions, proposing that the gathering of individual stories creates a powerful unified voice.

Story Rug as an Indigenous Research Framework

Metaphors were integral to this research, as metaphors evoke imagination and ancient wisdom. I found the use of metaphors a natural part of my thinking and writing as metaphors provided a space to visualize and connect difficult thought processes and assert the Navajo way of life. I continued to envision writing like weaving. In Indigenous Storywork, Archibald utilized a metaphorical basket to conceptualize research, and I visualized a Navajo rug—I visualized a story rug.

As I worked to create the story rug, I became more attuned to the knowledge and experiences that go into weaving a Navajo rug. On my trips home to the Navajo Reservation, my family and I would often visit with the Malone family. Bill Malone was a former trader at the historic Hubbell Trading Post located in my hometown of Ganado (Berkowitz, 2011). They now own their own store in Gallup, New Mexico, located on the outskirts of the Navajo Reservation. Since I was a youth, Bill and his wife, Minnie, and their children have been a part of our family's life. Minnie is a remarkable rug weaver. During a recent visit, I was immediately taken with the stunning Navajo rugs that hung from the walls and that were displayed over tables. I heard the gentle thumping sound of a weaving comb. Minnie was diligently working on a rug. I sat near Minnie and observed her hands patiently and meticulously pull charcoal colored wool through the warp. She shared with me stories about weaving, love, and relationships. In listening to her, I began to formulate clearer insights that connected weaving a rug to weaving a dissertation.

Figure 5.1. Eye Dazzler rug woven by my husband's maternal grandmother, Marie Tacheeney

The story rug I wove in my dissertation work has six parts that coincide with components of Navajo weaving. I will briefly explain each part here and then go into more detail throughout this chapter. In chapter 1 of the dissertation, I built the loom (Introduction): I provided a preview into the foundational features of the overall story rug including the purpose, research questions, methods, and significance. In chapter 2, I warped the loom (Literature Review): I presented the literature that shaped my understanding. I provided an overview of Native and Navajo educational attainment and the theoretical frameworks employed. In chapter 3, I gathered the weaving tools (Methodology): I described the methodological design including the interpretative strategies of Indigenous Storywork and narrative analysis, collection of stories, and the analytical process. In chapters 4 and 5 I wove the story rug (Findings). Throughout both chapters, I shared individual and collective stories of the ten Navajo students who participated in the study. Moreover, in chapter 4 I presented the Twin Warriors Story, a Navajo traditional oral story, and discussed how the Twin Warrior story applied to the students' journeys toward college. In chapter 6, I cared for the story rug (Conclusion): I offered implications for practice and recommendations for the future care of the story rug.

In the next sections, I will describe the connection between traditional forms of dissertation chapters (e.g., introduction, literature review, methodology, findings, and conclusions) and the rug weaving process (e.g., building the loom, warping the loom, gathering of story rug tools, weaving stories, and caring for the story rug), which provides a story rug framework for research.

Building the Loom: Introduction

To begin I built the story rug loom. A loom is the frame that holds the rug as it is woven. The loom is constructed using foundational features such as being solidly built with heavy construction materials like wood and metal, allowing the weaver easy access to the loom and positioning it accurately for weaving to occur (Bennett & Bighorse, 1971). In essence, the loom is well constructed in order to withstand the tugs of the weaving process.

In a dissertation, the introduction sets the basis of the overall research. Therefore, I viewed the introduction similarly to building a loom. In this story rug, the loom needed to be well constructed by positioning foundational features. Therefore, in building the story rug loom I included introduction elements such as an articulation of the purpose of the research where I elaborated on the centrality of Native students' experiences. I also articulated the research questions, an overview of the methodology, the significance of the study, and organization of the study as it relates to weaving a rug.

Warping the Loom: Literature Review

Before any creation of weaving begins, the warp needs to be put into place. The warp is thin, tightly spun yarn that is strung up and down in a vertical position throughout the loom. Basically, it is what secures all the strands (weft) together. Setting the warp can be a difficult task, as it needs to be strung tightly to withstand the tension of the weaving process. I see the warp as the binding groundwork upon which the weaver builds. In my research, setting the warp was similar to laying down prior knowledge that eventually helped to shape the story rug.

The purpose of chapter 2 (generally known as the literature review) acknowledges the literature that assisted in explaining how Native students navigate through educational systems and negotiate through challenges that they may experience. I presented an overview of Native educational attainment and the theoretical frameworks, Tribal Critical Race Theory (Brayboy, 2005), Cultural Resilience (Heavyrunner & Marshall, 2003), and Cultural Threads (Tachine, 2015), that guided my research approach.

Warping yarn on a loom can be a strenuous task, as you have to ensure that the warp is wrapped suitably. This process is very similar to crafting a literature review, because pulling together various research pieces into a concise, organized layout can be labor-intensive and tedious. Yet, the process is crucial for creating a well-woven rug.

Gathering of Story Rug Tools: Methods

In preparing to begin the weaving process the weaver gathers tools, which are the key instruments to creating a rug. The tools include the battens which are used to separate the warp sets for easier access; a weaving fork or comb that is used for pounding the weft (horizontal yarn) into position; sacking needles to help with the weaving near the ending stage; and yarn used to create the overall tapestry (Bennett & Bighorse, 1971). Often a mother or grandmother gives these tools to a weaver, as several weavers believe that, "To lend a tool to someone is to give your power. . . . a gift of energy and ideas as well" (p. 10).

I believe that we are given ideas and gifts from scholars and students to help us create a story rug. Chapter 3 served as the process of gathering the story rug tools (methodology) where I described the tools that helped to shape the story rug. The gathering of story rug tools chapter included the interpretative strategies of Indigenous Storywork and narrative analysis, collection of student stories, and my positionality in weaving the students' stories.

Weaving in Students' and Traditional Oral Stories: Findings

Weaving a Navajo rug is a strenuous process for both body and mind. As a beginner in rug weaving, my body is often sore after a day of weaving because it takes much discipline and strength to sit in front of a loom and patiently thread wool in and out of the warp. I not only try to maintain a sense of balance with my body, I am also concentrating on the delicate process of ensuring each single thread is woven just right to create an overall design. In that process, many thoughts dance in my mind as I recognize that my being is connected to the loom and those around me. Maintaining a sense of direction and diligence with the mind is important to the rug weaving process.

Similarly, sifting through student interviews and creating an overall story rug requires much toil for the body and mind. By using a story rug framework, I was able to process through the findings section and maintain the individuality of each of the student stories as well as gather students' experience into collective "designs." And in this example the designs created the themes the students shared in common. I saw the individual story as a single strand in the story rug. I then saw the gathering of student stories as a way to prominently display the designs in the story rug.

In weaving students' stories (findings chapters) I included three sets of stories as a way to capture their individual journeys. The first set is titled the "Student Introduction Stories" where I provide a brief biographical account of the ten students, including where they and their families are from. In the second set of stories, "Students' Schooling Stories," I share the students' schooling experiences, including how they saw themselves as a student, type of schools they attended, and their involvement within their schools. I then included the "Students' College Entrance Stories," as the last sets of stories. Those stories comprised a recollection of when students first thought about college, how many colleges they applied to, and what fields they were interested in studying. These sets of individual stories were threaded throughout the dissertation as a way to maintain the integrity of their experiences. To illustrate an example of the individual story threads, I included a sample of Sarah's story.

Sarah's Story. As I mentioned earlier, I introduced the ten Navajo students by providing a brief biographical account of who they are, where they are from, and their families. This introduction is the customary way for Navajo people to introduce themselves. However, to protect the anonymity of the student, I did not disclose Navajo clans as would be expected from a Navajo perspective. Respectfully, names and towns located on the Navajo Reservation are pseudonyms.

> Sarah had long hair that was usually coiled in a tight bun. She often wore blue jeans, a college t-shirt with a Nike zip-up sweatshirt, and worn running shoes. Her black-framed glasses sat comfortably on her smiley face as she had one of those faces that naturally formed into a warm smile. Sarah was born and raised on the Navajo Nation Reservation, in a small rural town called Purple Hills with roughly 1,200 residents. There were three gas stations, a tiny post office,

a small hospital/clinic, a school campus, and a handful of state/tribal offices sprinkled throughout the town. Modest homes, mobile trailers, and hogans (Navajo traditional dwellings) were spread throughout Purple Hills. Sarah loved to roam through the reservation land riding on her horse. She could spend the entire day riding her horse, travelling to visit friends and family, stopping by the general store, and then spending time alone, feeling free. The youngest of four children, Sara was raised by a "strong" single mom, "loving" maternal grandma, and a "tough" maternal grandpa. Until she was 10 years old, she lived in a hogan that had no running water or electricity. For Sarah, there were fond memories of living in that home. She smiled as she remembered sleeping with her mom and siblings in a full-size bed. Providing loving words when times were rough and celebrating in moments of joy, Sarah believed that "family is the backbone of everything." She recalled always being with her mom and grandma because she did not want to miss an opportunity to learn something from them. Most days Sarah walked nearby to her grandparents' home to ensure that her grandma remembered to take her insulin medicine and that her grandparents were both well and fed. Her four older siblings would jokingly tease her by calling her "the baby" because of her close connection to her grandparents and mom. Although her siblings teased her, they provided a sense of loving protection for Sarah. Sarah's family instilled a value for education in her. For example, Sarah cherished hearing her grandma say, "Nizhónígo [Go in Beauty], Nizhónígo, you're going to school, keep at it." Those words from her grandma were carried close in Sarah's heart as a reminder to strive for education, for she was the first in her family with high aspirations to go to a university. Sarah's purpose in going to college was to one day return to Purple Hills and take care of her grandparents and mom because they were "everything to me."

Navajo Traditional Story: The Twin Warriors Story. In addition to weaving the students' stories, I also included a Navajo traditional oral story of the Twin Warriors story. The story rug was guided, organized, and constructed parallel to the Twin Warriors. I will share the traditional oral story of the Twin Warriors (also referred to as the Monster Slayers) and then I will elaborate on the woven connection between the Twin Warriors and the ten Navajo students.

Changing Woman (Asdzą́ą́ Nádleehé), a central figure in Navajo history and culture, gave birth to twin sons, Born for Water (Tóbájíshchíní) and Monster Slayer (Naayéé' Neizghání). When they reached adolescent age, the twins wanted to know who their father was so they went on a journey to find him. They were guided with favor by gods who created a holy trail paved with rainbows. On their journey, they met Spider Woman (Na'ashjé'ii Asdzą́ą́)

> who shared with the twins that their father was the Sun (Jóhonaa'éí). Spider Woman gave Born for Water and Monster Slayer tools and a prayer to aid them on their quest to find their father. The twins were grateful for Spider Woman's assistance and continued on. As they travelled to find their father, they encountered four different obstacles. They survived each treacherous obstacle because of the tools and prayer that Spider Woman provided and that helped them to stay alive and continue on their journey.
>
> When they finally reached their father's home, Sun put the twins through various tests as a way to determine whether the twins were indeed his. The twins were guided by Wind (Níłch'i) and therefore the twins succeeded each test. Sun then asked, "Now, my children, what do you ask of me?" The twins sought help from their father, requesting that he provide them with weapons to slay the monsters (Naayéé) who were killing the Navajo people. Father Sun provided his children with weapons. The twins were grateful for their father's help and went on their way to face the monsters.
>
> The twin warriors first confronted the Big Giant (Yé'iitsoh) who was very big and powerful. The twins waited for the Big Giant to arrive at a lake which they were told was a place the monster went to daily. The Big Giant came to the lake to drink water and it was there that the twins struck the monster with lightning and arrows. The Big Giant fell down and died. The second confrontation was with the Horned Monster (Déélgééd) who was said to be hard to kill. With the help of Gopher (Na'azísí) and the weapons provided by father Sun, the Horned Monster was defeated. The third conquest was with Bird Monster (Tsé Nináhálééh) and the fourth monster defeated was Who Kills With His Eyes (Bináá' yee Aghání).
>
> After the twins conquered each monster, they returned home to their mother, Changing Woman, to share the news. Changing Woman rejoiced with her two sons and told the great news to the Navajo people. Through their valiant and courageous efforts, the twin warriors were considered heroes to the Navajo people.[1]

In my first interview with one of the ten students, Cecilia, she mentioned the traditional Navajo story of the Twin Warriors as she remembered a high school experience. Cecilia and a classmate gave a presentation on alcoholism among Native Americans to a group of community members. It was at that time that a respected elder commented to her and her co-presenter that they were like the Navajo Twin Warriors. Cecilia recalled, "One of the elders in the group stood up and said, 'You guys are like the epitome of the Twin Warriors. The Twin Warriors traveled from one world to the next to slay monsters and bring knowledge back to the people. You guys are just like the twin warriors, that's amazing, you are bringing knowledge back to community.'" In sharing this experience Cecilia conceptualized how she joined other Native students who were embarking on attending college. And as they navigate through that journey, they are recreating a contemporary version of the Twin Warriors story.

In acknowledging Cecilia's connection to the Twin Warriors story and valuing the role that traditional oral stories have in Indigenous methodology, I included the Navajo Twin Warriors story in my dissertation by highlighting the contemporary "monsters" (challenges) and "weapons" (sources of strength) that influenced the ten Navajo students as they journeyed to college (Tachine, 2015).

Caring for the Story Rug: Conclusion

My mother-in-law, Alta Wauneka, is known in our family as a skilled rug weaver, so I spoke with her about the ending stages of rug weaving. She is patient and kind as she teaches me about Navajo weaving. With her wisdom and insight she shared a beautiful way of caring for the story rug. She told me that once a weaver has completed a Navajo rug, they carefully take it off of the loom by using a needle to unravel the strands that held the rug to the loom. Once the rug is off of the loom, finishing touches are applied to complete the rug. Some Navajos get a damp rag and wipe the rug. In that process, the rug becomes more flexible and is therefore gently stretched into a square or rectangle. Long ago, some Navajos would dig a hole in the ground, dampen the ground with water, and place the rug in the hole to rest. After a day, the weaver would take the rug out of the ground and stretch it in place. The purpose of the water is to nourish the rug, so that it becomes more flexible and thereby more easily stretched into form.

For the conclusion chapter, I took the story rug off of the loom and added finishing touches to ensure that it too would be properly cared for. The final chapter included a "stretching process" where I discussed implications for policy, practice, and research as well as critically examined the monsters and weapons concepts and their contributions to the literature. Then, I "left a strand out" as a way to culturally care for the story rug and for the future story rugs to come. The concept of leaving a strand out is an important distinction of the story rug; therefore, I describe that beautiful significance.

"Leave one strand out." When a rug is finished, Navajo weavers often say, "leave one strand out," meaning that you never close your rug. Alta told me that while weaving, all your thoughts go into the rug, the good thoughts and even the bad ones. Thus, when you are done with your rug, you should leave one strand out because you do not want those thoughts to be trapped. They need to go, to be free. That way you are able to focus on your next rug. With that cultural teaching, my story rug did not close with a typical conclusion; I left a strand out.

Freeing the Strand: Finishing Thoughts

Including metaphors and traditional stories were important steps in reclaiming Indigenous research in higher education. Connecting contemporary students' experiences with the ancient Navajo Twin Warriors story provided a space where research could come to life, meaning illustrating and embodying monsters and weapons created a visual representation that I hope offered a deeper awareness of the connection between spirit and knowing. Contextualizing the dissertation as a rug weaving process not only helped me to organize my thoughts, but allowed individual and collective student stories to be tightly connected and yet individually honored.

Few studies center Indigenous perspectives and methodology in research. I believe that we as researchers create a systematic scholarship hierarchy whereby Native experiences and Indigenous inquiry continue to dwell at the bottom because of the sheer absence of Indigenous scholarship and lack of awareness about its rigor and value. There is a popular thought, "out of sight, out of mind," suggesting that when we do not provide Indigenous experiences, perspectives, and methodology into the discourse, they will continue to be ignored and forgotten.

We need to raise awareness, through research, of an important group of people. This research needs to be done carefully with people who incorporate theories and methods that align with Native values and epistemologies. Working with Tribal nations and Native peoples can help to get a better sense of the type of research needed and the culturally nuanced research protocols to keep in mind. The research process may take longer as there would be another layer of people and number of protocols involved, but the outcome would be worth the time and effort.

Non-Natives can help by encouraging and advocating for Indigenous scholarship. I give much appreciation and credit to my dissertation advisor Dr. Jenny Lee who gently and critically nudged me to "dig deeper" in my research development. As a non-Native, she surrendered control by allowing me to lead in engaging with Indigenous methodology whereby she recognized her place in stepping back, which ultimately sparked the story rug framework. With her support and sincere belief in diverse knowledge production perspectives, I learned about the intellectual beauty and sacredness that Indigenous research offers.

NOTES

I am grateful to Dr. Jo-ann Archibald and Dr. Catherine Riessman for providing a space to allow stories to emerge by respecting the stories that are shared, valuing the knowledge gained through the analytical meaning-making process, and recognizing the interconnectedness between storyteller and listener.

1. Navajo traditional stories including the Twin Warriors story are often told by a male and during the winter months. To honor the students in this study, I share the story in a respectful manner so as to not insinuate that I'm an expert in the Twin Warriors story or in Navajo traditional oral stories. In my attempt to abbreviate a version of the Twin Warriors story, I acknowledge that I sought guidance from various books meant for a range of audience members, from children to adults (Iverson, 2002; Locke, 1992; Mabery, 1991; Austin,

2009). Additionally, as a Navajo, I recall learning this story at various points in my life through oral storytelling in school settings, community meetings, and at occasional social functions with family and friends. Through these multiple sources and experiences, I share the Twin Warriors story in an abbreviated format. Oral storytelling acknowledges that there are various ways to share a story and multiple ways to interpret it; therefore, this version of the Twin Warriors story may be shared and interpreted differently based upon the person telling and the person listening. I encourage further reading and learning of the intricate teachings wrapped within Navajo traditional stories such as the Twin Warriors story, as these stories provide evolving life lessons.

REFERENCES

Archibald, J. (2008). *Indigenous Storywork: Educating the Heart, Mind, Body, and Spirit.* Vancouver, BC: UBC Press.

Austin, R. (2009). *Navajo Courts and Navajo Common Law: A Tradition of Tribal Self-governance.* Minneapolis, MN: University of Minnesota Press.

Bennett, N., & Bighorse, T. (1971). *Working with Wool: How to Weave a Navajo Rug.* Flagstaff, AZ: Northland Press.

Berkowitz, P. D. (2011). *The Case of the Indian Trader: Billy Malone and the National Park Service Investigation at Hubbell Trading Post.* Albuquerque, NM: University of New Mexico Press.

Brayboy, B. (2005). Toward a Tribal Critical Race Theory. *The Urban Review, 37*(5), 425–446.

Cajete, G. (1994). *Look to the Mountain: An Ecology of Indigenous Education.* Durango, CO: Kavaki Press.

Cook-Lynn, E. (2008). History, myth, and identity in the new Indian story. In N. Denzin, Y. Lincoln, & L. Smith (Eds.), *Critical and Indigenous Methodologies* (pp. 329–346). Thousand Oaks, CA: Sage Publishing.

Denetdale, J. (2014). The value of oral history on the path to Dine/Navajo sovereignty. In Lloyd Lee (Ed.), *Dine Perspectives: Revitalizing and Reclaiming Navajo Thought* (pp. 68–82). Tucson, AZ: The University of Arizona Press.

Emerson, L. (2014). Dine culture, Decolonization, and the Politics of Hózhó. In Lloyd Lee (Ed.), *Dine Perspectives: Revitalizing and Reclaiming Navajo Thought* (pp. 49–67). Tucson, AZ: The University of Arizona Press.

HeavyRunner, I., & Marshall, K. (2003). "Miracle Survivors": Promoting resilience in Indian students. *Tribal College Journal, 14*(4), 15–18.

Iverson, P. (2002). *Dine.* Albuquerque, NM: University of New Mexico Press.

Kovach, M. (2009). *Indigenous Methodologies: Characteristics, Conversations, and Contexts.* Toronto: University of Toronto Press.

Locke, R. F. (1992). *The Book of the Navajo.* Los Angeles, CA: Mankind Press.

Mabery, M. V. (1991). *Right after Sundown.* Tsaile, AZ: Navajo Community College Press.

Meyer, M. (2001). Our own liberation: Reflection on Hawaiian epistemology. *The Contemporary Pacific, 13*(1), 124–148.

Meyer, M. (2008). Indigenous and Authentic. In N. Denzin, Y. Lincoln, & L. Smith (Eds.), *Critical and Indigenous Methodologies* (pp. 217–232). Thousand Oaks, CA: Sage Publishing.

Riessman, C. K. (2008). *Narrative Methods for the Human Sciences.* Thousand Oaks, CA: Sage Publishing.

Smith, L. (1999). *Decolonizing Methodologies: Research and Indigenous Peoples.* Dunedin, New Zealand: University of Otago Press.

Tachine, A. (2015). Monsters and weapons: Navajo students' stories on their journeys toward college (Doctoral dissertation). Retrieved from Pro-Quest.

Wilson, S. (2008). *Research Is Ceremony: Indigenous Research Methods.* Nova Scotia, Canada: Fernwood Publishing.

CHAPTER 6

Stealing Horses

INDIGENOUS STUDENT METAPHORS FOR SUCCESS IN GRADUATE EDUCATION

Sweeney Windchief (Assiniboine)

What is your metaphor for education? This question is asked for the specific purpose of prompting what scholars have termed "self-authorship" (Magolda & King, 2008; Pizzolato, 2003; Torres & Hernandez, 2007), in this case specifically through the internal creation of metaphor, with the intent of considering cultural context in successfully navigating graduate education. If you are an Indigenous graduate student this question is for you! Self-authorship assists students in moving from feeling unsatisfied through the development of their own internal perspectives to feeling in control of their own educational destinies. Self-authorship facilitates student self-definition as they internally define their own perspectives in guiding action and knowledge construction (Magolda, 2001). In other words, by metaphorizing their own educational experiences, students are taking ownership of their own education and participating while simultaneously maintaining Indigenous identity.

Owning one's own experience, in any endeavor, is an important part of success. By stating their metaphors, Indigenous students aspiring toward a graduate degree will be better able to protect their Indigenous identities against the problematic phenomenon of assimilation. Education has historically been, and continues to be, experienced as an assimilative practice by Indigenous students. The foundations of this phenomenon are located in assimilation era (1824–1879) policies that were intentionally created to move Indigenous peoples away from aboriginal ontological space and unique cultural identity (Calloway, 2004). The assimilation era was rooted in a political landscape that is historically constructed, and subtly continues to promote assimilation, which is challenging because it erases Indigenous experiences from the educational environment. The literature in the field of American Indian education documents the Western educational institution's role in the homogenization of cultures, as recently stated by Sims: "The policies developed for the Indian education system at the time reflected society's beliefs in a racial hierarchy and in a national identity of progress that was achievable through individual industry. A system of schools for Indigenous students was developed both on and off reservations that would purportedly help students assimilate into the civilized nation and abandon their backward ways" (Sims, 2013, p. 81). Though Indigenous communities are no longer experiencing the official "Assimilation Era" of American history, the assertion of this chapter is that "incidental assimilation" is a current phenomenon and postsecondary educational institutions maintain these practices of assimilation.

"Active" and "passive" assimilation are the potential result of participating in the modern educational paradigm. "Active" assimilation is evident when an Indigenous student willingly turns away from their Indigenous identity in order to be successful in higher education. This is characterized by knowingly disregarding that which makes them Indigenous, including participating in aboriginal community events, forgoing community contributions and responsibilities, and severing their familial connections in order to become successful in the academy. In relation to "active" assimilation, "passive assimilation" occurs when a student experiences the conflict between community and academic expectations, and in order to be successful in school, plays by the rules, and graduates while uncritically accepting a majoritarian perspective in their given academic field.

These phenomena call for an Indigenous response that serves as a critique of the higher educational system in the United States, as well as the implementation of practices that can be utilized by Indigenous students in the successful and culturally conscious navigation of graduate education. The critique of the American educational system comes in terms of relatable curriculum that is well documented in the literature around culturally responsive pedagogy (Belgarde, Mitchell, & Arquero, 2002; Brayboy & Castagno 2009: Carjuzaa & Ruff, 2010; Castagno & Brayboy, 2008; Pewewardy & Hammer, 2003) which is primarily focused on primary-secondary education. In the context of postsecondary education, connections with Indigenous professors and a direct connection between the work that is accomplished in class and its relationship to one's community of origin empowers students in their academic pursuits. The focus of this chapter is to share Indigenous student metaphors applied in the realm of graduate education toward success, defined here as the successful navigation of graduate education while maintaining a strong sense of Indigenous identity.

If the goal for Indigenous students is indeed the attainment of an education that preserves a suitable quality of life and supports the perpetuation of North American Indigenous societies, Indigenous educators and students alike must strive to construct an educational paradigm that is relevant and culturally responsive (Castagno & Brayboy, 2008; Ladson-Billings, 1995; Pewewardy &

Hammer, 2003) to their own lived experiences. Among other practices, this includes adequate preparation for engaging in the culture of higher education, while simultaneously developing the wherewithal to maintain one's Indigenous identity in an often xenophobic campus climate (Flynn, Duncan, & Jorgensen, 2012). In order to combat this phenomenon, scholars have evaluated American Indian retention in college. Guillory and Wolverton's (2008) qualitative study on the experiences of 30 American Indian college students shares that the essential factors for college retention were campus social support, social events, and tribal support. This statement leads the author to offer an additional line of support for Indigenous students, albeit one that is internally constructed in juxtaposition to the external support systems constructed for the purpose of creating an environment for these students' success. Though the efforts made by institutions of higher learning are indeed helpful, it cannot be assumed that these support systems are implemented at all institutions attended by Indigenous students; therefore, internal constructs and concepts that motivate student success are both empowering and necessary, particularly if the students are attending a university where there are few Indigenous students in attendance and consequently few structural support systems in place. This chapter offers a strategic way of reframing Indigenous graduate student experiences toward success regardless of institutional efforts.

Theoretical Foundation

The theoretical grounds for this chapter include the integration of *Decolonizing Methodologies* (Smith, 1999), *Red Pedagogies* (Grande, 2004), and *TribalCrit* (Brayboy, 2005). The question posed in *Decolonizing Methodologies*, "For whom is this work being done?" (Smith, 1999), is the foundation of this chapter. In accordance with Indigenous methodologies, the intention here is to serve Indigenous peoples. Consequently, many of the sources used in this chapter purposely serve Indigenous peoples. With the resolve of not leading scholars into believing that the Indigenous experience is the same for all, the author reiterates that maintaining cultural specificity is essential, as is the intentional participation in transcendent collaborations as Indigenous peoples (Grande, 2004). *Red Pedagogy* calls for Indigenous peoples reaching out to one another to serve Indigenous communities beyond one's own. Also imperative to this chapter is TribalCrit (Brayboy, 2005), particularly the tenets related to storytelling: "Stories are not separate from theory; they make up theory and are, therefore, real and legitimate sources of data and ways of being" (p. 430). Brayboy also states, "Tribal philosophies, beliefs, customs, traditions, and visions for the future are central to understanding the lived realities of Indigenous peoples, but they also illustrate the differences and adaptability among individuals and groups" (p. 429). The author uses these tenets to promote adaptability and pragmatic work particularly within the context of education by encouraging students to create metaphors for their educational journey.

The literature on metaphor as it relates to education shows that though there are many articles pertaining to the field in general (Aubusson, Harrison, & Ritchie, 2005; Botha, 2009; Stofflett, 1996), very few address Indigenous peoples (Cajete, 1999; Henze & Vanett, 1993). Relatable to educational experiences are the practical approaches that focus on actions seeking a construction and consideration of metaphorical notions (Schmidt, 2005). Consciously integrating Indigenous and non-Indigenous scholarship is an investment in higher education while intentionally maintaining cultural integrity.

Indigenous Inquiry

The methodological approach applied in this study was Indigenous action research. Essentially, this is an approach that combines Indigenous research methodologies and action research, which weaves together the practical concerns of Indigenous peoples in a challenging place for the purpose of finding various solutions within a mutually acceptable ethical and sociocultural framework. Thus, from an Indigenous paradigm, one must be able to share how these methods are connected to Indigenous community (Wilson, 2008). These methods help to build respectful relationships between Indigenous education, the author, and the respondents by honoring Indigenous graduate student voices and perspectives through metaphor.

In conversation, the author described the concept of metaphor construction to the participants. This prompted Indigenous students' reflection on their experiences through the creation of their own metaphors. Relating respectfully to the participants helped form a stronger relationship with the ideas that we collectively share.

As the researcher in these interactions, the author's responsibilities included reciprocating by sharing examples of other metaphors as well as his own. It was essential to subsequently return to the respondents to share the finished work to assure that what they said is indeed what they intended to say, and to confirm that it could be made public through this chapter. In fulfilling the author's role and obligation to the participants, he was compelled to consider, "What am I contributing?" In reflecting on the study and in the spirit of connecting it to Indigenous inquiry paradigms, it is paramount to share that this work was done through Indigenous invitation, authorship, and respondent participation. This chapter and the entire book provide an opportunity to share, grow, and learn from various perspectives, including the editors, the authors, the participants, and the readership.

Data Sources

As stated by Denzin and Lincoln (2008), "All observation involves the observer's participation in the world being studied" (p. 49). The research data collection includes a combination of observations, personal conversations, and discourse analysis focusing on three groups of students, some of which overlap: (1) Those who are a part of the author's professional network, (2) Indigenous students taking a course on Indigenous methodologies at a predominately non-Native institution in the intermountain Western United States, and (3) Indigenous students enrolled in a program at the same university whose purpose is to certify and place Indigenous educators into administrative positions at schools with high populations of Indigenous students. All participants are indigenous graduate students, and the gender ratio of the respondents was approximately two-thirds female and one-third male. The time period for data collection and analysis was between April 2013 and February 2015.

The essential question asked of the participants is, "What is your metaphor for education?" This study then used an Indigenous conversational method (Kovach, 2010) through unstructured conversations with students. Subsequent analyses focused on Indigenous graduate student persistence and the connections between Indigenous ontologies and educational experiences. Analyses included related stories, examples, and explanations in reframing education within an Indigenous cultural context.

Through the metaphorization of their experiences, respondents make their own education applicable and meaningful. This process is internally created and expresses student experiences in an ethnocultural context serving to reframe education as a lifelong and meaningful experience. Reflexively, the observations and subsequent assertions are only one interpretation of many, albeit from the perspective of an American Indian male who works in higher education. Being mindful not to inappropriately essentialize or romanticize Indigenous peoples, the author recognizes Indigenous peoples, contemporary peoples who are members of sovereign nations with a long-standing genealogical connection to North America. What follows shows the variability and adaptability of student experiences from culturally unique perspectives.

In the rich conversations with the respondents, multiple metaphors emerged. The majority of responses were positive; however, there were examples that spoke of education as something not to be trusted, those that expressed disdain and reflected a deficit model discourse that is all too prevalent in academic literature, and those that lacked a clear connection to Indigenous conceptualizations of identity. In choosing which participant contributions to share, four criteria were used in alignment with community-centered inquiry for the purpose of doing research "in a good way" (Ball & Janyst, 2008). The criteria were as follows.

- Contributions included would reflect various tribal affiliations and identities.
- The metaphors shared would clearly be centered in an Indigenous paradigm.
- The metaphors described would not reflect deficit model discourse.
- The participant was provided the manuscript and agreed to the inclusion of their contributions in the chapter submission.

As a result, this chapter shares five examples.

Indigenous Student Responses

Given the dearth of applicable curricula, Indigenous students are burdened with the responsibility of making education relevant in their own context. Although there are classes that are aligned with their identity, these courses are viewed primarily as electives by colleges and universities, and the majority of courses taken in disciplines related to education are not centered in Indigenous ontological space. In other words, Indigenous curriculum is missing and students are creating culturally congruent space for themselves in addition to meeting the demands of their academic programs of study.

An Ed.D. candidate in Educational Leadership and Policy from the Fort Belknap Reservation in Northern Montana describes education as if it were horses.

> Education today is like horses back in the day. It's our job to attain horses for the purpose of being able to provide a good life for our families. There was honor in stealing horses and proving oneself in conflict with other tribes. So if we are able to sneak into the enemy camp, capture these horses, and work with them our way, we will be able to travel further, hunt more efficiently, and eventually improve the way that our whole community lives. That means that if we get an education, even though it was not ours to begin with, it will help us live better. The key is that we have to be able to work with it our way . . . an Indian way.

In the quote above the student understands graduate education to be like horses taken from the enemy, which is undoubtedly difficult. Graduate students experience stress, fear, and tension, as educational attainment can be a difficult and dangerous endeavor. Drawing on his own Indigenous ontological reality, the student created a metaphor that connects him to his community and purposefully leans on Indigenous systems of being and community-specific history. He reframes education in a way that centers Indigenous identity, and articulates academic knowledge into social and economic capitol. By viewing and experiencing education in this way he is treating it respectfully and caring for it intentionally, as he would a stolen horse; thus helping provide for his community and family.

A Hopi student from Arizona, pursuing a Ph.D., uses the analogy of corn to describe the relationship between the students and their education.

> It is like planting corn in the Hopi tradition. It is not just about the planting but the process of the preparation of the corn and the land and the prayers that link all of this together. We see our corn as our children, and as children need nurturing and guidance so does the corn. So like the corn, we're the seeds. As little seedlings coming out of the ground you watch for the wind. When the wind comes, you go and you take care of the seedlings and you carefully set up windbreaks so that wind won't dry out those plants. The outcome then is having produced healthy corn that is shared with the community. Education can be like this, if we take care of our students and guide them when needed and necessary, the outcome is reciprocated to community.

In this metaphor, the respondent describes how students should be cared for during the process of pursuing education. Corn is very symbolic for Hopi peoples and cared for in a very unique manner. The student's relationship with corn falls within the context of a very specific community practice. This metaphor is related to a way of life connected through ceremony and community ontology. Out of respect for community knowledge, the author actively chooses not to disclose the traditional ceremonies that this story comes from. The intention is not to over-disclose; rather, the intent is to appreciate the way Indigenous students are analogizing educational spaces, places, and things as their own. To use this analogy in explaining education is reminiscent of an example that defines survival for Indigenous peoples while protecting knowledge that is held by community.

In a third example, a Dakota Ed.D. student metaphorizes education as if it were buffalo.

> Education is like buffalo . . . If we live together with it, if we take care of it like my relatives did in the past, it will take care of us . . . like harvesting buffalo, you get out of it what you put in. Harvesting buffalo is hard work. But if you take care of the animal it will take care of you, it is a community thing you know? Little kids up through the elders are a part of this. We do it together. You know . . . we could honor education by representing it on our dance regalia . . . some people bead their mortarboards when they graduate. We could honor education for helping take care of us by putting some designs in our powwow regalia.

From the students' perspective, they feel that it is okay to share this metaphor because of a deeply felt familial and historical connection with the animal. The students persist in school because they know that if students are able to harvest (complete) respectfully, it will feed our families and provide the things our children need. This student is also a very skilled artist who has put buffalo into the designs of relatives' powwow regalia, connecting to the animal using what Meyer calls "Indigenous common sense"[1] (2013) by knowing buffalo in a mental, physical, and spiritual way while suggesting we do the same with education.

Education as a Weapon: An Apsaalooké Ed.D. student uses his language in metaphorizing education.

> For me the metaphor I have I had for education is the word weapon, which comes from Chief Plenty Coups' encouragement that education is our most powerful weapon. "iilihchilahkuxsuua" is the Crow word he used for weapon in regards to education, which literally means "how to help yourself." I see it as a way to prevent oppression, to preserve a way of life and protect the future. Not to conquer or harm anyone. In order to use a weapon one has to train in order to use it properly and one must be able to respect it because if used improperly it could possibly cause harm. So one must undertake education, and educating others with a sense of responsibility knowing the importance it has in our lives today.

This student uses his own understanding of his language and ancestral teachings to think about education. In his response he illuminates the preservation of a specific way of life to serve future generations in his community. In addition he discusses the responsibility that comes with a formalized education. Education is to be used carefully because if it is used improperly, it can cause harm. Potential harm could be the result of teaching, thinking, and researching in a way that does not consider Indigenous community experiences. If Indigenous community experiences are not considered, practitioners, teachers, and researchers run the risk of teaching the settler colonialism that is deeply embedded in current curricula and in educational knowledge production (Calderon, 2014) that alienates Indigenous students from engaging in contemporary educational constructs.

A Sqelixʷ student looks to the landscape in creating her metaphor.

> The bitterroot—a delicate but hardy plant that survives and thrives in drought, hardship and difficult climates while maintaining beauty and grace. The bitterroot was given, by Tupye, to the Sqelixʷ as a form of sustenance from the self-sacrifice of one of our elder women during a time of famine and hardship for our people. Although the root is bitter and difficult to enjoy initially, we learn to love what is offered—a simple food source that provides a number of medicinal and health benefits. It can provide sustenance for many of our people independently or when joined with other food sources to form a stronger, more enjoyable meal.

> The bitterroot is a metaphor for education because the journey through education can be difficult, lonely, and isolating. However, maintaining beauty, grace, dignity, and strength through those sacrifices leads to a better understanding of what is necessary to provide nourishment, leadership, and so many other benefits for our communities. Education provides the skills necessary to navigate between our own communities and those of the dominant society in order to rise as leaders, promote, and take hold of sovereignty, and continue to further our thriving tribal nations.

This student speaks very colorfully of survival, beauty, and success, in an unforgiving environment. Self-sacrifice and hardship can be difficult, but those hardships can also sustain a community. Thriving in a graduate program is a sacrifice. By engaging in doctoral study, students are often removed from their community, isolated in predominately Non-native institutions, and must navigate inhospitable landscapes in order to succeed. This student's example speaks of the many sacrifices that one must make to graduate. By combining Indigenous ontological space with academic space, it also illuminates leadership, community development, and tribal self-determination in juxtaposition with majoritarian society and political connotation as she relates her metaphor to the phenomenon of tribal sovereignty.

Significance of the Study

Couched in these metaphors are important values that emerge to assist students' participation and persistence in graduate education. They are constructed in a way that Indigenous students can accept the challenges that come with graduate school experiences and thrive. More importantly, by constructing metaphors, the respondents introduce significant ideas that bring deeper meaning to their own education by:

1. Recognizing education as coming from outside the community but working with it in culturally specific ways for the improvement of a community's quality of life. (Horses)
2. Acknowledging a relationship with education so that it is cared for, taking the responsibility to serve as a steward so that the community grows strong. (Corn)
3. Developing a relationship with knowledge and honoring it in a way that considers the mental, physical, and spiritual nature of knowledge acquisition. (Buffalo)
4. Training and using education responsibly for the good of the community, to provide for one's self, family, and community. ("*Iilihchilahkuxsuua*")

5. Providing sustenance, working through difficult situations, and combining education with ancestral teachings in order to rise as leaders. It promotes tribal self-determination and tribal sovereignty, to continue flourishing as tribal nations. (Bitterroot)

In reflecting upon these examples, these metaphors have power in their potential to connect to a larger community of students to help current and future students reframe the relationship they have with the educational experience using their own cultural context.

Discussion

Indigenous research must be guided by certain principles (Atkinson, 2001, p. 10) as cited in Wilson (2008). Centering relationships is part and parcel of enacting Indigenous methodologies. In this research, relationships with the respondents were established prior to the beginning of the conversations related to metaphor. Once conversations began, sharing, hearing, listening, and reciprocal conversations were central to the research. The students themselves approved of the research and the research methods in conversation about metaphor; as a result, students were engaged in conversation on a personal level in ways that consider specific communities and the unique nature that each individual brings to the conversation. These two-way conversations included the principles of reciprocity and responsibility through shared story. The researcher went beyond reflective nonjudgmental consideration of what was being seen and heard, to honor the students and their metaphors. Having learned from the conversations, a purposeful plan was informed by collective sharing, wisdom, and acquired knowledge. Finally, research respondents were shown the final manuscript prior to sharing publicly in a way that respected student contribution, tribal representation, and confidentiality. Because these relationships are rooted in more than mere research, a mindful connection between intellect and spirit was crucial. Listening, observing, and sharing were accomplished while reflecting on both respondents' and the author's lived experiences. The stories that were shared were received through a community-connected and subjective lens leading to a deeper appreciation of the students' experiences and an obligation to contribute to their success.

History has shown that students will need to adapt to new and constantly changing technologies and environments in order to succeed in graduate education. Regardless of the various structures that are intended to support Indigenous success in higher education, the author asserts that Indigenous students navigating higher education benefit from the intentional development of internal motivation and confidence through self-authorship, which can be done by creating culturally meaningful metaphors. Creating and sharing stories with one another generates student confidence in ways that preserve cultural integrity. The conversational method used (Kovach, 2010) allows for meaningful participation by the storyteller and the researcher simultaneously challenging traditional academic research in higher education while maintaining authenticity in research specifically for Indigenous peoples in higher education. This research is intended to reclaim Indigenous research in higher education to serve Indigenous communities.

NOTE

1. Indigenous common sense according to Meyer (2013) is the simultaneous and cyclical process of body, mind, and spirit in the act of learning, which is also known as a holographic epistemology.

REFERENCES

Aubusson, P. J., Harrison, A. G., & Ritchie, S. M. (Eds.). (2005). *Metaphor and Analogy in Science Education* (Vol. 30). Netherlands: Springer Science & Business Media.

Ball, J., & Janyst, P. (2008). Enacting research ethics in partnerships with indigenous communities in Canada: "Do it in a good way." *Journal of Empirical Research on Human Research Ethics, 3*(2), 33–51.

Belgarde, M. J., Mitchell, R. D., & Arquero, A. (2002). What do we have to do to create culturally responsive programs?: The challenge of transforming American Indian teacher education. *Action in Teacher Education, 24*(2), 42–54.

Botha, E. (2009). Why metaphor matters in education. *South African Journal of Education, 29*(4), 431–444.

Brayboy, B. M. (2005). Towards a tribal critical race theory in education. *The Urban Review, 37*(5), 425–446.

Brayboy, B. M. J., & Castagno, A. E. (2009). Self-determination through self-education: Culturally responsive schooling for Indigenous students in the USA. *Teaching Education, 20*(1), 31–53.

Cajete, G. A. (1999). *Igniting the Sparkle: An Indigenous Science Education Model.* Skyland, NC: Kivaki Press.

Calderon, D. (2014). Uncovering settler grammars in curriculum. *Educational Studies, 50*(4), 313–338.

Calloway, C. G. (1999). *First peoples: A documentary survey of American Indian history.* Boston: Bedford/St. Martins.

Carjuzaa, J., & Ruff, W. G. (2010). When Western epistemology and an Indigenous worldview meet: Culturally responsive assessment in practice. *Journal of the Scholarship of Teaching and Learning, 10*(1), 68–79.

Castagno, A. E., & Brayboy, B. M. J. (2008). Culturally responsive schooling for Indigenous youth: A review of the literature. *Review of Educational Research, 78*(4), 941–993.

Denzin, N. K., & Lincoln, S. (Eds.). (2008). *Collecting and Interpreting Qualitative Materials* (Vol. 3). Thousand Oaks, CA: Sage.

Evans-Campbell, T. (2008) Historical trauma in American Indian/Native Alaska communities: A multilevel framework for exploring impacts on individuals, families, and communities. *Journal of Interpersonal Violence, 23*(3), 316–338.

Flynn, S. V., Duncan, K., & Jorgensen, M. F. (2012). An emergent phenomenon of American Indian postsecondary transition and retention. *Journal of Counseling & Development, 90*(4), 437–449.

Grande, S. (2004). American Indian geographies of identity and power. In *Red Pedagogies; Native American Social and Political Thought.* Lanham, MD: Rowman & Littlefield.
Guillory, R. M., & Wolverton, M. (2008). It's about family: Native American student persistence in higher education. *The Journal of Higher Education, 79*(1), 58–87.
Henze, R. C., & Vanett, L. (1993). To walk in two worlds—or more? Challenging a common metaphor of Native education. *Anthropology & Education Quarterly, 24*(2), 116–134.
Joseph, D., & Windchief, S. (2012). Nahongvita: A Model to Support American Indian Youth in Their Pursuit of Higher Education. Research Forum: Advancing Knowledge and Scholarship in Higher Education. National Indian Education.
Kovach, M. (2010). Conversation method in Indigenous research. *First Peoples Child & Family Review, 5*(1), 40–48.
Ladson-Billings, G. (1995). Toward a theory of culturally relevant pedagogy. *American Educational Research Journal, 32*(3), 465–491.
Magolda, M. B. (2001). *Making Their Own Way: Narratives for Transforming Higher Education to Promote Self-Authorship.* Sterling, VA: Stylus Publishing.
Magolda, M. B. B., & King, P. M. (2008). Toward reflective conversations: An advising approach that promotes self-authorship. *Peer Review, 10*(1), 8.
McCarty, T., Borgoiakova, T., & Gilmore, P. (2005). Indigenous epistemologies and education—self-determination, anthropology, and human rights. *Anthropology & Education Quarterly,* 36(1), 1–111.
Meyer, M. A. (2013). Holographic epistemology: Native common sense. *China Media Research, 9*(2), 94–102.
Nagel, J. (1995). American Indian ethnic renewal: Politics and the resurgence of identity. *American Sociological Review,* 947–965.
Pewewardy, C., & Hammer, P. (2003). Culturally responsive teaching for American Indian students. *ERIC Clearinghouse on Rural Education and Small Schools,* 1–9. ERIC Number: ED482325.
Pizzolato, J. E. (2003). Developing self-authorship: Exploring the experiences of high-risk college students. *Journal of College Student Development, 44*(6), 797–812.
Schmitt, R. (2005). Systematic metaphor analysis as a method of qualitative research. *The Qualitative Report, 10*(2), 358–394.
Sims, C. D. L. (2013). Disrupting race, claiming colonization: Collective remembering and rhetorical colonization. In *Negotiating (Native) American Identities in the US.* Doctoral dissertation, University of Colorado-Boulder.
Smith, L. T. (1999). *Decolonizing Methodologies: Research and Indigenous Peoples.* London and New York: Zed Books.
Stofflett, R. (1996). Metaphor development by secondary teachers enrolled in graduate teacher education. *Teaching and Teacher Education, 12*(6), 577–589.
Swisher, K. G. (1996). Why Indian people should be the ones to write about Indian education. *American Indian Quarterly, 20*(1), 83–90.
Torres, V., & Hernandez, E. (2007). The influence of ethnic identity on self-authorship: A longitudinal study of Latino/a college students. *Journal of College Student Development, 48*(5), 558–573.
Wilson, S. (2008). *Research Is Ceremony: Indigenous Research Methods.* Winnepeg, Manitoba, Canada: Fernwood Publishing.

CHAPTER 7

Predictors for American Indian/Alaska Native Student Leadership

Theresa Jean Stewart
(San Luis Rey Band of Mission Indians, Gabrieliño/Tongva)

During the first year of my doctoral program, I faced the onslaught of core courses essential to partially satisfying my degree requirements. The goal of program requirements was to prepare students for the field of higher education—equipping us with foundational knowledge from the field, as well as research training. Like other Native graduate students, this year forced me to confront the dehumanizing nature of education and question my place in academia. I was fortunate, however, to be uniquely positioned at an institution that rested squarely within my ancestral homelands; an institution that was also my academic and professional home for nearly ten years. These connections gave me strength. Ever present, the relationships that I fostered with the land, local tribes, and on-campus community were a constant challenge in my thinking as a Native researcher in higher education.

The greatest obstacle that I encountered during this time was navigating research methodologies. Independently, I decided to enroll in a healthy balance of qualitative and quantitative courses—determined to develop a base knowledge in both methods. However, I struggled immensely in quantitative methods the entire year. Progressing to more advanced quantitative methodologies courses, I continued to have difficulty. As a Native woman, working with quantitative data felt incredibly impersonal. And, while qualitative research became increasingly instinctual, my mastery of quantitative methods grew more and more foreign. Pushing against my instincts to forego any further empirical research courses, I enrolled in Computer Analysis of Empirical Data in Education during the spring quarter. The objective of the course was to conduct an original study using a large-scale longitudinal dataset from the UCLA Cooperative Institutional Research Program (CIRP), which is the foundation of this chapter. The first few weeks of the quarter were painful, but I persevered by drawing on my relationships.

Fortunately, the professor and teaching assistant were incredible allies—always ensuring I understood the material. Early in the quarter, we discovered that the class dataset did not have a representative sample of American Indian students to conduct an adequate study. The professor, who was extremely supportive of my passion to work with American Indian/Alaska Native (AIAN) communities, provided me with a unique dataset that ensured I could conduct a study on American Indian students. This led to my first major breakthrough in quantitative research. From there, I pushed the traditional boundaries of quantitative research to conceptualize a study that coincided with my worldview as a Native woman.

This chapter reviews a longitudinal study that was conducted during the first year of my doctoral program. More importantly, woven throughout the chapter I have provided my perspective, rationale, and thinking while conceptualizing the study design, selecting the theoretical framework, and examining results—giving insight on how quantitative research can be shaped by an Indigenous worldview and demonstrating the necessity of reclaiming Indigenous research in higher education.

Problem Statement and Research Questions

When thinking about research, I reflect on my reason for pursuing graduate studies—to ensure the prosperity of our tribal communities. Contextualizing the state of Indian education and tribal communities can be worrisome. American Indian/Alaska Native (AIAN) students account for less than 1% of the college student population (Shotton, Lowe, & Waterman, 2013). Moreover, the national six-year graduation rate for AIANs is 39.4% for first-time, full-time freshmen at four-year institutions (IPEDS, 2012). This rate continues to be the lowest in the country, and equally concerning when reflecting on the evolving state of tribes across the United States. Many Native scholars contend, and I would agree, that educational attainment is a critical component of the future of tribal communities, with AIAN students playing a pivotal role in protection and strengthening tribal sovereignty, self-determination, and self-reliance (Brayboy, Fann, Castagno, & Solyom, 2012; Shotton et al., 2013).

The increasing social, political, and, in many places, economic pressures facing tribes today forces them to rely on human capital. This places many tribes and tribal organizations in precarious situations—venturing outside of their communities for support. My intention is not to critique tribal administrative decisions or AIAN academic achievement. Rather, my intention is to illuminate a real issue impacting the future of tribal communities—the readiness of Native people to lead tribal communities. If we aspire, as Native people, to advance the building of tribal nations (i.e., to Nation Build), what Brayboy et al. (2012) identify as "the conscious and focused application of indigenous people's collective resources, energies, and knowledge to the task of liberating and developing the physical pace that is identified as their own," we need to develop tribal members culturally, intellectually, and personally (p. 12). The aim is not to privilege Western or institutionalized education over traditional knowledge. Academic training and the ability to navigate mainstream institutional systems is tantamount to cultural competence. I argue, however, that higher education provides an avenue for fostering intellectual and personal skills. Therefore, it would be advantageous for Native communities to understand what promotes skill development during college.

The goal of this longitudinal quantitative study was to best understand how AIAN students develop leadership skills during college. Leadership skill development was selected because these skills were identified in the survey instrument to assist individuals when leading groups and organizations, or, in this case, tribes. Using the CIRP 2004 Freshman Survey (TFS) and 2008 College Senior Survey (CSS), this study explored the concept of "higher education for nation building and self-determination" by examining how pre-college characteristics and college experiences of AIAN in postsecondary education impact the development of leadership skills. The research questions for this study were: (1) What pre-college and institutional characteristics are the strongest predictors for American Indian/Alaska Native college leadership skills? (2) What in-college experiences and attitudes are the strongest predictors for American Indian/Alaska Native college leadership skills?

Background and Theoretical Framework

Prior research on AIAN higher education has focused on understanding student persistence and graduation because of low academic achievement. Much of this literature touches on the social, educational, cultural, and institutional barriers that stall degree completion (Brayboy et al., 2012). While there is a breadth of literature on student leadership development in postsecondary education, few sources intentionally include Native students (Minthorn, 2014; Minthorn, Wanger, & Shotton, 2013; Williams, 2012).

The existing research on AIAN leadership indicates that a dichotomy exists between Western and Indigenous values and approaches to leadership. According to Badwound and Tierney (1988), and Warner and Grint (2006), Western society approaches leadership hierarchically, where leadership is identified by an individual leader heading an organization or community. Conversely, AIAN communities are noted to approach leadership as situational and relational rather than rooted in individuals (Komives, Mainella, Longerbeam, Osteen & Owen, 2006; Warner & Grint, 2006). Although individuals argue that colonization and assimilation have altered leadership styles in Native societies, many traditional leadership practices continue to this day inside and outside of academia.

Building on notions of AIAN leadership, Johnson (1997), and Harris and Wasilewski (1992), examine Native leadership in academic settings, each reporting on core values of AIAN leadership as examined in tribal colleges and among tribal community leaders. Both present major themes that embody Native leadership—commitment to serving the community, demonstrating the necessity of education for cultural survival and self-determination, bridging the relationship between diverse groups, maintaining a sense of balance, being a good relative, inclusive sharing, contributing to the common good, and noncoercive leadership. These themes are important, as Minthorn and Chavez (2014) point out that non-Native Colleges and Universities (NNCU) continue to operate from models and theories that exclude or fail to incorporate Native college populations (Minthorn & Chavez, 2014; Williams, 2012).

The theoretical framework used to design this study was the Social Change Model for Leadership Development (figure 7.1). Developed by Astin and Astin (1996), this model emphasizes two leadership development principles: (1) leadership is tied to social responsibility and creating change at an institution or on

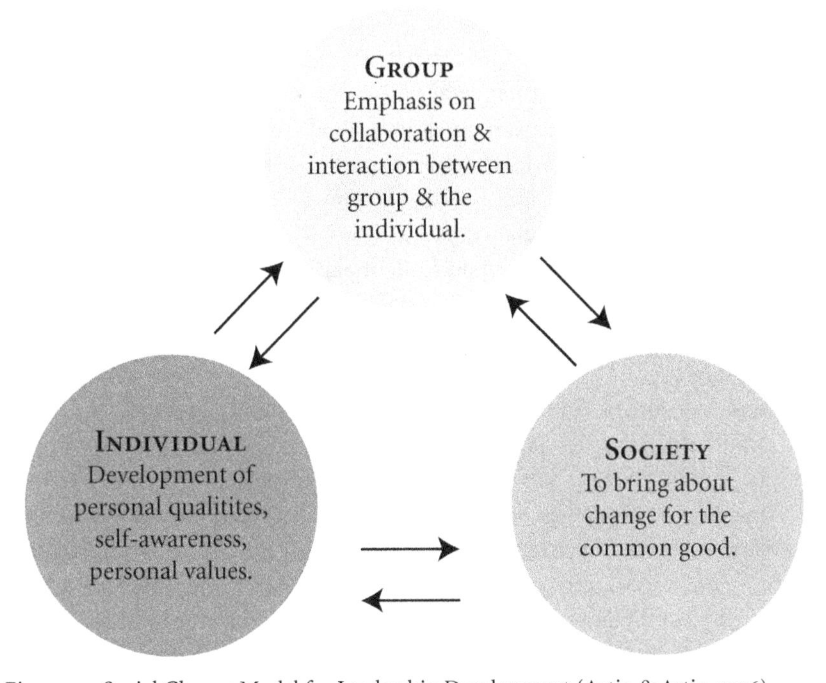

Figure 7.1. Social Change Model for Leadership Development (Astin & Astin, 1996)

the community, and (2) leadership is founded on increasing an individual's self-knowledge and being able to work collaboratively with others. These two principles focus on students' growth across seven values of leadership: consciousness of self, congruence, commitment, collaboration, common purpose, controversy with civility, and citizenships (Astin & Astin, 1996).

A primary reason this model was selected was because it is extremely malleable and interpretative when adapting it to examine AIAN values of leadership. In the model, the seven values interact and overlap across the three levels: the individual, group, and society (Astin & Astin, 1996). When applying this model to AIAN students, I accounted for elements of the AIAN community at each level and conceptually wove these elements into the model. For example, the societal/community level consists of a student's desire to bring about change for the common good. When interpreting this level to explicitly include AIAN elements, I thought of it to also mean "the desire to influence change within the American Indian community overall or within their specific tribal communities," who are often the target of AIAN student efforts.

Research Design

Sample

The data for this study came from the CIRP 2004 TFS and 2008 CSS, which is administered by the UCLA Higher Education Research Institute. The TFS is administered before the fall quarter/semester to first-year students, and consists of items pertaining to personal and academic background, pre-college characteristics, attitudes, expectations, and values. Similarly, the CSS is administered to the same cohort in the spring quarter/winter semester during the student's senior year. The CSS consists of items related to college experience, including academic performance, student-faculty interaction, co-curricular activities, and perceptions. Based on student participation in the fall 2004 TFS, the final dataset used for this study totaled 591 self-identified AIAN undergraduate students from 150 participating institutions from a total sample of 18,002 students.

Descriptive statistics indicated that 68.4% of the sample are female (n = 404), with 31.6% being male (n = 187). In addition, 98.6% of the students were enrolled full time, and 95.4% were between 19 and 20 years of age. Only 15.1% of students were first-generation college students, with 52.1% reporting their father as having college degree or higher, and 55.1% reporting their mother as having a college degree or higher. A large portion (40.3%) of respondents reported their parents' annual income range to be between $60,000 and $149,000, which is above the national median income for AIAN families (Akee & Taylor, 2014). Notably, these descriptive statistics present several puzzling characteristics that deviate from current demographics on AIANs in postsecondary education. While this was concerning when I was preparing this study, I pressed forward, understanding the limitations of the sample but also the implications for using a nationwide dataset with significant representation of AIANs.

Variables

The dependent variable (DV) for this study was leadership skills. The DV was a composite variable generated from five variables in the CSS (see table 7.1). This variable closely resembles recent CIRP construct leadership skills, created in later surveys, which is defined as "a united measure of students' beliefs about their leadership development, leadership capacity and experiences as a leader." The Cronbach's alpha for these five items is 0.685 (see table 7.1 for constituting factor).

The independent variables for this study include pre-college and institutional characteristics. In addition, the theoretical framework provided an approach for selecting predicting variables. In other words, variables related to college student experiences and perceptions were identified based on how they fell into individual, group, and community levels (Astin & Astin, 1996). Variables were blocked into five groups in order to examine how they influenced DV. (See appendix 7.A for coding scheme.)

The first two blocks consist of pre-college and institutional characteristics that control for student leadership skills prior to examining in-college experiences. This method is aligned with Astin's Input-Environment-Outcome (IEO) model (1970), which suggests that inputs have can directly predict students' outcomes but also have bearing on student experience (Astin & antonio, 2012). Controlling for these inputs establishes a baseline for understanding the role of college experiences on leadership development. Block one examines students' pre-college characteristics. This block included: sex, parental income, high school grade point average, self-rated leadership ability, and ambition to be a community leader. Block two examines the impact of institutional characteristics, such as institutional control and selectivity.

TABLE 7.1
ITEMS CONSTITUTING DEPENDENT VARIABLE

Leadership (Cronbach's alpha = 0.685)	*Factor Loading*
Change in leadership ability	0.68
Self-rated leadership ability at senior year	0.62
Participated in leadership training in college	0.56
Satisfied with leadership opportunities	0.55
Career Concern: Leadership Potential	0.53

Blocks three, four, and five are intented to be congruent with the three dimensions of leadership development identified in the social change model for leadership development—individual, group, and institution/community (Astin & Astin, 1996). These variables relate to students' in-college experiences and end-of-college perceptions and attitudes regarding individual, group, and community leadership development. Reflecting Astin & Astin's model for leadership development (1996), the block examining individual student characteristics during college seeks to examine personal qualities, self-awareness, and personal values. These variables include: student self-rating of cooperativeness, self-confidence, self-understanding, understanding of others, and self-rated change in interpersonal skills.

Blocks four and five emphasize collaboration and group interactions between the students, and groups or group members. Thus, variables examining participation in student organizations were included. Of particular interest is the impact of student organizations on leadership because the impact of such organizations on the college outcomes for Native and non-Native students varies (Antonio, 2001; Lundberg, 2007). Finally, the last block seeks to examine attitudes toward goals or career aspirations based on in-college experiences on leadership. This block includes the following variables: goal of becoming a community leader, participating in a community action program, influencing social values, and career concerns related to working for social change and leadership potential.

Analysis

Analysis consisted of an initial examination of frequencies and descriptive statistics that permitted significant descriptive information on the sample because of its size. This process influenced the selection of particular variables for cross-tabulation. Cross-tabulations were then used to examine any unique occurrences in the data. A linear regression was conducted to examine the relationship between the DV and independent variables. The five blocks of variables were entered into the regression using forced entry. Pre-college characteristics entered first, followed by institutional characteristics and then individual, group, and community. A p-value of less than 0.05 was used as a cutoff to measure statistical significance.

Limitations

Although this study offers unique insights into the development of AIAN leadership skills quantitatively, it is important to note study limitations. First and foremost, it is critical to mention that data used for this study were acquired from a nationwide survey. As such, the measures were not designed or normed for a study explicitly done on AIANs. Along these lines, many of the variables have been interpreted so as to best understand or explain pre-college and in-college AIAN student experiences and perceptions. For example, when examining the role of student organizations on leadership development, we can only suggest that students in the sample participated in Native student organizations, but we cannot confidently make this claim. Regardless, these measures help us to understand the role of pre-college and in-college experiences and perceptions. Second, the conceptual design and theoretical framework were adapted and interpreted to allow us to examine AIAN students. Therefore, we are unable to directly link study results to the larger issues of "higher education and self-determination for Native Nation Building."

Results

Tables 7.2 and 7.3 present the final results of the regression analysis. Table 7.2 displays changes in variance as each block of variables is entered into the model. The final model explains a total variance of 54.1%. Block one, accounting for 18.7% ($p < 0.001$) of the variance, suggests that pre-college characteristics had a significant role on student leadership. Block three, contributing 26.3% ($p < 0.001$) of the variance in the entire model, reflects the impact of students' attitudes toward cooperativeness, social self-confidence, self-understanding on leadership development. According to Astin and Astin (1996), the greater the self-awareness, the greater likelihood of students developing leadership skills at the individual level.

The smallest changes in variances can be attributed to blocks two, four, and five. Block two (0.3%) had no statistically significant impact on the total variance, which suggests that institutional type and selectivity has little to no bearing on AIAN student leadership. Blocks four and five added 4.9% ($p < 0.001$) and 4% ($p < 0.001$) of variance to the total model, respectively, for a total of 8.9%. Block four examined student experiences with leading a group, as well as experience interacting and collaborating with others. The significance of this block suggests that participation in campus organizations, whether student government,

TABLE 7.2.
R^2 CHANGE AND SIGNIFICANCE BY BLOCK

Block	*R^2 Change and Test of F change*
1. Pre-college Characteristics	0.187***
2. Institutional Characteristics	0.003
3. Individual	0.263***
4. Group	0.049***
5. Community	0.040***
Total Model R^2	0.541

*$p < 0.01$, **$p < 0.005$, ***$p < 0.001$

academic organizations, fraternities and sororities, or ethnic organizations, do not have as great an impact on leadership development as other factors. The same applies for block five, which accounted for a student's intention to engage with the community to bring about social change.

Table 7.3 displays the standardized and unstandardized regression coefficients for each variable, as well as the statistical significance of variables after all five blocks are entered into the model. Similarly, Table 7.4 displays the regression coefficients for the variables as each block is entered, as such we can witness observable changes in the statistical significance of beta coefficients at each block entry. The advantage of this perspective is witnessing when variables become significant and identifying what blocks or potentials variables impacted the changes in the model as blocks were entered in to the model. Again, a p-value of 0.05 or lower was used to assess the significance of the variables in each block. The findings of this study offer unique insights, while also echoing some existing literature, on the leadership development of AIANs enrolled in postsecondary institutions nationally. Given the topic studied, this knowledge may benefit tribal leaders who look to higher education as a mechanism for nation-building and self-determination, as well as university faculty, administrators, practitioners, and researchers. Thus, the following section discusses findings and implications for tribal and educational practice.

Pre-college and Institutional Characteristics

After all variables are entered into the model, only one pre-college variable remained statistically significant in relation to AIAN student leadership skills—self-rated leadership ability at 0.23 ($p < 0.001$). Based on these results, we can conclude that high self-perception of leadership ability prior to college has a significant and positive impact on their AIAN student leadership development. Therefore, it would also be to the best interests of tribal communities, reservation and urban, to offer leadership opportunities to its members prior to college (Williams, 2012).

The goal of becoming a community leader was an additional variable that held statistical significance throughout the model until the final block was entered. This suggests that students have an orientation toward community leadership prior to college, which changes during college for one reason or another. For these reasons, Native communities should consider orienting their members with leadership roles and professional careers where there is a specific need before college. Generally, many tribal communities, and students themselves, promote the return of members pursing postsecondary education to their respective tribal communities following graduation. Tribes are also becoming increasingly reliant on the support of Native and non-Native people with the skills and knowledge to operate developing tribal infrastructures. It would be to the advantage of tribal leaders and Native communities to better understand how pre-college and in-college experiences impact student leadership development so that they

TABLE 7.3
FINAL STANDARDIZED AND UNSTANDARDIZED REGRESSION COEFFICIENTS PREDICTING LEADERSHIP FOR AMERICAN INDIAN/ALASKA NATIVE STUDENTS

Variable	*Standardized Beta-weights*	*Unstandardized Beta-Weights*
BLOCK 1: PRE-COLLEGE CHARACTERISTICS		
Sex: Female	-0.05	-0.19
High School GPA	0.01	0.01
Parental Income	0.05	0.03
Performed volunteer work in high school	0.03	0.10
Self-rated leadership ability	0.23***	0.45
Goal to be a community leader	0.00	-0.01
BLOCK 2: INSTITUTIONAL CHARACTERISTICS		
Selectivity	0.01	0.00
Institution Control	-0.01	0.02
BLOCK 3: INDIVIDUAL		
Cooperativeness	0.05	0.11
Social Self-Confidence	0.13**	0.24
Self-Understanding	0.10*	0.23
Understanding of others	-0.32	0.08
Interpersonal skills	0.28***	0.65
Understanding of problems facing your community	0.12**	0.27
BLOCK 4: GROUP		
Joined a social fraternity or sorority	0.02	0.08
Participated in student government	0.09*	0.50
Participated in an ethnic/racial student organization	0.12***	0.48
Joined an organization related to major	0.06	0.21
Performed volunteer work in college	0.08*	0.22
BLOCK 5: COMMUNITY		
Desire to influence a political structure	-0.08	-0.16
Desire to influence social values	-0.03	0.07

(*continued*)

TABLE 7.3
FINAL STANDARDIZED AND UNSTANDARDIZED REGRESSION COEFFICIENTS PREDICTING LEADERSHIP FOR AMERICAN INDIAN/ALASKA NATIVE STUDENTS
(continued)

Variable	*Standardized Beta-Weights*	*Unstandardized Beta-Weights*
BLOCK 5: COMMUNITY		
Desire to become a community leader	0.27***	0.53
Desire to participate in a community action program	0.00	0.00
Desire to work for social change	-0.02	-0.03
Plans to participate in a community service organization	-0.04	-0.22
Final R^2	0.541	

*p < 0.01, **p < 0.005, ***p < 0.001

TABLE 7.4
REGRESSION COEFFICIENTS PREDICTING LEADERSHIP FOR AI/AN STUDENTS

	Standardized Regression Coefficients					
Variables	MODEL 1	MODEL 2	MODEL 3	MODEL 4	MODEL 5	*B*
BLOCK 1: PRE-COLLEGE CHARACTERISTICS						
Sex: Female	0.00	-0.01	-0.04	-0.05	-0.05	-0.19
High School GPA	0.00	0.01	0.04	0.02	0.01	0.01
Parental Income	0.03	0.03	0.02	0.03	0.05	0.03
Performed volunteer work in high school	0.10*	0.10*	0.07*	0.04	0.03	0.10
Self-rated leadership ability	0.33***	0.33***	0.26***	0.23***	0.23***	0.45
Goal to be a community leader	0.13*	0.12*	0.09*	0.08*	0.00	-0.01
BLOCK 2: INSTITUTIONAL CHARACTERISTICS						
Selectivity		-0.04	0.00	0.01	0.01	0.00
Institution Control		0.06	0.05	0.02	-0.01	0.02

(continued)

	Standardized Regression Coefficients					
Variables	Model 1	Model 2	Model 3	Model 4	Model 5	*B*
BLOCK 3: INDIVIDUAL						
Cooperativeness			0.08*	0.05	0.05	0.11
Social Self-Confidence			0.14***	0.14**	0.13**	0.24
Self-Understanding			0.08	0.10*	0.10*	0.23
Understanding of others			0.01	-0.01	-0.32	0.08
Interpersonal skills			0.29***	0.29***	0.28***	0.65
Understanding of problems facing your community			0.20***	0.16***	0.12**	0.27
BLOCK 4: GROUP						
Joined a social fraternity or sorority				0.02	0.02	0.08
Participated in student government				0.11**	.09*	0.50
Participated in an ethnic/racial student organization				0.11**	.12***	0.48
Joined an organization related to major				0.05	.06	0.21
Performed volunteer work in college				0.12**	.08*	0.22
BLOCK 5: COMMUNITY						
Desire to influence a political structure					-0.08	-0.16
Desire to influence social values					-0.03	0.07
Desire to become a community leader					0.27***	0.53
Desire to participate in a community action program					0.00	0.00
Desire to work for social change					-0.02	-0.03
Plans to participate in a community service organization					-0.04	-0.22
Final R^2	0.187	0.19	.453	.502	0.541	

*p < 0.01, **p < 0.005, ***p < 0.001

can begin to promote the ideas of leadership, sovereignty, self-determination, and self-reliance at the earlier stages of their students' academic, personal, and professional development.

As mentioned, the block consisting of institutional variables did not add any significance variance to the model nor did the variables changes in significance throughout the model. These results suggest that institutional control and selectivity had no bearing on the leadership development of AIAN students. In other words, leadership development of AIAN students is not dependent on where the student attends school.

Individual

Block three examined the impact of students' attitudes and perceptions on leadership, after controlling for pre-college and institutional characteristics. These variables coincide with the model of social change for leadership development in that they examine the students' self-awareness at the individual level. As mentioned, this block added the most variance to the model at 26.3%. Social self-confidence had a positive relationship with the DV at 0.13 ($p < 0.005$). Similarly, self-understanding had a positive relationship with the DV at 0.10 ($p < 0.05$). This variable became significant after block four was entered into the model, which may suggest that participation in groups influenced students' understanding of self. Interpersonal skills proved to have the strongest predictive power of any variable in the final model at 0.28 ($p < 0.001$). These findings are congruent with the social change model for leadership development. Astin and Astin (1996) assert that leadership development is nonhierarchical and that all students have an opportunity to develop. They argue that self-awareness is key in developing leadership characteristics. From this study, we see that self-rated social self-confidence, self-understanding, and interpersonal skills had a strong relationship with the DV. Based on the social change model we can conclude that in-college experiences shape a student's level of self-awareness, therefore impacting their leadership at the individual level.

Group

Block four consisted of variables measuring in-college group experiences, including participation in student government, ethnic/racial organizations, fraternities or sororities, or academic organizations related to a major. Participation in student government had a positive relationship, with leadership at 0.09 at entry ($p < 0.01$). In addition, participation in a racial/ethnic student organization also had a strong relationship with the DV at 0.12 ($p < 0.001$). These findings yield intriguing results because they coincide most directly with previous research. Both Astin (1984) and Minthorn (2014) argue that college is an important time in the development of student leadership skills for Native and non-Native students. Astin (1984) asserts that students are most engaged during their college years, developing these foundational skills. On the other hand, Minthorn (2012) finds that student involvement in Native student organizations, including fraternities and sororities, not only has implications for leadership development but also helps to instill Native values of leadership that may have been lost due to colonization and assimilation. This block also included a variable that examined the impact of performing volunteer work during in college. This variable remained significant at 0.08 ($p < 0.01$). Therefore, students who reported performing volunteer work in college were likely to develop leadership characteristics.

Community

The final block examined the desire and plan to bring about social change within society, or in the case within tribal communities. Only one variable proved to be significant—the desire to become a community leader. The standardized regression coefficient for desire to become a community leader was 0.27 ($p < 0.001$), having a positive relationship with the DV. We can assert that the desire to become a community leader had a positive and significant impact on the leadership development of AIAN students in this sample.

Discussion

This study provides an empirical examination of AIAN college student leadership development using a nationwide sample of Native college students. While limitations can be attributed to the dataset, findings provide valuable insight and implications for understanding what experiences foster AIAN student leadership skills before and during college, which is important to those committed to the prosperity of tribal communities. Additional areas of exploration are also highlighted through conceptual and theoretical models, such as examining the role of variables on social agency, as social agency may be a more appropriate predictor for nation-building. This nuanced examination may be helpful in understanding AIAN students' inclination toward post-college involvement with their tribal communities. Based on demographic findings, another area to explore would be the impact of income and financial aid on leadership.

Equally important, this chapter illustrates several opportunities for reclaiming quantitative research in higher education. The study shared in this chapter offers a specific example on how one can reclaim Indigenous research in higher education by reorienting theoretical models, in this case Astin and Astin's (1996) Social Change Model for Leadership Development, using an Indigenous lens to develop quantitative research conceptually, theoretically, and analytically. For example, when conceptualizing the study design, as mentioned, I considered existing issues and challenges in the AIAN community so that the research would be relevant to Native communities. When using specific measures and the theoretical framework, I also interpreted each to also signify what it would mean to Native communities based on existing AIAN literature. While this was not the measure given in the survey or the intention explained in the selected framework, these interpretations helped to make the research relevant and applicable to AIAN communities. Finally, in analyzing the results, I was conscious of interpreting findings and presenting implications that would be useful to AIAN communities despite the limitations of the dataset.

It is also important to address the ways that this study addresses ethical considerations in improving Indigenous research in higher education or highlights progress already made, such as the importance of Native people conducting research on or with AIANs, including quantitative research and the use of large datasets. Other scholars, such as Swisher (1996), have previously shared the opinion that educational research on American Indians should be conducted by Native researchers. For example, Swisher (1996) expressly stated, "in the spirit of self-determination, Indian people should be the ones to write about Indian education" (p. 85). Over the last several decades, Native scholars have overwhelmingly responded to this clarion call. Moreover, they have responded by ensuring scholarship addresses community needs and issues, is inclusive of Indigenous methodologies and frameworks, is respectful of Indigenous knowledge, and includes Native voices. This study builds on that work, in that I am a Native researcher examining a nuance of tribal community prosperity, which is student leadership skill development, and using an Indigenous lens.

Thinking about the future of Indigenous research in higher education, there continue to be areas in the field of education that can work to ensure Indigenous voices and perspectives are included in empirical research, including studies done using large datasets. First, researchers can conduct research that is relevant to Native communities. Second, scholars can collaborate with communities to understand what information is important to them and how they want to be represented by data. Finally, scholars can be conscious of the implications of their research, and avoid research that is damage-centered or deficit-oriented, but rather identifies the strengths of AIAN students. Moreover, individuals working within higher education and institutional research using "big data" can collaborate with Native educators in the construction of survey measures to ensure they are inclusive of Native communities. Along these lines, research can also develop quantitative measures that meet the needs of AIAN scholars, but more importantly, of community members.

APPENDIX 7.A
VARIABLE DEFINITIONS AND CODING

Dependent Variable—Leadership	
Change: Leadership ability	5 point scale; 1=much weaker, 5=much stronger
Self-rating: Leadership ability	5 point scale; 1=lowest 10%, 5=highest 10%
Act in College: Participated in leadership training	3 item scale; 1=not at all, 2=occasional, 3=frequently
Satisfaction: Leadership opportunities	6 item scale; 1=can't rate/no experience, 6=very satisfied
Career Concern: Leadership potential	4 point scale; 1=not important, 4=essential
Independent Variables	
BLOCK 1: PRE-COLLEGE CHARACTERISTICS	
Sex	1=male, 2=female
What was your average grade in high school?	8 item scale; 1=D, 8=A–A+
Parental Income	14 point scale; 1=less than $10,000, 14=$250,000
Act in Past Year: Performed volunteer work	3 item scale; 1=not at all, 2=occasional, 3=frequently
Self-rating: Leadership ability	5 point scale; 1=lowest 10%, 5=highest 10%
Goal: Becoming a community leader	4 point scale; 1=not important, 4=essential
BLOCK 2: INSTITUTIONAL CHARACTERISTICS	
Institution Control	1=public, 2=private
Selectivity	Based on reported median SAT Verbal + Math scores; ACT composite scores; Other comparable sources
BLOCK 3: INDIVIDUAL	
Self-rating: Cooperativeness	5 point scale; 1=lowest 10%, 5=highest 10%
Self-rating: Self-Confidence (Social)	5 point scale; 1=lowest 10%, 5=highest 10%

(*continued*)

APPENDIX 7.A
VARIABLE DEFINITIONS AND CODING
(continued)

Block 3: Individual	
Self-rating: Self-Understanding	5 point scale; 1=lowest 10%, 5=highest 10%
Self-rating: Understanding of others	5 point scale; 1=lowest 10%, 5=highest 10%
Change: Interpersonal skills	5 point scale; 1=much weaker, 5=much stronger
Change: Understanding of problems facing your community	5 point scale; 1=much weaker, 5=much stronger
Block 4: Group	
Act in College: Joined a social fraternity or sorority	Dichotomous variable; 1=no, 2=yes
Act in College: Participated in student government	Dichotomous variable; 1=no, 2=yes
Act in College: Participated in an ethnic/ racial student organization	Dichotomous variable; 1=no, 2=yes
Act in College: Joined a club or organization related to your major	Dichotomous variable; 1=no, 2=yes
Act in Past Year: Performed volunteer work	3 item scale; 1=not at all, 2=occasional, 3=frequently
Block 5: Community	
Goal: Influencing a political structure	4 point scale; 1=not important, 4=essential
Goal: Influencing social values	4 point scale; 1=not important, 4=essential
Goal: Becoming a community leader	4 point scale; 1=not important, 4=essential
Goal: Participating in a community action program	4 point scale; 1=not important, 4=essential
Career Concern: Working for social change	4 point scale; 1=not important, 4=essential
Plans to participate in a community service organization	2 item scale; 1=marked, 1=not marked

REFERENCES

Akee, R., & Taylor, T. (2014). Social & Economic Change on American Indian Reservations: A Databook of the US Censuses and the American Community Survey 1990–2010. Unpublished manuscript. http://taylorpolicy.com/us-databook/

Antonio, A. L. (2001). Diversity and the influence of friendship groups in college. *The Review of Higher Education*, 25(1), 63–89.

Astin, A. (1984). Student involvement: A developmental theory for higher education. *Journal of College Student Personnel*, 25, 297–308.

Astin, A. W. (1970). The methodology of research on college impact (Part I). *Sociology of Education*, 43, 223–254.

Astin, A. W., & antonio, a. l. (2012). *Assessment for Excellence: The Philosophy and Practice of Assessment and Evaluation in Higher Education*. Lanham, MD: Rowman & Littlefield.

Astin, H. S., & Astin, A. W. (1996). *A Social Change Model of Leadership Development Guidebook*, version 3. Los Angeles, CA: Higher Education Research Institute, University of California, Los Angeles.

Badwound, E., & Tierney, W. G. (1988). Leadership and American Indian values: The tribal college dilemma. *Journal of American Indian Education*, 28(1), 9–15.

Brayboy, B. M. J., Fann, A. J., Castagno, A. E., & Solyom, J. A. (Eds.). (2012). *Postsecondary Education for American Indian and Alaska Natives: Higher Education for Nation Building and Self-Determination: ASHE*, 37(5). Wiley.com.

Fox, M. (2005). Voices from within: Native American faculty and staff on campus. In *Journal of Leadership Education*, M. J. Tippeconnic Fox, S. C. Lowe, & G. McClellan (Eds.), *Serving Native American Students* (pp. 49–60). San Francisco, CA: Jossey-Bass.

Guillory, R. M. (2009). American Indian/Alaska Native college student retention strategies. *Journal of Developmental Education*, 33(2), 12.

Harris, L., & Wasilewski, J. (1992). *This is what we want to share: Core cultural values*. In Americans for Indian Opportunity Contemporary Tribal Governance Series.

Johnson, V. (1997). Weavers of change: Portraits of Native American women educational leaders. (Doctoral dissertation). Dissertation Abstracts International, 59(01), 36A. (University Microfilms No. AAT98–22466).

Komives, S. R., Mainella, F. C., Longerbeam, S. D., Osteen, L., & Owen, J. E. (2006). A leadership identity development model: Applications from a grounded theory. *Journal of College Student Development*, 47(4), 401–418.

Kuh, G. D. (2001). Assessing what really matters to student learning: Inside the National Survey of Student Engagement. *Change*, 33(3), 10–17, 66.

Lundberg, C. A. (2007). Student involvement and institutional commitment to diversity as predictors of Native American student learning. *Journal of College Student Development*, 48(4), 405–416.

Minthorn, R. (2014). Perspectives and values of leadership for Native American college students in non-native colleges and universities. *Journal of Leadership Education*, Spring 2014, 67–95. doi:10.12806/V13/I2/R4

Minthorn, R., & Chavez, A. F. (2014). *Indigenous Leadership in Higher Education* (Vol. 3). New York, NY: Routledge.

Minthorn, R., Wanger, S., & Shotton, H. (2013). Developing Native student leadership skills: The success of the Oklahoma Native American Students in Higher Education (ONASHE) Conference. *American Indian Culture and Research Journal*, 37(3), 59–74. doi:10.17953/aicr.37.3.01843v2733240715

Nagel, J. (1997). *American Indian Ethnic Renewal: Red Power and the Resurgence of Identity and Culture*. New York, NY: Oxford University Press.

Oxendine, D., Oxendine, S., & Minthron, R. (2013). Historically Native American fraternity and sorority movement. In H. Shotton, S. C. Lowe, & S. J. Waterman, (Eds.), *Beyond the Asterisk: Understanding Native Students in Higher Education*. (pp. 67–80). Sterling, VA: Stylus.

Portman, T., & Garrett, M. (2005). Beloved women: Nurturing the sacred fire of leadership from an American Indian perspective. *Journal of Counseling & Development*, *83*, 284–291.
Shotton, H., Lowe, S. C., & Waterman, S. J. (Eds.). (2013). *Beyond the Asterisk: Understanding Native Students in Higher Education*. Sterling, VA: Stylus Publishing.
Swisher, K. G. (1996). Why Indian people should be the ones to write about Indian education. *American Indian Quarterly*, *20*(1), 83–90.
Tierney, W. G. (1992). *Official Encouragement, Institutional Discouragement: Minorities in Academe—The Native American Experience*. Norwood, NJ: Ablex Publishing.
U.S. Department of Education, National Center for Education Statistics, Integrated Postsecondary Education Data System (IPEDS). (2012). Percentage of first-time full-time bachelor's degree-seeking students at 4-year institutions who completed a bachelor's degree, by race/ethnicity, time to completion, sex, and control of institution: Selected cohort entry years, 1996 through 2005. [Data file]. Retrieved from: http://nces.ed.gov/programs/digest/d12/tables/dt12_376.asp
U.S. Department of the Interior. (2012). Indian Affairs—Frequently Asked Questions. Retrieved from: http://www.bia.gov/FAQs/index.htm
Warner, L. S., & Grint, K. (2006). American Indian ways of leading and knowing. *Leadership*, *2*(2), 225–244.
Williams, R. S. (2012). Indigenizing leadership concepts through perspectives of Native American college students. (Doctoral dissertation). Oklahoma State University.

CHAPTER 8

Tribal College Pathways

David Sanders (Oglala Sioux Tribe)

Matthew Van Alstine Makomenaw
(Grand Traverse Bay Band of Ottawa and Chippewa Indians)

"Why don't our students survive when they come to your universities?" (Taylor, 1999, p. 4). This was the question asked about Tribal College and Universities (TCUs) transfer students by a TCU president. The question posed back in 1999 is still important today. Since their inception in 1968 TCUs have been effective in educating postsecondary American Indian/Alaska Native (AIAN) students. The question for TCUs and those concerned with TCU success is what happens to the students who choose to transfer and attend a four-year mainstream institution. AIAN students in 2009–10 represented 1.2% of degrees conferred for all associate's degrees and 0.8 percent of all bachelor's degrees conferred in the United States (U.S. Department of Education, 2012). What is not fully known is the success rate and pathways of TCU transfer to four-year degrees. The current study used descriptive quantitative data to examine the success and pathways of TCU transfer students through two cohorts of American Indian College Fund Full Circle scholarship recipients.

Tribal College Purpose and History

TCUs began to develop in the late 1960s, Navajo Community College being the first, with the belief that tribal nations should have a role in the education of their citizens (Dejong, 1993). TCUs have unique missions tied to their tribal nation's culture, language, and history (Benham & Stein, 2003). While open to everyone, TCUs must have at least 51% enrollment of AIAN students to maintain federal funding. In order for TCUs to count students as American Indians, those students must be enrolled members of a federally recognized tribal nation. There are currently 37 TCUs, 35 of which are fully accredited. The 35 TCUs comprise the group of TCUs that are full members of the American Indian Higher Education Consortium (AIHEC), a support network for TCUs on a national level (AIHEC, 2016).

Tribal College Transfer Data

A limited amount of information is available on TCU transfer student success and pathways. Data from a 2011 cohort of 21 two-year TCUs showed an average transfer out rate of 13%, with the lowest TCU rate being 3% and the highest, 21% (National Center of Educational Statistics (NCES), 2016). It should be noted that six of the 21 two-year TCUs did not report any transfer out rates. In addition, a 2008 cohort of 13 four-year TCUs embodied an average transfer out rate of 20%, with the lowest TCU being 6% and the highest, 32% (NCES, 2016). Of the 13 four-year TCUs, nine did not report any information on transfer out rates. Of the 34 TCUs in the NCES, only 19 reported any information on transfer out rates. The challenge is that there is still a large amount of data missing on TCU transfer out rates.

In comparison with the average transfer out rate of 13% for two-year TCUs and 20% for four-year TCUs, the average transfer out rates for community colleges in general for the cohort entering fall 2007 was 18.8%, and 17.8% for the cohort entering in fall 2010 (American Association of Community Colleges, 2015). The transfer out rates of TCUs and community colleges paint a certain picture and beg the question of why two-year TCUs have a lower transfer out rate. However, transfer out rates do not tell us the success rate of transfer students and what type of institutions transfer students attend. Some institutions, albeit very few, will post on their websites how many TCU students are enrolled, but do not post how many of the TCU transfer students graduate. There is a need and usefulness to understand the pathways and success of TCU transfer students at four-year institutions. Transfer out data do not allow for an analysis of student level progress to postsecondary success.

A Need for Accurate and Complete Data on TCUs

The U.S. Department of Education launched the College Scorecard, designed to inform students and families about the value of degrees from various colleges and universities primarily based on cost, graduation rate, and employment. The College Scorecard is designed to assist students and families in making their college choice in an era of so many college options. The College Scorecard, however, does not consider transfer rates or bachelor degree completion for transfer students. Data and information on TCU transfer students are significant and critical to tribal colleges in an era of accountability and value. In addition, databases such as the National Student Clearinghouse (NSC) and Integrated Postsecondary Education Data System (IPEDS) are great places to find data, but they have limitations as related to AIAN students and TCUs. Data on transfer out rates and transfer student bachelor degree completion would strengthen TCUs as a college choice.

National Student Clearinghouse

National Student Clearinghouse is a nonprofit, nongovernmental agency whose work involves educational reporting, data exchanges, enrollment and graduation verification, and research services to organizations and educational institutions. More than 3,600 colleges and universities participate in NSC reporting. Currently 17 TCUs submit data to NSC. More than 98% of all students in public and private U.S. institutions participate in NSC reporting (see http://www.studentclearinghouse.org/about/).

The NSC Research Center has produced numerous reports on postsecondary student transfer, pathways, and mobility among other important topics and speaks to the role of two-year institutions in students' successful completion of four-year institutions. Signature Report 9: Transfer & Mobility: A National View of Student Movement in *Postsecondary Institutions, Fall 2008 Cohort* (July 2015) is the latest report offered by NSC that describes the transfer and mobility pathways of 3.5 million first-time students entering in fall 2008. Despite the commendable attempt at describing differences in transfer rates and pathways based on a number of different characteristics including gender, starting institution type, multiple transfers, out-of-state/in-state transfers, timing of transfers, enrollment intensity (full-time part-time, mixed), etc., data in the NSC do not allow for an analysis based on race, nor are tribal colleges included as a category in institution type. Thus, transfer and mobility pathways of AIAN attending both mainstream institutions and TCUs are missing. Our study will attempt to offer complementary data concerning a sample of AIAN students attending both TCUs and mainstream institutions.

Accurate data on AIAN transfer rates and mobility pathway trends, especially those attending TCUs, are important for a few reasons. It can allow TCUs to better inform their processes with regard to student success, persistence, and completion. Enrollment and graduation information regarding alumni can inform TCUs about the types of institutions their students are attending and may allow an avenue to partner with other institutions. How many students transfer to other TCUs, for instance? Are there articulation agreements in place within the TCU system to accommodate student transfers? How much of student success at four-year institutions can be attributed to TCUs? What types of degrees are earned by students transferring to four-year institutions and should this impact the types of degree programs TCUs offer? Oftentimes transfer is associated with students attending a two-year institution first, then enrolling in a four-year institution. Transfer and mobility data can inform TCUs about the number of students who transfer to their institutions from other types of mainstream institutions which may in turn foster the development of a transcript audit, which essentially is an institutional analysis of a student's incoming transcript to determine whether a student has enough credits to be awarded an associate's degree. Finally, how many students enroll during the summer and could this have an impact on the way a TCU can serve AIAN students? Without an accurate description of AIAN transfer and mobility pathways, TCUs are at a loss in describing aspects of their own impact on their role in the success of AIAN students and are missing important information with regard to assisting transfer students more effectively.

TCU Transfer Experiences

The literature on TCU transfer student experience at four-year institutions is scarce and often focuses on student experience at four-year institutions. A three-year study on TCU transfer students to Non-Native Colleges and Universities in science fields revealed personal/cultural/social support as factors in a successful transition (Lee, 2007). A study examining the acculturation of AIAN students from tribal lands to non-Native institutions showed discrimination and racism as a major obstacle in the transition process (Flynn, Olson, & Yellig, 2014). TCU transfer students at four-year institutions identified the need to find a Native American community on the four-year institution's campus as a factor for success (Makomenaw, 2012). Studies on the student experience share a glimpse of what is happening when TCU transfer students attend four-year institutions, but they do not include success rates.

Moreover, much of the research on TCU transfer students consists of qualitative studies. A qualitative study of TCU transfer students to four-year institutions indicated that the participants would not have enrolled in a four-year institution if not for attending a TCU first (Brown, 2003). Dell's (2000) qualitative study on TCU transfer students to four-year institutions found that finances and family are key factors in student retention for transfer students. While qualitative studies provide valuable insight, they do not provide a complete picture of the success rate of TCU transfer students at four-year institutions.

The American Indian College Fund Scholarship Programs

The American Indian College Fund (the College Fund) has been providing scholarships to American Indian/Alaska Natives (AIAN) college students since its inception in 1989. The College Fund has two scholarship programs: (1) the TCU Scholarship Program, and (2) the Full Circle Scholarship Program. The TCU scholarship program funds students attending TCUs. Recipients are selected and awarded by each TCU. In contrast, the Full Circle Scholarship Program recipients attend both mainstream schools and TCUs. Recipients of this scholarship are selected by College Fund staff. In academic year (AY) 2013–2014, the College Fund awarded 780 Full Circle applicants and funded 3,558 TCU applicants.

A large percentage of the overall AIAN students enrolled in postsecondary institutions attend TCUs. Approximately 15,000 AIAN students enroll annually at TCUs. In fall 2013 there were 147,800 undergraduate AIAN enrolled in postsecondary institutions (http://nces.ed.gov/programs/digest/d14/tables/dt14_306.10.asp). Thus, approximately 11% of all undergraduate AIAN students attended a TCU. The College Fund's 3,558 scholarship recipients comprised 23% of all TCU students and 2.5% of all AIAN undergraduate students in AY 2013–2104. For the Full Circle Scholarship recipients, whose data became distinct from the TCU scholarship recipients in AY 2009–2010, there were 2,535 scholarship recipients since then. From AY 2002–2003 there were a total of 27,239 TCU and Full Circle unduplicated student scholarship recipients.

Due to the increasing demand for data and evidence of impact, the College Fund has taken on the task of providing important information about student scholarship recipient outcomes. The College Fund built a scholarship recipient and applicant internal database to house student demographic information. In addition, the College Fund is utilizing the National Student Clearinghouse tracking services. The College Fund has been able to submit tracking queries to NSC and obtain enrollment and degree verification information on approximately one-quarter of its scholarship recipients. With only one-quarter accounted for and a desire to gain a greater understanding of student outcomes, the College Fund has identified two causes for the lack of available tracking information on scholarship recipients: First, the College Fund's early capacity for collecting scholarship recipient data was not as great as it is now. Thus the early years of data contained less demographic data, including certain specific data needed for tracking inquiry submissions to NSC. This led to obtaining a smaller percentage of tracking information on students receiving funding during the AY 2002–2003 through 2008–2009. And second, many TCUs have only recently begun submitting enrollment and degree verification data to NSC. Currently 17 of the 35 TCUs are submitting this data. Thus, even if the College Fund had all necessary demographic data on all of its scholarship recipients for submission of tracking queries, it would obtain only 40% of the overall tracking information of its scholarship recipients. To mitigate some of these issues the College Fund directly contacts TCUs to verify enrollment of TCU and Full Circle Scholarship recipients each semester they receive funding. In addition, the College Fund obtains graduation verification of scholarship recipients attending TCUs. With the NSC tracking enrollment and degree verification and the direct verification of enrollment and degree information from TCUs, the College Fund is in an enviable position to potentially describe the enrollment patterns and degree attainment information of a sizeable portion of AIAN postsecondary students.

Indigenous Methodology

Indigenous research methodology is the infusion of Indigenous culture, language, self-determination, and history into research and approach to data. The purpose of an Indigenous methodology is to provide a counter-narrative of Indigenous peoples grounded in social justice and healing (Smith, 1999). Indigenous research should be more than theoretical—it should have practical implications for Indigenous communities (Meyer, 2003). In addition, Indigenous methodology requires researchers to be accountable to Indigenous communities by sharing useful findings and data with the communities from which they were collected (Kahakalau, 2004). Our study on the TCU transfer student pathway incorporates tenets of Indigenous methodology by recognizing and honoring tribal sovereignty through tribal enrollment and focusing on AIAN student success rather than student failures.

A political and controversial question for AIAN people involves who is able to identify as AIAN. Native Americans since the Dawes Rolls of 1887 have been subjected to blood quantum as a means to determine who is and who is not Native American (Garroutte, 2003). The federal government and many AIAN tribal nations often use one-quarter blood quantum to qualify for programs and tribal enrollment. Universities and U.S. census use self-identification as a means to determine who is counted as AIAN. Honoring tribal sovereignty means honoring the right for tribal nations to determine their own citizenship. There are issues and challenges with using blood quantum and tribal enrollment as indicators of who is or who is not AIAN, but tribal enrollment, which honors tribal sovereignty, is more accurate than self-identification as a means to determine who is AIAN. The American Indian College Fund requires that its scholarship applicants be enrolled members of a state or federally recognized tribal nation, or have the ability to show that they are a descendant of an enrolled parent or grandparent of a state or federally recognized tribal nation. Therefore, the participants in the current study are tribally enrolled or direct descendants of tribally enrolled members, whereas the national dataset includes those who self-identify as AIAN; this therefore may actually inflate the AIAN student count and may not actually be a very accurate measure of who is or isn't actually AIAN.

The Native American authors in the current study aim to gather information on student success and data useful to TCUs and communities. A critique of researchers conducting studies on AIAN communities is that they often involve helicopter research (gathering data from a community and leaving) and the research produced is purely theoretical and does not provide any practical service for AIAN communities. This study is part of a larger organizational research agenda and data sovereignty push. The Office of Research and Sponsored Programs (ORSP) was created as a new department within the College

Fund in 2013 and was designed to address important data capacity issues within the organization as well as to support the data capacity efforts of TCUs. To date the College Fund has presented to the American Indian Higher Education Consortium (AIHEC) board, which consists of TCU presidents, information about the importance of submitting data to NSC and the advantages it offers to their institution. The analysis for this study (and others like it) is meant to serve as an illustration to TCUs demonstrating possible uses of this type of data and to offer a platform for discussion about providing data to inform their own work. ORSP continues to do research in the quantitative sphere around scholarship recipients but also provides qualitative research to highlight the important work occurring at TCUs. In addition, we have created avenues for funding research projects focusing on TCUs, disseminating research conducted at TCUs by TCU faculty/ students (with the publication of the *Tribal College and University Research Journal*) and the hosting of annual research conferences. The researchers in this study, in particular, will highlight achievement and useful information to inform educators so they are able to make policies and decisions that help AIAN communities and students.

NSC's Signature Report 9 defined transfer as "any change in a student's institution of enrollment irrespective of the timing, direction, or location of the move, and regardless of whether any credits were transferred from one institution to another" (p. 5). This definition highlights the importance of inclusion of a diversity of transfer type. Typically transfer assumed a move from a two-year community college to a four-year institution or across four-year institutions. "The transfer rate reported here considers the student's first instance of movement to a different institution, before receiving a bachelor's degree and within a period of six years. For those students who began at two-year public institutions, we also include transfers that happened after receiving a degree at the starting two-year institution" (p. 6). For our analysis we defined transfer as a change in institution, regardless of direction of transfer, before receiving a bachelor's degree. We did not focus on first-time students, nor did we focus on a time frame of six years as did NSC; instead our students were included if they were funded in either the 2009–2010 or 2010–2011 academic years. In addition, we looked at their enrollment patterns over the time spanning fall 2001 through fall 2015. Thus, two cohorts of Full Circle scholarship recipients were the focus of this inquiry into the transfer and mobility pathways and degree attainment of College Fund scholarship recipients. These two cohorts were chosen specifically because they would have had at least five years to graduate (if their first year of postsecondary enrollment was in either of these two academic years) from a postsecondary institution and because a relatively large proportion of Full Circle scholarship recipients in these cohorts started their postsecondary journey at mainstream institutions. The inclusion of both TCU and mainstream scholarship recipients allows the opportunity to compare transfer rates, pathways to success, and graduation information between those who started at a TCU with those who started at both two-year and four-year mainstream institutions.

There were 278 and 562 Full Circle scholarship recipients in AY 2008–2009 and AY 2009–2010, respectively. Combining these two cohorts and eliminating those students receiving scholarships both academic years yielded 793 students. 222 students were not submitted to NSC for tracking due to a lack of necessary demographic data required by NSC. 531 students were submitted for tracking inquiries to NSC. Further reduction of the overall number of students analyzed in this study included eliminating those who did not receive any type of degree (these degrees included technical degree, certificate, diploma, AA, AAS, BA, BS). 271 of the 793 students received a degree.

NSC provides the opportunity to those seeking degree and enrollment verification the ability to determine the desired year and semester to begin the tracking of enrollment and degree attainment. We decided to include the years starting fall semester of 2001 and ending fall 2015. Since we were able to obtain the tracking data earlier than the semesters/years our scholarship recipients were funded, we were able to eliminate from analysis those students who obtained a bachelor's degree very near fall semester of 2001 since there was no enrollment information prior to that date. Also we decided to analyze only those students receiving up to a bachelor's degree, thereby eliminating those students whose enrollment information contained only information leading to master's degree attainment. After eliminating students based on these criteria, the number of students analyzed in this inquiry settled at 232.

Findings

Graduation

Of the 531 students submitted for tracking purposes to NSC, 271 had earned a degree (obtaining at least one of the following: diploma/technical degree/certificate, AA/AS/AAS, BA/BA, MA/MS, PHD/MD/JD or an unspecified degree [other]) for a graduation rate of approximately 49%. A total of 380 degrees were earned by the 271 graduates. Table 8.1 illustrates the breakdown of degrees earned by institution type (TCU/Mainstream) and degree type. As might be expected, the vast majority of degrees earned from TCUs were associate's degrees, while the vast majority of degrees earned from mainstream institutions were bachelor's degrees (most TCUs are two-year institutions). Of the 271 students, 113 earned multiple degrees. Twenty-nine of the 271 students earning degrees earned degrees at both TCUs and mainstream institutions.

TABLE 8.1
DEGREES EARNED BY INSTITUTION TYPE

Institution Type	*TD/ Certificate/ Diploma*	*AA/AS/ AAS*	*BA/BS*	*MA/MS*	*PHD/ JD/MD*	*Other*	*Totals*
TCU	18 (50%)	103 (74%)	20 (13%)				141
Mainstream	18 (50%)	36 (26%)	134 (87%)	35	11	5	239
Totals	36	139	154	35	11	5	380

Transfer and Mobility

Students included in this analysis exhibited much movement from institution to institution. Thirty-eight percent of the 232 students included in this analysis started at a TCU. 143 (62%) students started at a mainstream institution (mainstream being a non-TCU institution) with 45 of these starting at two-year mainstream institutions. In all, the 232 students attended a total of 474 institutions for an average of 2.04 institutions enrolled during their undergraduate years. Sixty-six percent of these students transferred at least once during their undergraduate years, with 91 students transferring once, 42 transferring two times, 22 transferring three times, seven transferring four times, and two transferring five times.

What is the rate of transfer for those starting at a TCU versus those starting at a mainstream institution and for those starting at two-year mainstream institutions? As shown in table 8.2, transfer rates are roughly the same for those starting at TCUs and those starting at mainstream institutions. Disaggregated further we see that the transfer rates for those starting at two-year mainstream institutions jumps dramatically to 98%, while for those starting at four-year mainstream

TABLE 8.2
TRANSFER RATES FOR STUDENTS BY STARTING INSTITUTION TYPE

Starting Institution	*Number of Students Starting at*	*Number of Students Transferring at Least Once*	*Percentage of Students Who Transferred at Least Once*
TCU Institution	89	55	62
Mainstream Institution	143	99	69
Two-Year Mainstream Institution	45	44	98
Four-Year Mainstream Institution	98	55	56

institutions it drops to 56%. Students transferring after earning a degree transferred at a rate of 42%. Many students who transferred after earning a degree did not transfer immediately, nor was the transfer always from a two-year institution to a four-year institution (as will be seen below).

Seventy percent of scholarship recipients were female, 30% were male. Were there differences in the transfer rates of male and female AIAN student scholarship recipients? Table 8.3 shows that generally speaking there were small differences in transfer rates across genders. Sixty-five percent of males and 67% of females transferred at least once during their undergraduate years. Males generally started their postsecondary enrollment in greater numbers than females at TCUs, 44% to 35%. A greater proportion of females enrolled started at mainstream institutions, 65% to 56%.

Was there a difference in the transfer rates of males and females who started at a TCU versus a mainstream institution? Table 8.4 illustrates the differences in transfer rates across genders for those starting at mainstream institutions and TCUs. Men starting at TCUs transferred at a higher rate than females starting at a TCU. Conversely, women starting at a mainstream institution transferred at a slightly higher rate than men starting at mainstream institutions. Men and women starting at two-year mainstream institutions transferred at very high rates: All males transferred and 92% of women transferred.

Taken as a whole, there is much movement of AIAN scholarship recipients regardless of starting institution type and gender across institutions.

AIAN Pathways to Success

Now that we know the percentages of scholarship recipients transferring based on a number of criteria, can we describe the pathways students take to completion? Do we know, for instance, where they start, where they go, and where they might be coming from? The beauty of the National Student Clearinghouse data is that they provide this information. They provide student enrollment history at

TABLE 8.3
MALE/FEMALE STARTING INSTITUTION AND TRANSFER RATES

	Male	*Female*
Total number of students	70	162
% of overall	70	30
% transferred	65	67
% started at TCUs	44	35
% started at mainstream	56	65
% started at two-year mainstream	14	16

TABLE 8.4
TRANSFER RATES BROKEN DOWN BY GENDER AND STARTING INSTITUTION

	Men	*% Transferred*	*Women*	*% Transferred*
Overall number	70	65	162	67
Number starting at TCUs	31	71	56	58
Number starting at mainstream	39	64	105	70
Number starting at four-year mainstream	10	100	25	92

each institution they are enrolled each term. This section describes the pathways our students took to completion based on starting institution type. What we were able to see is noteworthy. First, four-year mainstream starters transferred to TCUs and four-year mainstream institutions at relatively high rates, with the majority of transfers to TCUs at 49%. Second, very few transferred to other two-year mainstream institutions. This was not true of TCU starters, where the majority of transfers went to four-year mainstream institutions. Similarly, students starting at four-year mainstream institutions tended not to transfer to a two-year institution (only 8%), whereas the majority went to four-year mainstream institutions with about one-fifth of transfers attending TCUs. In short, two-year institutions were not destinations, generally speaking, for AIAN scholarship recipients.

Low Rate of TCU Student Mobility

Students who started at TCUs did not demonstrate a high level of mobility in comparison to two-year and four-year institution starters. Fifty-four percent of four-year starters who transferred, transferred a second time, while 40% of those transferred a third time compared to 41% of two-year mainstream starters who transferred and 54% of those second-time transfers transferred a third time. For TCU starters a second transfer occurred only 30% of the time, while 41% of second transfers transferred a third time.

TCUs in Pathways

TCUs are included in the pathways of AIAN students who started at two-year and four-year mainstream institutions. Twenty percent of four-year mainstream starters transferred to a TCU, while 49% of two-year starters did so. The same cannot be said of TCU starters—only 4% transferred to other TCUs.

The data we analyzed for this study brought to light the varying pathways our AIAN scholarship recipients take to completion. In some cases it confirmed our initial thoughts regarding the movement of AIAN students. For instance, we expected TCU students to transfer to and complete their studies at mainstream institutions more than the reverse. The data confirmed this, showing that four-year institutions became the ending destination for many AIAN scholarship recipients, especially those transferring multiple times. Eighty-six percent of four-year starters ended at a four-year mainstream institution after three transfers, as did 45% of TCU starters. In other ways the data revealed interesting points to consider in their pathways to success: (1) Our AIAN students tended to transfer back to places of institutional familiarity; 40% of four-year mainstream starters transferred back to their original institution after their first transfer out, as did 18% of TCU starters; (2) Summer enrollment seems to be an integral component in the pathways to success. Eighty-three percent of all scholarship recipients have enrolled in at least one summer session; and (3) There is some transfer movement of AIAN scholarship recipients across state lines, approximately 33% of scholarship recipients having done so.

Discussion: Comparison to NSC

How does the information gleaned from this descriptive analysis of scholarship recipient data compare to national data? Put another way, are our funded students different from other students when it comes to transfer and mobility? Unfortunately, as we pointed out above, there does not exist AIAN student-level transfer and mobility data that we can use for comparison. NSC has produced an extensive look at transfer and mobility, but the methods used were entirely different from what we were able to employ. For one, their data centered on first-time entering students, while ours did not. Second, this cohort of students entered in the fall of 2008. In addition, the time span was six years. Our study was not cohort-based since our data were not reliable enough to determine first-time entering students. Instead, we focused on a "cohort" of students who were funded in 2009–2010 and 2010–2011. In addition, our time span ranged from fall 2001 through fall 2015.

The limitations of data in regard to student-level AIAN students play a major part in our inability to say anything substantive in the context of transfer and mobility. We have a small sample of Full Circle Scholarship recipients who may or may not reflect the AIAN students enrolled at TCUs and mainstream institutions. In addition, we are cognizant of the fact that TCUs are not currently submitting data to the NSC system that would allow our work the ability to compare against other like-situated postsecondary students. Given these limitations and shortcomings associated with the data we can say something about our scholarship recipients (and we have). We can also make some tentative comparisons with the NSC study on transfer and mobility with the understanding that what we will be putting side by side below needs to take into account all the different methods and types of students and institutions reported in the results of their work and ours. Finally, showing NSC data and our Full Circle data side by side can help illustrate the types of information each system can offer and also show where additional information is needed.

The data in tables 8.5 and 8.6 suggest that AIAN students transfer and have greater mobility than non-AIAN students. Our male students transferred at a 67% rate while our female students transferred at a 65% rate, compared to the NSC male students who transferred at a 37% rate and females at a 39% rate. In the NSC data, the rate of transfer for students starting at two-year institutions and four-year institutions differed little, 40% to 37%, whereas for our students, those who started at two-year institutions transferred at an extremely higher rate, 98% versus those who started at four-year institutions and TCU, 56% and 62%, respectively.

Recommendations for Research and Practice

Four recommendations for research and practice arise from our analysis of AIAN TCU and Full Circle Scholarship recipients: One, given the number of students transferring multiple times, more research is needed to understand why students transfer multiple times and the challenges associated with multiple transfers. Is there a longer time to completion, for instance, and how does this impact financial aid? Two, the transfer pathways indicate that many students transfer back to their original institution. Given this phenomenon, four-year institutions

TABLE 8.5
NSC AND FULL CIRCLE RECIPIENT DEMOGRAPHIC DATA

	NSC	*Full-Circle*
Overall Number of Students	3.5 billion	793 (unduplicated) 232 analyzed
STARTING INSTITUTION TYPE FALL 2008 COHORT		
2-year public	48.2%	19.4%
4-year public	32.2%	42.2%
Tribal Colleges and Universities	—	38.4%
GENDER		
Male		30.2%
Female		69.8%

TABLE 8.6
TRANSFER RATES FOR SELECTED NSC AND FULL CIRCLE DATA POINTS

	NSC (%)	*Full Circle (%)*
Starting Institution Type		
Two-year public	39.8	98
After receiving associate's	3.9	—
Four-year public	36.5	56
Tribal Colleges and Universities	—	42
Gender		
MALE	36.8	67
Starting at a TCU	—	72
Starting at a four-year mainstream	—	44
Starting at a two-year mainstream	—	100
FEMALE	39	65
Starting at a TCU	—	56
Starting at a four-year mainstream	—	59
Starting at a two-year mainstream	—	97
Out of State		
Two-year public	18.5	33
Four-year public	24.0	39
Tribal Colleges and Universities	—	36
MALE		
Two-year public	—	38
Four-year public	—	35
Tribal Colleges and Universities	—	32
FEMALE		
Two-year public	—	31
Four-year public	—	40
Tribal Colleges and Universities	—	31

(*continued*)

	NSC (%)	*Full Circle (%)*
Timing of Transfer		
Second year	36.6	—
Third year	24.4	—
Destination of Transfer		
Two-year public to four-year public	42.2	—
Two-year public to two-year public	36.5	—
Four-year public to four-year public	35.7	—
Four-year public to two-year public	38.1	—

should develop a resource guide or department for transfer students on what courses they should take at another institution in the event they plan to or end up transferring back to original institution. TCUs should evaluate transcripts and courses from transfer students to determine if they have enough credits to receive an associate's degree. Three, mechanisms can also be put in place to assist TCUs in submitting data to national databases, specifically NSC, but also encourage the use of data at the institutional level to assist TCUs in their work in following students outside their own institutions. Four, institutions should be encouraged to require AIAN students to submit proof of tribal enrollment or lineal descent. This additional work and specification of AIAN students should be reflected in national postsecondary datasets such as IPEDs or NCES which would allow TCUs to underscore their impact on the overall success of AIAN nationally.

Using an Indigenous research methodological lens to assist in the analysis of quantitative data like that included in this study proposes a solution to this problem. It points to an integration of tribal enrollment and sovereignty policy. It allows tribes to verify members in an area that typically sees no value in doing so. In essence, inclusion of this data makes it clear that Indian identification is a very important contested, political ground—who defines citizenship and how is it defined? As it currently stands, the individual student self-identifies as AIAN with no proper method of verification. Verifying student tribal enrollment (whether it be in federally or state-recognized tribes) through additional mechanisms would open avenues in higher education institutions for discussion and possible collaboration with tribal entities. In essence, it would create a place within higher education institutions for tribal educational officials to interact and share concerns. With regard to the data specifically, the inclusion of verified tribal enrollment data allows for a more nuanced comparison of AIAN data across institution type. Researchers would be able to make more valid comparisons regarding student enrollment, persistence and retention rates between TCUs and mainstream institutions, for instance. Further disaggregation of data would make the data more tribal-specific, thus better informing tribes, tribal higher education departments and potentially state-level policy regarding the pathways students take to postsecondary success.

Conclusion

In this chapter, we were able to illustrate the pathways AIAN College Fund scholarship recipients took to completing postsecondary degrees. We highlighted the types of data available to the College Fund organization that are not currently available to other organizations/institutions. The data the College Fund has access to include information on verifiably tribally enrolled students, a marker not typically used in postsecondary AIAN information. In addition, most of these students attend TCUs whose transfer data are typically incomplete. With this descriptive analysis we were able to produce some important preliminary findings that suggest AIAN exhibit much more movement in their journey to postsecondary success than their non-Native counterparts. We were able to quantify transfer rates for our students and eventually were able to "compare" these findings to national student data found in a National Student Clearinghouse report. What became painfully clear is that there are some serious holes in both our dataset and the NSC data (and other national datasets) that preclude the possibility of making valid comparisons of our students to AIAN students nationally. Our ability to make important statements about the movement of postsecondary undergraduate AIANs is hampered by the inability to make these comparisons across institution type. One of the main points of contention factoring into the inability to make valid comparisons is the fact that national datasets do not require AIAN to verify tribal enrollment. This is a huge obstacle because we do not know if we are actually comparing like groups.

An Indigenous research focus allows us to highlight these discrepancies and illustrate the need for more nuanced classifications of AIAN students. Doing so allows us to show the practicality of inclusion of additional information as well as the pragmatic uses of this data. In addition, we hold ourselves accountable to the data, paying special attention to our understanding of the potential impact and uses of our data—the aim is to describe the AIAN postsecondary experience more succinctly and efficiently and also to tell the TCU and AIAN student story more fully. This in turn can be used for the benefit of tribes, tribal colleges, and AIAN communities and organizations.

REFERENCES

American Association of Community Colleges. (2015). Community College Completion. Retrieved from http://www.aacc.nche.edu/AboutCC/Trends/Documents/completion_report_05212015.pdf

American Indian Higher Education Consortium. (2016). Retrieved from http://www.aihec.org

Benham, M. K. P., & Stein, W. J. (Eds.). (2003). *The Renaissance of American Indian Higher Education: Capturing the Dream.* Mahwah, NJ: Lawrence Erlbaum Associates.

Brown, D. (2003). Tribal colleges: Playing a key role in the transition from secondary to post-secondary education for American Indian students. *Journal of American Indian Education,* 42, 36–45.

Dejong, D. H. (1993). *Promises of the Past: A History of Indian Education.* Golden, CO: North American Press.

Dell, C. A. (2000). *The first semester experiences of first semester American Indian transfer students* (Doctoral dissertation). Montana State University, Bozeman, MT.

Flynn, S. V., Olson, S. D., & Yellig, A. D. (2014). American Indian acculturation: Tribal lands to predominately White postsecondary settings. *Journal of Counseling & Development,* 92(3), 280–293.

Garroutte, E. M. (2003). *Real Indians: Identity and Survival of Native America.* Berkeley, Los Angeles, London: University of California Press.

Kahakalau, K. (2004). Indigenous heuristic Action research: Bridging western and Indigenous research methodologies. *Hūlili: Multidisciplinary Research on Hawaiian Well-Being,* 1. Honolulu: HI: Kamehameha Schools, 19–33.

Lee, T. S. (2007). Successes and challenges in higher education transitions. *Tribal College,* 19(1), 30.

Makomenaw, M. V. A. (2012). Welcome to a new world: Experiences of American Indian tribal college and university transfer students at predominantly white institutions. *International Journal of Qualitative Studies in Education,* 25(7), 855–866.

Meyer, M. A. (2003). *Ho'oulu Our Time of Becoming: Hawaiian Epistemology and Early Writings.* Honolulu, HI: Ai Pohaku Press.

National Center of Educational Statistics (2014). http://nces.ed.gov/programs/digest/d14/tables/dt14_306.10.asp

National Center of Educational Statistics (2016). http://nces.ed.gov/collegenavigator/ Smith, L. T. (1999). *Decolonizing Methodologies: Research and Indigenous Peoples.* London and New York: Zed Books Ltd.

Taylor, J. S. (1999). *America's first people: Factors which affect their persistence in higher education.* ASHE annual meeting paper. ERIC documents.

U.S. Department of Education, National Center for Education Statistics. (2012). The Condition of Education 2012 (NCES 2012–045), Indicator 47.

CHAPTER 9

Moving beyond Financial Aid to Support Native College Students

AN EXAMINATION OF THE GATES MILLENNIUM SCHOLARS PROGRAM

Natalie Rose Youngbull (Cheyenne and Arapaho Tribes of Oklahoma)

The Gates Millennium Scholarship Program (GMSP) was founded in 1999 and promised to fund 20,000 high-achieving, community-oriented, and engaged scholars in 20 years. The Gates Millennium Scholarship is both merit-based and need-based; recipients demonstrated high academic merit and involvement throughout high school and proved substantial financial need. As high-achieving and low-income students, recipients are able to attend their first choice institution with the scholarship funding. GMSP quickly became recognized as one of the most competitive and prestigious scholarships to receive, and those recipients of the scholarship were welcomed into the Gates family. Annually, 1,000 scholars were awarded the scholarship and 150 of those scholars were American Indian. Every year, Indian Country celebrated the incoming class of American Indian Gates Millennium Scholars (AIGMS) for their accomplishments and potential influence within higher education and their respective tribal communities. AIGMS carried the hopes and dreams of their families and communities as they embarked on their journeys into higher education. Throughout the years, the GMSP has achieved an impressive overall five-year graduation rate of 82.2% among all four racial/ethnic cohorts (GMSP website, n.d.). Yet, of the four racial/ethnic cohorts, the American Indian cohort boasted the lowest overall graduation rate (S. Abbott, personal communication, fall 2009).

Thus far, existing research has identified several factors that play into an American Indian student's persistence within higher education, such as family support, involvement with the Native community on campus, and maintaining spirituality (Jackson, Smith, & Hill, 2003). What has not been thoroughly examined in previous studies is the influence of academic merit on the persistence of American Indian students as incoming freshmen to institutions of higher education. Literature focusing on high-achieving American Indian students is lacking, as the American Indian college student population traditionally has been considered to be too small a group to partition out into specific groups. Lack of academic preparation has been noted as a nonpersistence factor for American Indian students (Brown & Kurpius, 1997; Fann, 2002), but research is necessary to show if this has the same meaning for high-achieving American Indian students. Another area that has not been explored as a major factor of nonpersistence is American Indian students' financial aid status. Financial difficulties have also been linked to the attrition of American Indian students (Guillory & Wolverton, 2008), but there is a need to study the impact of substantial financial aid on American Indian students' nonpersistence in college. Academic merit and financial aid are two important aspects for all students' success in their journey through higher education (Perna, 2006; Roderick, Nagaoka, & Coca, 2009), and are especially important factors to take into account when an American Indian student decides to leave college before graduation. Though the GMSP addresses two of the largest barriers identified for Native students, some AIGMS still do not persist. The issues of nonpersistence of American Indian Gates Millennium Scholars have yet to be explored. The purpose of this study was to gain a greater understanding of why 20 American Indian college students who were high-achieving and received the Gates Millennium scholarship did not persist to graduation. To achieve this greater understanding from an Indigenous perspective, it was important to utilize existing theoretical frameworks developed by Native scholars that employed critical, culturally sensitive lenses for the analysis. Additionally, centering on the participants' stories was an Indigenous methodological approach used to focus on building relationships and sharing knowledge to understand participants' experiences.

Review of Literature

American Indian College Student Educational Pathways

This section provides an insight into the current statistics of American Indian college student enrollment trends, educational achievements, and the type of institutions attended. Overall, the enrollment of American Indian college students has more than doubled over the past 30 years (Devoe, Darling-Churchill, & Snyder, 2008). The rates of American Indians who have attained a bachelor's degree range from 4% to 9.3%, while 20–27% of the general population has attained the same degree (Jackson & Turner, 2004; Native American Higher Education Initiative, 2005). In sum, American Indian students are matriculating to college at a higher rate than ever before, yet still lagging behind in representation and completion within institutions of higher education.

Examining the type of institutions American Indian college students are attending is important to understanding overall enrollment trends. Brayboy, Fann, Castagno, and Solyom (2012) acknowledge that a hierarchy exists among institutions of higher education and proximity is an issue for many Native students. Lowe (2005) addressed the lack of change in enrollment trends for American Indian students: "Even though progress has been made in aggregate Native American enrollment over the past twenty years, little has changed with respect to the types of institutions at which Native American students are enrolled. Data show that Native Americans continue to be underrepresented both in the more prestigious private and four-year sectors of higher education and overrepresented in the less prestigious public and two-year sectors" (p. 34).

In the next few sections, financial aid and campus racial climate literature will be discussed to provide a better understanding of the barriers faced by American Indian college students on their educational pathways.

Impact of Financial Aid

Eighty-six percent of American Indian college students received financial aid and 46.5% were first-generation, low-income students (U.S. NCES, 2015). As the federal Pell grant continues to decrease in its ability to cover students' cost of attendance (Shea, 2003), the majority of American Indian college students will be affected. Additionally, low-income students are significantly affected by the shift in financial aid policy from need-based aid to merit-based aid (Shea, 2003). Thus, low-income and minority students today are faced with the challenges of rising tuition and greater competition for access to grants and scholarships to help alleviate some of the burden of paying for college (Heller, 2003). As a result, American Indian students have to seek other funding options, but often experience a lack of access to information on additional financial aid sources (Cunningham, McSwain, & Keselman, 2007; Guillory & Wolverton, 2008; Tierney, Sallee, & Venegas, 2007). The Gates Millennium Scholarship served as an additional source of financial aid for American Indian students, as it was need-based first and then merit-based.

It is important to examine the impact of financial aid upon American Indian students, as unmet financial need has been identified as a key factor in the persistence of this particular student population (Guillory & Wolverton, 2008; Tierney et al., 2007). Additionally, understanding the funding opportunities for American Indian college students helps to negate the general assumption that Native college students have guaranteed full funding to attend the college of their choice. In her dissertation on the impact of tribal financial aid on American Indian student college-going, Nelson (2015) underscored a major financial aid assumption made about American Indian college students—increased financial aid as an indicator of higher persistence to graduation rates. This research study also challenges this assumption as the participants were recipients of substantial financial aid and did not persist to graduation with the generous funding.

Campus Racial Climate

Campus racial climate is defined as the general racial atmosphere within a college campus that directly impacts access, persistence, and graduation rates of minority students (Solorzano, Ceja, & Yosso, 2000). Within the existing campus racial climate literature, there are limited studies focused on American Indian college students. However, there are several studies on American Indian student retention and persistence that have identified nonpersistence factors that are linked to the campus racial climate, including feelings of invisibility and/or isolation and a lack of sense of belonging on campus (Brayboy, 2004; Gloria & Kurpius, 2001; Jackson et al., 2003; Wells, 1997). Brayboy's (2004) study on American Indian students' issues with (in)visbility in Ivy institutions did not address stereotype threat directly, but the study revealed how these particular students dealt with issues of visibility by employing strategies to be more invisible on campus to lessen the possibility of problematic experiences. Castagno and Lee (2007) examined one university's policy regarding Indian mascots and the lack of a policy concerning ethnic fraud. Though the university claimed to be dedicated to promoting diversity and increasing the number of American Indian students and faculty, it did not fully eradicate the use of Native mascots on campus, nor did it implement a policy to guard against ethnic fraud. The university received a formal request from a group of Native faculty, staff, and students to implement a policy to require self-identified Native students to provide proof of tribal enrollment before receiving financial support from the university. The university responded by claiming that it is not within the institution's purview to institute policy and procedures to identify enrolled members of tribal nations.

In previous studies, campus racial climate has tended to be generalized to the overall campus. Though not directly linked to the overall campus racial climate, one study found American Indian students' nonpersistence correlated with the lack of comfort and disconnect felt on campus (Gloria & Kurpius, 2001). This finding sustains previous research that found American Indian students' perceptions of college were influenced by experiences of marginalization and alienation on campus (Lin, Lacounte, & Eder, 1988; Huffman, 1991). These factors are directly related to an institution's campus racial climate that impacts American Indian students' persistence.

Methodology

This study utilized a phenomenological qualitative approach guided by an Indigenous research paradigm. A phenomenological qualitative approach centers on the experience and the interpretation through the senses, with emphasis on the knowledge and understanding we gain from our experiences (Merriam, 2009). A qualitative design is more culturally responsive to the American Indian population, as an Indigenous paradigm recognizes that knowledge is built upon the relationships created with the people and all that surrounds us (Wilson, 2001). Through an Indigenous paradigm, knowledge is not created or owned; rather, it is relational and shared (Wilson, 2001). To center on relationship, one-on-one interviews were conducted with participants to gain in-depth knowledge and understanding about the experiences of AIGMS's nonpersistence within institutions of higher education. Through interviews, AIGMS shared their stories and journeys through higher education. Utilizing stories is not new to qualitative methodology; as Seidman (2006) stated, "stories are a way of knowing" (p. 7). According to Kovach (2009), though, the means by which story is used are culturally specific, and for Indigenous peoples, stories contain knowledge and wisdom while at the same time demonstrating relationships. In her dissertation research, Tachine (2015) utilized two Indigenous methodologies, Indigenous Storywork (Archibald, 2008) and Narrative Inquiry (Riessman, 2008), for their emphasis on story as an instrumental mode of inquiry. These Indigenous methodologies assisted Tachine (2015) in illuminating the influential pre-collegiate experiences of ten successful Navajo college freshmen. Kovach (2009) described stories as "active agents within a relational world, pivotal in gaining insight into a phenomenon" (p. 95). Sharing stories is congruent with the building of knowledge through relationships within American Indian communities.

A qualitative methodological approach was appropriate for this research because it sought to gain understanding of the experiences of American Indian Gates Millennium Scholars who did not persist to graduation, including identifying factors from both inside and outside higher education institutions. To align the qualitative methodology with an Indigenous approach, three theoretical frameworks—Tribal Critical Race Theory (TribalCrit) (Brayboy, 2005), Cultural Models of Education (Fryberg & Markus, 2007) and the Family Education Model (FEM) (HeavyRunner & DeCelles, 2002)—were utilized. TribalCrit was developed out of a need for a theoretical framework to specifically explore American Indian lived experiences with cultural distinction since European contact, including American Indian persistence and retention in institutions of higher education (Brayboy, 2005). Cultural models of education were utilized to prove that Native American college students understood education to be a tool for success for the community significantly more than their comparison groups, and were more likely to put their family and community concerns ahead of academic concerns. FEM utilizes the concept of the family structure to improve student persistence to graduation rates at Tribal Colleges and Universities. Each framework was chosen for its ability to offer a critical, culturally sensitive lens in the analysis to gain a deeper cultural understanding of AIGMS's experiences.

In qualitative research, the researcher is the primary instrument. The researcher is essential for gaining an understanding of the phenomenon through collecting and analyzing the data (Merriam, 2009). Merriam acknowledged subjectivity as a major weakness in utilizing the researcher as the key instrument, but subjectivity cannot be separated from an Indigenous paradigm. "Tribal epistemologies are a way of knowing that does not debate the subjectivity factor in knowledge production—subjectivity is a given" (Kovach, 2009, p. 111).

Role of the Researcher

As an American Indian Gates Millennium Scholar alumna, this research inquiry was personally driven by the need to understand how other AIGMS's did not persist to graduation. I was fortunate to use the scholarship funding to receive my bachelor's and master's degrees and fund three years of my doctoral program. Knowing that I had the funding to cover my educational costs made it easier to continue on my educational journey. No one in my family had ever received such a scholarship, and I felt it was my responsibility to make the most of it. My successes were not my own, though. They were a product of the many mentors who guided and assisted me along the way. Like many of my study participants, I believed in maintaining relationships within and giving back to my community. Focusing my dissertation topic on AIGMS, a group that I also belong to, was my way of giving back not only to my community but also to the organization that provided a way for me to reach the highest level of education.

I firmly believe that these individuals also had to have reached a point where they were ready to share their stories. They spoke candidly about their experiences and exhibited the emotions associated with their struggles. That is why their stories are so rich. At the end of the interview, each participant thanked GMSP for the funding and thanked me for the opportunity to share their story and experiences. Sharing their experiences and stories was not just for their own personal closure, but more for the impact they could have on upcoming Native college students. That was their way of giving back in return for the opportunity they were given, even if they weren't able to utilize it to its fullest potential.

In qualitative inquiry, it is important for the researcher to identify herself in relation to the research topic (Creswell, 2009). Indigenous methodologies recognize the importance of identifying oneself in the research as it clarifies the perspective one has on the world (Hampton, 1995; Kovach, 2009; Meyer, 2004). Identifying the researcher's background may provide better understanding of the topic and interpretation of the data (Creswell, 2009). Through an Indigenous paradigm, Kovach (2009) acknowledged that "it is not only the questions we ask and how we go about asking them, but who we are in the asking" (p.111). As an AIGMS alum, I understood the process the participants endured to receive the scholarship and its impact upon participants' self-perceptions in college.

This insider perspective provided a common understanding between the participants and me that encouraged the participants to openly share their experiences without fear that I would misrepresent their words. "Indigenous people versed in their culture know that sharing a story in research situates it within a collective memory. Likewise, Indigenous researchers ought to know of the deep responsibility of requesting an oral history—i.e., an individual recounting of a particular happening. A researcher assumes a responsibility that the story shared will be treated with the respect it deserves in acknowledgment of the relationship from which it emerges" (Kovach, 2009, p. 97). In addition, my background as an AIGMS alum and experience as an administrator working in higher education gave me a unique perspective on this particular population.

Site/Source

The Gates Millennium Scholarship Program (GMSP) is a national scholarship program that serves racial minority students from across the nation. Annually, 1,000 incoming college freshmen were awarded through the scholarship program. Recipients belonged to one of four racial/ethnic categories—African American, American Indian/Alaska Natives, Asian and Pacific Islander American, and Hispanic American. Annually, 150 American Indian students were recipients of the scholarship program. Though GMSP boasts exceptional overall graduation rates among its scholarship recipients, the American Indian cohort possesses the lowest persistence to graduation rate of all the cohorts (S. Abbott, personal communication, fall 2009).

Research Participants

Twenty former AIGMS were recruited through purposeful sampling. Purposeful sampling was the chosen method based upon the criteria to be awarded a Gates Millennium Scholarship. The purposeful sample was drawn from the AIGMS who did not persist to graduation with the scholarship funding. The exact number of AIGMS who fall into this category is currently unknown. Yet through my interactions with the American Indian Graduate Center (AIGC) staff, the nonprofit organization that houses the American Indian cohort of the Gates Millennium Scholarship, I was told that there is a considerable number of AIGMS who fit this category.

Relationships were central to connecting with each of the participants for this study. Margaret Kovach (2009) expounded on the importance of this factor in gathering participants: "there has to be evidence that the Indigenous researcher is approaching this work respectfully. Because of the relational factor in sampling, it is not simply a matter of the researcher choosing participants. This process is more reciprocal" (p. 126). Personally, I knew of a handful of former AIGMS who fit the criteria. Beyond personal associations, I utilized my extended network of family, friends, and professional contacts to connect with seven other former AIGMS. I am immensely indebted to my network as they personally outreached to each of these participants and vouched for my credibility and genuine approach to this research. An example of relationality employed in this research study is gaining a participant through my mother's outreach to her contacts. The remaining eight participants were reached through social media; they were recommended through professional networks who heard about my research and knew of a former AIGMS who fit the criteria.

Data Collection

Purposeful sampling was chosen to intentionally investigate the student population that significantly relates to the theoretical frameworks that were utilized (Maxwell, 2005). Each participant filled out a participant questionnaire form and was interviewed one-on-one. Seidman (2006) stated that interviewing "is deeply satisfying to researchers who are interested in others' stories" (p. 14). Fifteen of the 20 interviews were conducted over the phone, as these participants were located all across the nation. I was able to conduct five in-person interviews with participants who lived within driving distance from my location. These interviews were conducted in spaces chosen by the participants and included the participant's office, a conference room, a local coffee shop, a tribal college library, and a grandmother's dining room.

Through an Indigenous methodology, it was important to ensure that respect was embedded throughout the protocol (Kovach, 2009). The design of the interview protocol was guided by the tenets of Tribal Critical Race theory, with each question related to one or more of the tenets. It was important to begin each interview by establishing connection and familiarity with the participant. So I introduced myself and shared my background as a former AIGMS, then I asked participants to tell me about themselves in the way they felt most comfortable. In relation to the importance of identity and acknowledging oral histories as legitimate sources of data/theory, I asked the participants to identify themselves and to share an experience from their adolescence when they realized education was important to them. To underscore how colonization is endemic to society and assimilation as part of the educational process, the next few questions focused on their experiences on campus including their transition during their first year. Related to the tenets of understanding knowledge, power, and culture through a Native lens, I inquired about their relationship with their family while on campus. In regard to the importance of acknowledging the vast, unique, and evolving backgrounds of American Indians, I focused a question on the source of inspiration that led the participants to college. The closing questions focused on their correspondence with the GMSP, advice about college from similar students, and the factors involved in their decision to leave college.

The participant questionnaire form collected basic demographic information and important values of participants. One-on-one interviews ranged between 45 minutes to two hours in length and were transcribed within one to two weeks of the interview date. All interviews were audio recorded and transcribed verbatim. Each participant received a transcribed copy of their interview, for the purpose of acknowledging that their stories and experiences belong to them and not me, as well as being able to follow up to clarify any vague information from the interview. Descriptive notes were taken during the interviews and I wrote a memo after each one detailing salient and notable information.

Data Analysis

Since my research objective is to uncover reasons behind the nonpersistence of American Indian Gates Millennium Scholars from institutions of higher education, the data analysis was guided by category construction, which allows for any piece of the data to be considered important to answering the research questions (Merriam, 2009). Category construction permitted a fluid process for data analysis to take place concurrently throughout the data gathering period. Continually asking questions during this period about the data was important to the overall analysis, as Corbin and Strauss (2008) affirmed that "asking questions and thinking about the range of possible answers helps us to take the role of the other so that we can better understand the problem from the participant's perspective" (p. 70). Open coding was utilized to remain as open about the data as possible. Next, analytical coding facilitated the process of grouping the codes into categories through interpretation and reflection on meaning (Merriam, 2009). Throughout the analysis I wrote memos to flesh out connections among the codes, record emerging themes, and to reach for deeper meaning and understanding of the data. "The very act of writing memos . . . forces the analyst to think about the data. And it is in thinking that analysis occurs" (Corbin & Strauss, 2008, p. 118). And finally, I had the opportunity to share preliminary findings with a group of Native scholars who provided critical feedback on the emergent themes. These processes were central to the authenticity of the findings.

Findings

American Indian Gates Millennium Scholars' persistence in college was affected by factors related to both institutional and personal issues. On campus, AIGMS's experiences were impacted by their institutions' campus racial climate. The first emergent theme discusses exclusion and lack of belonging. The second part of the findings elaborates on the condition of the Gates Millennium Scholarship Program that impeded AIGMS's persistence to graduation. The second emergent theme discusses the inflexible deferment policy.

Exclusion and Lack of Belonging

I did feel like a foreigner, you know. I didn't feel comfortable.

—David

David chose his institution based on location; it was located in his own tribal community. Yet he did not feel a sense of belonging on campus. TribalCrit's sixth tenet identifies governmental and educational policies as problematic due to their overall goal of assimilation (Brayboy, 2005). As a result of these policies, mainstream campuses do not reflect Native ways of being. AIGMS expressed feelings of marginalization, isolation, and invisibility within their campus experiences. They felt tokenized and unacknowledged on campus. They also discussed the impact of lack of Native representation among faculty.

Marginalization, Isolation, and Invisibility. Bailey wishes she would've put more thought into her choice of institution. In retrospect, she realized that being near her family was vital to her well-being. She acknowledges that this is an important factor among other Native college-bound students. Particularly, she came from a tight-knit community where everyone acknowledged each other—either verbally or with a wave, handshake, or hug. This is what she was used to, so it made her re-consider her decision to attend that particular institution when she experienced the complete opposite on her campus.

> My family is essential to me. Being away from them was so hard. Like it's even hard that they actually can't visit me at college. It's something that I knew is very prevalent in other Native American students. It's being away from family and it's culture shock. You're so used to there being other Natives around and they feel like they don't have to hide or that they don't have to look down. One thing I really didn't like about [my university] was the fact that I felt ashamed to be myself, to be Native. It's not something you should ever be ashamed of. But I learned how to be ashamed of myself there. And it wasn't . . . because there were other students there that were tribal students and we banded together and we really did help each other. I'm pretty sure I would've went crazy if I didn't have them. But just walking on the campus and knowing that you can't look up because people are just staring at you and giving you weird looks and it's constant. And it's everybody that I talked with there saying this. So it was like literally hold your head down in shame and walk around them to go to class. And that was really hard for me to do. (Bailey)

On campus, Bailey felt marginalized when she tried to interact with people the way she was taught from home. Instead of acknowledgment, she was shrugged off, ignored, or rebuked for her efforts. And when she branched out to make connections with non-Native students, she was treated as a token to them. "They'd be like 'here's my Native friend,' but they'd never want to hear about my culture. That was hard to take, not being able to talk about it, like some big shameful situation." Interestingly, the majority of tribal students on campus that she bonded with were also Gates scholars. She discussed how they were a tightly knit group that came together to escape ostracism of the larger campus.

Isolation on campus was another issue discussed by AIGMS. Thomas connected with other students during the summer bridge program on campus, but lost touch when the fall semester began. "After that program was over and the actual semester started, you know how it is, everybody, the campus blows up big time." With no connections on campus, Thomas felt like he was disassociating from campus. Similarly, Rachel had mixed emotions about campus. "I was lost. I was in awe, like 'wow, I'm actually here.' Then again, I was alone. I felt alone . . . I was literally alone, standing there like watching the whole world spin around me and I'm just like 'what am I doing here?'" Thomas and Rachel both missed the deadline for housing in the residence halls, so they had to live in apartments during their freshman year. Thomas lived with two friends who were upperclassmen and Rachel rented a room in one of the student apartment complexes. Rachel never made connections on campus; she didn't reach out for any support and didn't finish the fall semester. Thomas, on the other hand, sought out the Native center on campus and made frequent visits there, but he never asked for help. It was difficult for him partly because, he said, "everything came naturally to me," but it was also tied to his cultural way of being.

> I guess maybe, you know how [my tribe], our culture, our demeanor, we're meant to be humble and kind of like the ones behind the scenes holding things up. And to be strong, I guess, but not to put ourselves out there or be flashy, or whatever. So those kind of things. So I would just be quiet and keep to myself and not really connect with people. (Thomas)

It was important for Thomas to carry those traditional teachings with him and continue to practice his cultural ways of being on campus, and he preferred to be recognized for his authenticity. "I wanted to be acknowledged, but off my own efforts . . . I wanted it to be genuine, somebody to take an interest, but I didn't want [it] to be like 'look at me, look at me, I did this' in a way." In accordance with other Indigenous scholars, TribalCrit asserts that Native ways of being and knowing are fundamental to self-determination and self-education (Brayboy, 2005; Barnhardt & Kawagley, 2005; Battiste, 2002; Lomawaima & McCarty, 2002). Though institutions of higher education may have Native studies departments or centers, AIGMS's feelings of isolation are directed at the larger campus. On campus, Thomas knew where to find support—the Native center, Native faculty and roommates. Outside of those specific spheres, he felt like just another face in the crowd and found it difficult to relate to his instructors, as most of them were international graduate students. There was a lack of connection that plagued Thomas as the semester progressed.

Nadine's institution had a multicultural center on campus and when she sought assistance through the center, her experience was unpleasant. She felt excluded and couldn't understand why she was treated in that way. She tried to shrug it off and attempted to develop a relationship with the staff and center, but it didn't resolve the exclusion she was feeling. Nadine wasn't afraid to advocate for herself and found support outside of campus at a local tribal college.

> It was weird. When I would go in and ask for help and stuff and they would just sit me there. And I would be sitting there for like 45 minutes and there would be four people who'd come in after me that would be seen before me. And I'd be like "what's going on here?" And then, I would go see a different counselor and everything would be taken care of right away. You know, they're like, "oh, let's do this." You need a tutor. We can set that up for you. And I was like "awesome!" And they tried to incorporate that into the multicultural center, but it was just like, it felt the same way. Every time I would go back it was really hard. I mean to feel comfortable going to that center. And then towards the end of one semester, I actually requested a, what do you call those, work studies with the multicultural center. Praying and hoping, you know, that I'd be able to connect with them on a more personal level and maybe build a more personal relationship off of that. But towards the end, it was just like, no it still doesn't feel right. People would treat me differently, and I was just like "why is that happening," you know? I didn't really understand. I would actually get help off of campus with, um, there's a different tribe around there. Oh, I can't remember their name. And I would actually go to their community college there. They had a community center there and I would be able to talk to other Natives and I actually felt accepted there. And they weren't trying to say, "oh, well you're doing all this other stuff. Why do you need help?" Stuff like that. And then, when I went there they were like, "yeah, don't worry about it, you can come whenever you want. Just let us know when you're here so we can help you out, pay attention. If you need a tutor, we're here for you." Stuff like that. It was so much more comfortable being there than on campus. (Nadine)

It was fortunate for Nadine that the tribal college was near her institution and that she was instinctive enough to look outside of campus for the support she needed; but that's not always the case for Native students at any particular institution. When Native students do not find the necessary support in the very centers that are supposedly designed to serve them, it's easy to understand how they can feel isolated on campus. Nadine also received flawed advice from the director of the multicultural center concerning her Gates scholarship and the purchase of a laptop. She ended up owing the institution.

Invisibility on campus was another issue for AIGMS. Brayboy (2005) explained that Native students face this problem on mainstream campus due to general society's lack of awareness and knowledge about Native peoples today. The Native student presence on campuses varies with the student population and location. Still, it was surprising for Dana to face this while she was a Native ambassador for her institution, especially given the substantial amount of tribal nations located in the area.

> Dealing with the fact that I'm this Native ambassador carrying this reign and then whenever I would go out, sometimes I would meet such ignorant people that didn't even know that Native people still existed. I met some people from [the city], some girls, some Caucasian women. They were like "oh so you're from India?" I'm like "no, I'm from here. Did you know there's 23 tribes here?" And they'd be like "no, I didn't even know there was Native people that still existed. I thought they were dead." That was an eye opener and something that was really hard to realize as a Native person. People don't even recognize our existence. They don't even care we exist. (Dana)

This experience was disheartening for Dana and negatively affected her sense of belonging at her institution. Dana, along with her fellow AIGMS, felt as though their experiences at their respective institutions did not meet their expectations. Beyond expectations of their Native background being embraced on campus, they thought the title, Gates Millennium Scholar, would be recognized among their faculty. However, their experiences proved to them that their presence, both as Native and a Gates Millennium Scholar, remained unacknowledged.

Lack of Native Representation among Faculty. Several AIGMS pointed out the lack of Native representation among faculty on their campuses. In particular, Freda and David experienced defining moments in their American Indian courses with non-Native faculty. Freda's institution had a well-established Native community, on campus including a Native studies program. In her first semester she was enrolled in a large American Indian studies course taught by a faculty member in the Anthropology department. The non-Native instructor dismissed the actions of the federal government upon Native peoples and the full impact of those actions in the first class session. This bold statement left Freda in disbelief and unsure of how to react.

> Being a Native American woman, I remember going into, it was an American Indian history class and the professor, I will never forget one of the first words that came out of his mouth during our first class was that genocide never

> happened on American soil. So, I think maybe that was the first encounter that I had that I totally disagreed with him and I felt like he was completely ignoring American Indian heritage and things that have happened on American soil. It was to the point where I thought he was being sarcastic, you know, but he was being serious. That is just what he truly believed. And I guess I was just appalled that he was teaching American Indian history. That he was telling students, because I feel, I know in fact, that I was maybe one of three Indian students in that class. So I guess that was probably the one that sticks out of my mind the most, is that I felt like that I wanted to tell him "you're full of crap," you know. (Laughs.) And how dare you, you know, is how I felt almost. How dare you say that to us. And how dare you be teaching this and as a white man. Yeah, I guess that was one of the major ones that I felt like my teachings and the things that I've learned and grew up with as a person, our way of life, that that was totally disrespected. But at the time being just an early student, it was like I was unsure of how to even approach that. I was unsure if I should automatically speak up, speak my mind and tell him you're full of it. That it's not true. I was very unsure, so I didn't say anything. But I remember the feeling. I remember the feeling. (Freda)

That feeling was full of mixed emotions for Freda, but the key moment in this experience was when she didn't respond. She was silenced by this non-Native instructor's bold statement, caught off-guard and unable to articulate her reaction. Fortunately, she knew the Native faculty in the Native studies department and they advised her to switch that course for another. They knew of this particular instructor's reputation, and advised their students to avoid taking his courses.

David purposely chose his institution for the location—it was located in his tribal community. He wanted to be a role model and positive example of a tribal member in higher education for the tribal youth coming up. When he enrolled in a Native studies course, he was interested to find out the tribal background of the instructor, to see what kind of influence that would have on the course content.

> I took a Native American studies class and it was a white man teaching it. (Laughs.) And excuse my language, but I was in class and this white man's up there. He's wearing aviator sunglasses and he's introducing himself. And then he starts speaking Kiowa. And then he says his name in Kiowa. And he couldn't—and there's two Kiowa boys in there with me. And then, there's a few Cherokees, few Cheyennes, a few Comanches in there. There's about forty of us in there. We were all freshmen I can tell you that much. And we're sitting there. I'm like I really hope this is a good Indian guy. And this white guy walks in. I'm like ok, he's Cherokee, you know. (Laughs.) You know, he's pale skinned. He's gotta be Cherokee. So he starts talking and he tells us he's Kiowa. The two Kiowa boys look at me, and I'm just like "hey." (Chuckles.) And this

> guy starts talking Kiowa. Introduces himself in his Kiowa name. And he says, "I just spent the summer on the Kiowa reservation here in Oklahoma" and blah, blah, blah, something else, and he says "I'm connected with my people." And I said "what tribe are you?" And he said "oh I'm not. I'm Caucasian. I'm from Ohio." And I said "well this is b—-s—t. I'm outta here." (Laughs.) And he said "what?" I said "man, you're not a real Indian. You're just one of those posers." I said "we call you posers." I said "I can't be in this class. You're not going to teach me anything." And I got the curriculum for the class and he gave us eight different books to read. And all of them were—a couple of them were written by fake Indians. You know, they want you to do vison quests and what not. And there was maybe one book that he gave me, and I think I still have it, that was actually written by a real Native. (Laughs.) But that kind of was just like "oh my gosh, why do they do this to me?" (David)

David was not afraid to express his disapproval of this non-Native instructor teaching a Native studies course. He felt it was disrespectful of the institution to hire a non-Native instructor to teach these courses when the institution was located in the heart of his tribal community. David thought there had to be a qualified Native faculty member to teach these courses. As a freshman transitioning to campus, this was a disappointing experience that impacted his sense of belonging. Unfortunately, David did not have anyone to guide him on campus like Freda did. So he walked away from that course and from the institution as a whole because he didn't feel he was wanted or belonged there.

In retelling the story of these defining encounters with their non-Native instructors, Freda and David both utilized humor in their descriptions. Humor holds a distinctive space within Native ways of being. Commonly, humor is used as a way to control social situations and to humble an individual rather than embarrass them publicly (Deloria, 1969). And in difficult situations, such as those experienced by Freda and David, it is used to balance discouraging emotions. Deloria (1969) affirms that humor is the glue that holds Native people together and, as a balancing agent, is central to their survival. For Freda and David, humor was the best outlet to describe their difficult and disappointing experiences.

Inflexible Deferment Policy

The Gates Millennium Scholarship Program is strict in its application guidelines—only incoming freshmen are awarded and there is no option to reapply. GMSP also abides by strict criteria from the application to the award time limit for each degree. In terms of the deferment period, GMS are granted one full academic year to defer. They can break it up into semesters or use it for an entire academic year. When AIGMS were faced with obstacles and needed to take a break from college, the majority of them utilized the deferment and planned to return to school. For several AIGMS, circumstances beyond their control kept them from returning within the strict time frame of the deferment. They mentioned reaching out to the AIGC staff for assistance and were told that if they didn't return to school after the end of their deferment period then they forfeited their scholarship. The American Indian cohort is one of the four cohorts funded by GMSP. The American Indian Graduate Center (AIGC) staff services the American Indian cohort, though GMSP oversees the structure of the program to serve each cohort in the same manner.

Some AIGMS fought to stay in college and keep the scholarship by breaking up their deferment periods and transferring to different institutions, but due to events beyond their control they eventually dropped out and lost the scholarship. These AIGMS faced serious medical issues, mental health issues, loss, and family obligations. Nadine took a semester off to grieve the loss of her younger sister, then returned to school only to have to return home and take care of her ailing mother because she was the eldest among her siblings. She notified AIGC of her second semester of deferment and was told that if she left school again, she would lose the scholarship. Bailey and Christine experienced life-threatening medical issues that caused them to defer. Christine was unable to return to college, but Bailey transferred to another university closer to home. Then she received a call from her mother while she was on her death bed and Bailey dropped everything to be by her side. She lost the scholarship because she didn't finish the semester. Rachel didn't transition well to her first institution, so she left and experienced a life-threatening accident that permanently impacted her mobility. She was able to defer the scholarship and return to another institution closer to her family, but due to lifestyle change as a result of the accident, she was unable to complete the semester and lost the scholarship. Michelle was dealing with mental health issues and transferred three times to try to stay in school, yet ultimately she was unable to completely focus on her studies.

> It's just, um, emotionally I was going through a lot. I had a lot going on during that time, because, um, from bad decisions on top of . . . just . . . some . . . other things, traumatic things that I was going through. I actually did defer my scholarship once because of a situation that I was in. And they granted me the deferment and it was fine, but then by the time I came back to school, I wasn't ready still. I was making really bad decisions. Additionally, I just wasn't, I couldn't get myself to go to class. I couldn't get myself to wake up in the morning. I couldn't get myself to go to bed at night. It was a bad situation that I was in. I just wasn't ready to go back to school but, you know, the deferment that I had processed was up and so it was time for me to go to school. That's how I ended up basically kind of losing my scholarship, because I don't feel like I was all the way emotionally ready to go back to school after everything that I had been through. (Michelle)

It was clear that Michelle needed counseling support and guidance. She utilized the services on campus, but it wasn't a good experience. She tried the Indian Health Services (IHS) off campus and found a connection with a counselor there, but her counselor's position was cut due to budget deficits. After losing her counselor, Michelle gave up on counseling because she felt she would not be able to make another connection with a different counselor. Michelle should not have had to look off campus for counseling support and guidance. She should have gotten the support and guidance from her campus's counseling services and/or program. There is need for culturally competent training for counselors to work with Native students and it is not only necessary for certain organizations, such as IHS, to have this cultural competency training. It is necessary on all campuses with Native students.

Jessica had an interesting situation and experience. She received the Gates scholarship, but enlisted into the military after high school graduation because she was burned out on school and needed a break before college.

> I went straight into the military right after high school instead of going to college. I was told about the deferment and so I did that. Then my enlistment got extended, so I stayed in a little longer than expected and I was told after I was done and everything that I could use my scholarship, called in and everything and they told me that I've lost it since I didn't defer it the whole time. And that they only defer twice or something like that. So, I didn't use the scholarship or anything. I pretty much lost out on it. (Jessica)

The AIGC staff didn't clarify the specific time frame of the military deferment period or the need to request an extension on her deferment until after she called in to request funding.

> Yeah, the first time I called them, I told them what I was doing and everything, and they told me to get my deferment papers, and they emailed it to me and I got them signed and everything by my command that I was at at the time. And I sent it in and I got approved. Then they didn't tell me that I had to do another deferment form again until I called them back saying "hey, I'm going to college in the service, can I use the scholarship?" And that's when they told me that I wasn't able to, because I didn't turn in my paperwork or anything like that. And that's when she told me that even if I had deferred again, it would've only been another two years covered, and since I did 5 years of active duty, it wouldn't have even worked so to speak, in a way, because it was that extra year. (Jessica)

Jessica was never able to use the Gates scholarship funding even though, by earning it, she was promised five years of funding for her undergraduate degree. In the end, she was penalized for serving the country before going to college.

These examples reveal that AIGMS deferred from their respective institution of higher education; they needed time off to tend to family issues, health and medical concerns, and military service. They did not walk away from higher education, nor did they fail to communicate with the AIGC staff concerning their issues. They checked in and turned in the necessary paperwork for deferment; unfortunately, the inflexible deferment policy resulted in many AIGMS losing the scholarship funding when they were ready to return. Interestingly, the deferment policy is not published on the GMSP website. The policy and paperwork were shared with AIGMS only when they contacted the AIGC staff concerning their issues.

Reframing American Indian Student Departure

This research project highlighted the stories of struggle for 20 American Indian Gates Millennium Scholars who did not persist to graduation within their respective institutions of higher education. I described their experiences as stories of struggle because they are the ones that go untold because they are not success stories. As incoming freshmen, these particular Native students were high-achieving and fully funded. Guillory and Wolverton (2008) compared and contrasted perceptions of persistence factors and barriers among American Indian students and university administrators. The researchers found that university administrators—including university presidents, board of higher education regents, and faculty—named sufficient financial support as the top persistence factor for American Indian students. "All institutions saw financial aid as the most important factor impacting persistence" (Guillory & Wolverton, 2008, p. 70). Conversely, the Native students identified family as their number one persistence factor, specifically that their educational attainment would improve the lives of their families. "It is a reflection of an Indigenous philosophy of putting community before individualism" (p. 74). AIGMS had sufficient funding, whereby the lack of financial resources was not a major theme for their nonpersistence. In addition, AIGMS identified family as a major motivation for them in their educational endeavors, yet they still did not persist within their initial institutions.

Prior literature on Native student attrition focuses on the student perspective and the factors involved. Well-known individual factors that impede Native student success include lack of academic preparation, homesickness, and feeling isolated on campus (Benjamin, Chambers, & Reiterman, 1993; Brown & Kurpius, 1997; Lin et al., 1988; Swanson & Tokar, 1991). When studies focus on the individual student perspective, they disregard the institutional impact upon the student experience. This project aimed to turn attention to the systemic and institutional factors that adversely affect American Indian student persistence. Based on the findings, AIGMS experienced systemic pushes from within the institutions. In essence, AIGMS had all the predictors of success when they entered college, but were not provided the necessary support and resources to persist to graduation from their respective institutions and scholarship program.

In approaching this research topic, my goal was to challenge the perspective of American Indian student departure from higher education. This study revealed that Native students do not always take a linear path in their educational journeys. Many start out with plans to go straight through to graduation. Yet, along the way their journeys drifted, possibly to other institutions, before achieving the ultimate goal of a college degree. Institutional data would label these students as departures because they did not go straight through on a linear path. Waterman (2007) highlighted the stories and experiences of 12 Haudenosaunee who took "complex" paths to degree attainment. Interestingly, Waterman (2007) found that "the participants managed a college degree while maintaining their cultural integrity even though it meant more work and effort" (p. 20). On average, the Haudenosaunee students took almost eight years to complete a bachelor's degree and attended more than one college along the way. These students remained connected to their tribal communities while striving for their degrees. In light of this research, "departure" does not seem to reflect the experiences of the participants. And the findings of this research project highlight institutional impact along with push and pull factors that describe how departure does not explain the AIGMS participants' experiences.

Departure became the leading term to describe student attrition, namely for American Indian students, due to Tinto's (1975, 1982, 1987) well-recognized theoretical framework that sought to be all-inclusive of individual factors to student attrition. Though Tinto argued that departure was a better term to describe student attrition because it was neutral in nature, the term is a cultural construct that does not align with American Indian cultural values and teachings (Tierney, 1992). This research challenged Tinto's departure framework because it broadened the focus from the individual student to the students' experiences within institutions of higher education, including students' interactions with the scholarship program. The AIGMS's nonpersistence within institutions of higher education places more responsibility on the institution and the scholarship program.

Conclusion

This phenomenological qualitative study explored the experiences and nonpersistence of 20 American Indian Gates Millennium Scholars (AIGMS). Instead of focusing on the student perspective, this study sought to highlight the institutional influence of the college upon participants' experiences. The purpose of this approach was to reframe departure for American Indian students. Departure speaks more toward the individual student perspective, as in how the student was not equipped to be successful in college. This viewpoint is problematic because it absolves the institution of any responsibility. TribalCrit (Brayboy, 2005) was the most culturally appropriate theoretical framework that provided a greater understanding of the specific, present-day societal issues and norms that affect American Indian college students. As these were stories of struggle, utilizing stories as an Indigenous methodological approach provided the space for AIMGS to freely share and describe their experiences in the way that they felt most comfortable. By valuing and utilizing stories as an Indigenous methodological approach, this research was able to highlight the institutional impact upon AIGMS's nonpersistence. AIGMS's educational pathways encompassed discouraging experiences from within the institution and with GMSP/AIGC. Their experiences with campus racial climate not only included feelings of exclusion, marginalization, and invisibility, but also comprised the lack of representation of Native faculty. Identifying and addressing the structural and institutional inconsistencies that affect Native college students is a main objective of TribalCrit (Brayboy, 2005). These experiences within campus racial climate led AIGMS participants to feel disconnected on campus when they did not see themselves represented within the classroom. Additionally, AIGMS did not receive the necessary support in the form of extended deferments from GMSP/AIGC. Fundamentally, this study underscored how AIGMS's respective institutions of higher education and the Gates Millennium Scholarship Program did not honor AIGMS's educational pathways.

REFERENCES

Abbott, S. (2009, Fall). Personal communication.

Archibald, J. (2008). *Indigenous Storywork: Educating the Heart, Mind, Body and Spirit.* Vancouver, BC: UBC Press.

Barnhardt, R., & Kawagley, A. O. (2005). Indigenous knowledge systems and Alaska Native ways of knowing. *Anthropology and Education Quarterly, 36*(1), 8–23.

Battiste, M. (2002). *Indigenous Knowledge and Pedagogy in First Nations Education: A Literature Review with Recommendations.* Ottawa, Canada: Indian and Northern Affairs Canada.

Benjamin, D. P., Chambers, S., & Reiterman, G. (1993). A focus on American Indian college persistence. *Journal of American Indian Education, 32*, 24–40.

Brayboy, B. M. J. (2004). Hiding in the Ivy: American Indian students and visibility in elite educational settings. *Harvard Educational Review, 74*(2), 125–151.

Brayboy, B. M. J. (2005). Towards a tribal critical race theory in education. *The Urban Review, 37*(4), 425–446.

Brayboy, B. M. J., Fann, A. J., Castagno, A. E., & Solyom, J. A. (2012). Postsecondary education for American Indian and Alaska Natives: Higher education for nation building and self-determination. *ASHE Higher Education Report, 37*(5).

Brown, L. L., & Kurpius, S. E. R. (1997). Psychosocial factors influencing academic persistence of American Indian college students. *Journal of College Student Development, 38*, 3–12.

Castagno, A. E., & Lee, S. J. (2007). Native mascots and ethnic fraud in higher education: Using tribal critical race theory and the interest convergence principle as an analytic tool. *Equity and Excellence in Education, 40*, 3–13.

Corbin, J., & Strauss, A. (2008). *Basics of Qualitative Research* (3rd ed.). Thousand Oaks, CA: Sage Publications.
Creswell, J. (2009). Research Design: *Qualitative, Quantitative, and Mixed Methods Approaches* (3rd ed.). Thousand Oaks, CA: Sage Publications.
Cunningham, A. F., McSwain, C., & Keselman, Y. (2007). *The Path of Many Journeys: The Benefits of Higher Education for Native People and Communities.* A report by the Institute for Higher Education Policy, in collaboration with the American Indian Higher Education Consortium and the American Indian College Fund. Retrieved from www.ihep.org
Deloria, V. (1969). *Custer Died for Your Sins: An Indian Manifesto.* New York: MacMillan.
Devoe, J., Darling-Churchill, K., & Snyder, T. D. (2008). *Status and trends in the education of American Indians and Alaska Natives: 2008.* NCES 2008–084. National Center for Education Statistics (ERIC Document Reproduction Service N. ED502797). Retrieved from ERIC database.
Fann, A. (2002). *Native college pathways in California: A look at higher education access for American Indian high school students.* Paper presented at the Association for the Study of Higher Education Annual Meeting, Sacramento, CA.
Fryberg, S. A., & Markus, H. R. (2007). Cultural models of education in American Indian, Asian American, and European American contexts. *Social Psychology of Education, 10,* 213–246.
Gloria, A., & Robinson-Kurpius, S. (2001). Influences of self-beliefs, social support and comfort in the university environment on the academic nonpersistence decisions of American Indian undergraduates. *Cultural Diversity and Ethnic Minority Psychology, 7,* 88–102.
GMSP website (n.d.). Retrieved from http://www.gmsp.org/gates-millennium-scholars-program/
Guillory, R. M., & Wolverton, M. (2008). It's about family: Native American student persistence in higher education. *The Journal of Higher Education, 79*(1), 58–85.
Hampton, E. (1995). *Memory comes before knowledge: Research may improve if researchers remember their motives.* Paper presented at the First Biannual Indigenous Scholars' Conference, University of Alberta, Edmonton.
HeavyRunner, I., & DeCelles, D. (2002). Family education model: Meeting the student retention challenge. *Journal of American Indian Education, 41*(2), 29–37.
Heller, D. (2003). *Equity and opportunity in state merit scholarship programs.* Mimeo, Penn State University.
Huffman, T. E. (1991). The experiences, perceptions, and consequences of campus racism among Northern Plains Indians. *Journal of American Indian Education* (January), 25–34.
Jackson, A. P., Smith, S. A., & Hill, C. L. (2003). Academic persistence among Native American college students. *Journal of College Student Development, 44*(4), 548–565.
Jackson, A. P., & Turner, S. (2004). Counseling and psychotherapy with American Indians. In T. Smith (Ed.), *Practicing Multiculturalism* (pp. 215–233). Boston: Allyn & Bacon.
Kovach, M. (2009). *Indigenous Methodologies: Characteristics, Conversations, and Contexts.* Toronto: University of Toronto Press.
Lin, R., LaCounte, D., & Eder, J. (1988). A study of Native American students in a predominantly White college. *Journal of American Indian Education, 27,* 8–15.
Lomawaima, K. T., & McCarty, T. L. (2002). When tribal sovereignty challenges democracy: American Indian education and democratic ideal. *American Education Research Journal, 39*(2), 279–305.
Lowe, S. (2005). This is who I am: Experiences of Native American Students. In M. Fox, S. Lowe, & G. McClellan (Eds.), *Serving Native American Students* (pp. 33–40). San Francisco, CA: Jossey-Bass.
Maxwell, J. A. (2005). *Qualitative Research Design: An Interactive Approach.* Thousand Oaks, CA: Sage Publications.
Merriam, S. B. (2009). *Qualitative Research: A Guide to Design and Implementation.* San Francisco, CA: Jossey-Bass.

Meyer, A. M. (2004). *Ho'oulu Our Time of Becoming: Hawaiian Epistemology and Early Writings*. Honolulu: Ai Pohaku Press.

Native American Higher Education Initiative (2005).

Nelson, C. A. (2015). *American Indian college students as Native nation builders: Tribal financial aid as a lens for understanding college-going paradoxes* (Unpublished doctoral dissertation). University of Arizona. Proquest.

Perna, L. W. (2006). Studying college choice. A proposed conceptual model. In J. C. Smart (Ed.), *Higher Education: Handbook of Theory and Research*, Vol. 21 (pp. 99–157). New York: Springer.

Riessman, C. K. (2008). *Narrative Methods for the Human Sciences*. Thousand Oaks, CA: Sage Publications.

Roderick, M., Nagaoka, J., & Coca, V. (2009). College readiness for all: The challenge for urban high schools. *The Future of Children*, *19*(1), 185–210.

Seidman, I. (2006). *Interviewing as Qualitative Research: A Guide for Researchers in Education and the Social Sciences*. New York, NY: Teachers College Press.

Shea, C. (2003, November 9). "Five Truths About Tuition." *New York Times*.

Solorzano, D., Ceja, M., & Yosso, T. (2000). Critical race theory, racial microaggressions, and the experience of Chicana and Chicano scholars. *Qualitative Studies in Education*, *11*(1), 121–136.

Swanson, J. L., & Tokar, D. M. (1991). College students' perceptions of barriers to career development. *Journal of Vocational Behavior*, *38*, 92–106.

Tachine, A. R. (2015). Monsters and weapons: Navajo students' stories on their journeys toward college (Unpublished doctoral dissertation). University of Arizona. ProQuest.

Tierney, W. G. (1992). An anthropological analysis of student participation in college. *Journal of Higher Education*, *63*(6), 603–618.

Tierney, W. G., Sallee, M. W., & Venegas, K. M. (2007). Access and financial aid: How American Indian students pay for college. *Journal of College Admission*, *197*, 14–23.

Tinto, V. (1975). Dropout from higher education: A theoretical synthesis of recent research. *Review of Educational Research*, *45*, 89–125.

Tinto, V. (1982). Limits of theory and practice in student attrition. *Journal of Higher Education*, *53*, 687–700.

Tinto, V. (1987). *Leaving College: Rethinking the Causes and Cures of Student Attrition*. Chicago: University of Chicago Press.

U.S. Department of Education, National Center for Education Statistics. (2015). Quickstats [Chart showing "Enrollment and Academic Expectations"]. NPSAS: 08 and NPSAS: 12 Undergraduate Students. Retrieved from http://nces.ed.gov/datalab/quickstats/createtable.aspx

Waterman, S. J. (2007). A complex path to Haudenosaunee degree completion. *Journal of American Indian Education*, *46*(1), 20–40.

Wells, R. N. (1997). *The American Indian experience in higher education: Turning around the cycle of failure II*. (ERIC Document Reproduction Service No. ED 414 108).

Wilson, S. (2001). What is an Indigenous research methodology? *Canadian Journal of Native Education*, *25*(2), 175–179.

CHAPTER 10

The Intersection of Paying for College and Tribal Sovereignty

EXPLORING NATIVE COLLEGE STUDENT EXPERIENCES WITH TRIBAL FINANCIAL AID

Christine A. Nelson (Laguna/Navajo)

> Amongst my Native American[1] peers, I was classified as a high achieving student in school. I attended pre-college access programs, had supportive parents, and received fairly good grades. College was always the next step for me, but why at the age of 20 was I attending my third college? And why was my tribal scholarship, which was my largest financial aid award, being denied?
>
> I can recall feeling overwhelmed with financial uncertainty. The individuals who worked their 9 to 5 jobs and came home to what appeared to be little worry became increasingly appealing and ideal for my future. I soon found myself erasing all the years of being indoctrinated with college-going messages and ending the childhood dream of becoming a veterinarian. Sixteen years later as a newly minted PhD, I can still recall the range of emotions I experienced during that time and often reflect upon the subsequent decisions I made when I lost my tribal scholarship. This loss of financial aid not only limited my access to college, it challenged how I perceived the benefits of college and most interestingly, it sent me on a long journey of defining what it meant to be an enrolled member of my tribal nation. (Christine, personal communication, October 20, 2015)

In my student affairs professional experience, I have witnessed many Native students confronted with various tribal financial aid conundrums. I cannot help but feel connected to them, as the personal narrative above explains—I know how it feels. As a higher education researcher, I assert that the current literature fails to fully explore the complexities of financial aid for Native students.

Financing or paying for higher education has been shown time and time again to be a challenge for Native students by limiting access to and persistence in higher education (Guillory & Wolverton, 2008; Swanson & Tokar, 1991). In 2010, approximately 85% of Native college students received some form of financial aid, with an average amount of aid being $10,900. This aid amount includes all grants, both need- and merit-based, from federal, state, and private entities, federal and state loans, and federal work-study (Aud, Fox, & KewalRamani, 2010). The amount of students receiving aid is promising and indicates Native college students are seeking various funding options to finance their education. However, the average amount of aid a Native college student received was $1,800 less than the overall average of other racial/ethnic groups (Aud et al., 2010). Juxtaposing the lower amount of aid received with the high recipient percentage complicates how we understand financial aid and provides an opportunity to explore the meaning of financial aid, particularly tribal financial aid, in a Native student's college experience. The following question guided this inquiry: "How do Native college students describe the role of tribal financial aid throughout their college-going process?" In this chapter, I posit that financial aid for Native students is unlike any other ethnic group by exploring the role of tribal financial aid through a Native Nation-Building lens. This Indigenous perspective on funding transcends the norm of researching financial aid merely as a lack of funding issue that impacts college access. Native Nation-Building asserts an opportunity to provide a more complete picture on the intersection of tribal sovereignty and college-going experiences. This chapter concludes by presenting the lived experiences of the students and implications on policy, practice, and future inquiries.

Financial Aid for Native Students

There currently exists a plethora of mainstream research showing the multifaceted impacts of financial aid, such as influence on college choice, student price perception, and retention (DesJardins & McCall, 2010; Perna, 2008, 2010). However, most mainstream research is irrelevant to the context of Native students due to statistical insignificance or complete exclusion. More notable to this discussion is how there are very few studies specifically focusing on the nexus between financial aid and Native students. The limited studies that do include Native students demonstrate that the lack of financial aid is a barrier to accessing and persisting in college (Carney, 1999; Guillory & Wolverton, 2008; Mendez, Mendoza, & Malcolm, 2011), but there continues to be a lack of understanding of why and how financial aid operates in the lives of students to influence their college-going decisions and behaviors.

In this inquiry, I focus on the role of tribal financial aid for two reasons. First, tribal financial aid is a unique funding stream that is only available to most tribally enrolled Native students. Tribal financial aid, or tribal scholarships, are granted to enrolled tribal members and generally administered by individual Tribal Education Departments (TEDs). If a tribe has a TED, this does not equate to the tribes awarding aid under similar criteria and protocol or that the tribe offers higher education financial aid (Nelson, 2015). Currently, it is unknown how many Native students receive tribal financial aid, but this does not mean tribal funding sources should be overlooked in financial aid discourse (Tierney, Salle, & Venegas, 2007).

The second reason is to acknowledge the political and historical relationship Native students have to financial aid. As early as the 1700s, various assimilation iterations emerged through the use of financial aid, such as relocation to urban cities through vocational programs (Carney, 1999; Reyhner & Eder, 2004; Szasz, 2003). These methods systematically used financial aid to dismantle tribal nations and their citizens' connections to their tribes. The development and administration of self-determined tribal financial aid and scholarships in the mid-1900s significantly altered the political implications of financial aid on the Native college-going experience (Brayboy, Fann, Castagno, & Solyom, 2012; Carney, 1999). Native college-going is now systemically influenced by tribal needs through financial aid. When centering tribal financial aid as a lens to understanding college experiences, the political status of being Native American is tethered to Native student experiences. To privilege Native identity as a relevant political status, I specifically used Native Nation-Building as a lens in which to frame student experiences.

Framing the Inquiry: Native Nation-Building

Generally, when discussing nation-building, one is referring to sustaining infrastructure and establishing economic stability to a nation. Nation-building, from an international perspective, looks at how a nation embodies a democratic unity of citizenship. Brayboy et al. (2012) note that nation-building is often rooted in creating a homogenized identity and notions of colonization where non-Western ideas are dismissed. Native Nation-Building or Tribal Nation-Building is an extension of nation-building that takes an anti-colonial approach to capacity-building. It addresses the historical injustices and political status of only Northern Native American tribes (Cornell & Kalt, 2010).

Native Nation-Building is a comprehensive plan and is more than creating jobs or economic wealth (Cornell & Kalt, 1998). The concept pushes tribal nations to broaden the definition of economic development and seek out "anybody with time or energy or ideas or skills or good will . . . who's willing to bet those assets on the tribal future" (p. 193). This includes many aspects of sovereignty, such as food, language, culture, health, and, most central to this study, educational sovereignty (Champagne, 2003; Gonzalez, 2008). To fully understand how sovereignty is engaged in the higher education process one must understand that tribal nations have a desire to remain distinct in their political status. While other marginalized groups within the United States have advocated for equality and access to the opportunities that the current democratic nation has to offer, tribal nations seek to remain distinct and sovereign entities (Brayboy et al., 2012). The premise behind Native Nation-Building is for tribes to become self-sustaining so the right to remain sovereign is preserved.

This inquiry's use of Native Nation-Building theory does not assume that all Native students understand, embrace, or are even aware of the concept. Rather, this study utilizes the Native Nation-Building lens to understand how students describe their understanding and relation to tribal financial aid through their college-going experiences. Since students are in contact with and applying for funding from their tribal nations, there is an assumption they have some connection to the tribe. This assumption is important when considering the purpose of the tribal funding, which is established and articulated to students by individual tribal nations. For example, one Southwest tribal nation states that it hopes the funding encourages their tribal citizens to return to the tribe to contribute to capacity-building of the tribe. Similar expectations can be found across other tribal nations (Austin, 2005). Beyond the tribal nations' motivations, Native Nation-Building has the potential to illuminate a different frame to explore how Native college students experience college-going.

The Place of Inquiry

Place is referenced to understand the context of this inquiry. From an Indigenous perspective place "[is] the relationship of things to each other" (Deloria & Wildcat, 2001, p. 23). Place is not only the physical location where the interaction occurs, but the relationship that develops from the interaction. The institutional and tribal contexts interact with students and help form experiences and develop understandings of those experiences. To maintain a level of focus and feasibility, the inquiry is limited to ten tribes that are allocated within the Southwest and have existing relationships with the two site universities.

To also understand place from an institutional and tribal perspective, two steps were taken to establish relationships between places (contexts). First, I sought out tribal financial aid officers to inform them of this study and to acknowledge and answer any questions they had. Second, I spoke with university officials (i.e., student services advisors, financial aid officers, faculty) at the two institutions to gain a professional's understanding of campus climate surrounding tribal financial aid. These two steps were instrumental to the research design as it aligns with Indigenous methods of inquiry that seek to redefine *place* as a site of relationship-building (NCAI Policy Research Center and MSU Center for Native Health Partnerships, 2012; Smith, 2007).

Students Informing the Inquiry

Thirty-seven undergraduate Native students, who applied for tribal financial aid and were academically persisting in college, were drawn from two four-year public research universities located in the Southwestern portion of the United States. At the time of the study, five were freshmen, four were sophomores, eleven were juniors, and seventeen were seniors. All 37 students had applied for tribal financial aid and received amounts ranging from zero to $8,000 per academic year, with a cumulative amount of tribal aid exceeding an average $150,000 per academic year. Students who received zero dollars were included in the study because their experience provided a valuable perspective on how Native college students pay for college and further demonstrated how tribal financial aid for students is not guaranteed funding. Including the three non-tribal aid recipient students, the participating students reflected the multiple dimensions found within the Native college student population. These dimensions included students who reside on and off their home reservations, the amount of aid received from tribes, gender, age, and the class standing in school. For example, 26 students described growing up on the reservation, but more than half either lived off the reservation at some point or felt their experiences were not limited to a rural, reservation life. On the same note, ten of the eleven students who never lived on the reservation still described a strong connection to their tribal community.

Collection of Student Experiences

Through one-on-one and open-ended discussions with students, I was able to gather key experiences that allowed participants to describe the context of their life, retell the experiences from their own lens, and reflect upon the essence of those experiences (Seidman, 2006). The context, details, and reflection provided by the student illuminated the intersection of tribal financial aid and student experience. Each session consisted of semi-structured interview questions and lasted approximately an hour to an hour and a half. Students were compensated for their time with a $20 university meal card. Providing students with compensation for their time and participation represents a critical point of relationship-building for Indigenous communities (Kovach, 2009), and the compensation allowed participation of students who may be struggling academically and/or financially, many of whom are commuting to college, to contribute to the diversity of the sample and make it more representative of the broader population of college-going Native students. Prior to meeting with each student, I reviewed the corresponding tribal nation's financial aid policies and goals. Tribal funding bylaws enriched the interviewing process and provided a clearer tribal context for each student. It also helped reveal if the student was aware of their tribe's financial aid intentions and protocols and if these aspects were relevant to the student's college-going experiences.

Processing Student Experiences

The initial process of analyzing the student experiences occurred in tandem with additional student conversations (Corbin & Strauss, 2008). Each interview was audio recorded, transcribed verbatim, and organized using Nvivo 10 software. Following each interview and throughout the remaining part of the study, memoing was used to expand upon the data analysis process and improve validity of the data (Corbin & Strauss, 2008, p. 118). The initial review of data, along with memoing, led to generating student profiles utilizing Seidman's (2006) recommendations on profiles. After each profile was situated with its varying personal dimensions, the process of open coding followed and served as a lens when conducting content analysis on the documents obtained from the tribal funding agencies. The tribal context helped triangulate the themes from the student's lived experiences. Once the tribal documents were analyzed again, the process of axial coding or connecting codes with the two sources of data was completed (Corbin & Strauss, 2008).

Institutional Context

The participants of this study were drawn from two Southwestern research-focused universities. Both institutions showed promising trends to define place in both a physical and nonphysical space. From a physical perspective, both institutions are located near defined tribal communities, and from a historical aspect, are located on lands that were appropriated from the original inhabitants of the land. From a relational perspective, both institutions have designated Native student support services, established financial aid protocols serving Native students, and recruited higher percentages of Native students, staff, and faculty when compared to other mainstream universities.

Tribal Context

A total of ten tribes, all located in the Southwestern portion of the United States, were represented in this study. Out of respect for tribal sovereignty and tribal IRBs, it was decided to not identify the tribal nations that were represented in this study. This decision was based on two factors: (1) this body of research acknowledges and privileges the sovereign rights of tribal nations, and (2) it is important for outsiders to understand the inherently complicated process to developing a respectful research design involving tribal communities. In order to protect the rights of tribal nations, a second internal review board (IRB) screening was conducted to determine if an external tribal IRB process was warranted. For this project, it was deemed unnecessary to initiate tribal IRBs because tribal identification was excluded from any formal publications, and all collection of student experiences was limited to campus locale.

Authenticity and Limitations of the Inquiry

In this study, I implemented strategies to help ensure that the most authentic point of view is represented in the findings. First, the interviewing protocol and techniques improved the likelihood of having rich and thick descriptive datasets. This "rich" data provided me with descriptions to more accurately understand the context of the participant's experience (Maxwell, 2005). The second strategy utilized member checking throughout the data collection and analysis process (Creswell, 2009). The third technique drew upon Indigenous methodologists that recognize the "researcher" as never being fully abstained from the process. I am both an insider and outsider in this process. As an insider and a former recipient of tribal financial aid, I have a unique understanding of tribal financial aid. Tightly connected to my insider status is the moral and cultural obligation I have to represent the students' voices in the most accurate way possible and to remain accountable to the Indigenous community as a whole (Wilson, 2001). As described in preceding sections, the concept of *place* established my connection to maintaining tribal accountability throughout the inquiry. Such safeguards included consultation with various Indigenous tribal communities and Indigenous researchers and following my institution's policy of having established Indigenous scholars review the IRB application for tribal considerations.

In terms of limitations of this inquiry, the knowledge gained from it is meant to provide a snapshot of how Native college students at two Southwest universities make meaning of the receipt of tribal financial aid. This qualitative inquiry is not meant to homogenize how students interact with or perceive their tribal nation's financial aid process, but is meant to expand the underlying dominant assumptions of higher education and how Native students make meaning of their experiences through a culturally relevant lens. Last, this inquiry is limited to students who have applied for tribal financial aid. Therefore, perceptions of financial aid may differentiate from students who have not applied for tribal financial aid.

Knowledge Acquired

The knowledge acquired through this inquiry begins to unpack the financial aid process for Native students. Through a tribal financial aid lens, I am able to explore a process that is solely unique for Native students. The findings are divided into two parts. The first section provides a classification of tribal financial aid. This is the first time the tribal financial aid process has been described in this manner. It demonstrates that the tribal financial aid process is not uniform across tribal entities. The second section reveals the lived experiences of Native students who applied for tribal financial aid. Through this process, we can begin to understand that meaning of tribal financial aid has implications on college experiences for Native students.

Tribal Financial Aid Classification

Through the review of publicly available information, themes emerged across the ten tribes represented in this study. All TED application processes required students to provide proof of tribal enrollment. Less consistent across tribes was an explicit message explaining the goal and purpose of TEDs providing tribal financial aid. The tribes that do state a purpose link their messaging to improving individual educational access so the individual can impact tribal capacity-building.

The ten tribal financial aid processes were categorized into three types to help contextualize student experience when applying and receiving tribal financial aid (see table 10.1 for overview). The classification of tribes into different types contextualized student experiences and further developed the process of paying for college as non-monolithic across all Native students. Need & Merit

TABLE 10.1
TYPE OF TRIBAL EDUCATION DEPARTMENT (TED)
CLASSIFIED BY AID AND SUPPORT PROVIDED

TED Type	*Applications Process*	*Type of Aid Awarded by TED*	*Supplemental Services*
Need & Merit TED (Type N&M)	• Application • Financial need analysis • Evidence of college enrollment admission • College transcripts • Proof of tribal enrollment	• Need-based aid • Merit-based aid • Need- and Merit-based aid	• Campus visits to universities within a close proximity
Need & Merit + TED (Type N&M+)	• Application • Financial need analysis • Evidence of college enrollment • College transcripts • Proof of tribal enrollment	• Need- and Merit-based aid	• Campus visits to universities within a close proximity • TED coordinates with other human services departments within the tribe to provide support
Merit TED (Type M)	• Application • Short essay • College transcripts • Proof of tribal enrollment	• Merit only	• Newsletter sent to scholarship recipients

TEDs (Type N&M) provided both need- and merit-based aid. The aid application process required a basic one- to two-page application, financial aid needs analysis, college enrollment verification and/or class schedules, proof of tribal enrollment, and updated transcripts. Need & Merit TEDs (Type N&M+) only provided need-based aid and the application process mirrored Type N&M's process. Type N&M+ differentiated from Type N&M in the supplemental support they provided students, hence the "plus" sign. Type N&M worked closely with students to provide additional economic and emotional support by visiting colleges and universities located within the state or neighboring states. Type N&M+ provided the same support, but also closely coupled their financial aid process with other social support services, such as TANF or WIC. Students who received funding from Type N&M expressed appreciation for the seamless process and one student mentioned the TED sent care packages throughout the academic year. Merit TEDs (Type M) provided merit-based awards/scholarships. The application process was most simple of all, with most of the process occurring online. Students had to submit a one- to two-page application, proof of tribal enrollment, transcripts, and generally a short essay describing their collegiate and career goals. Beyond financial support, Type M sent students periodic emails to remind them of deadlines and local events.

Tribal Financial Aid and College Perceptions and Decisions

The students' lived experiences revealed how their unique relationships with either their tribal educational officials and/or tribal citizens revealed a cyclical and negotiating process of college-going. As anticipated in my review of tribal financial aid public documents, the main purpose of tribal financial aid is to assist their tribal members with costs associated with attending institutions of higher education. The expectation that students would return to their tribal nation after graduating was less explicit in the documents, but an overwhelming amount of the participants thought it was expected. As students explained their perception of and experiences with tribal financial aid, the perceptions of tribal financial were mixed with both positive and negative experiences. Through those understandings, I was able to identify four areas related to how tribal financial aid intersected with the college-going experiences of the students.

Strengthened Relationships. Corina, a second-generation student who grew up both in and away from her tribal community, explained how her TED (Type N&M+) was instrumental to helping her stay connected with her tribe while she was in college.

> This past semester [the tribal financial aid director] held a luncheon . . . he had all the [scholarship recipient] students come . . . they had representatives from

> each department show up there too. He had us introduce ourselves and what we were doing and just to say hey, these guys are going to school so look out for them in the future if they ever plan on applying to help out . . . I think that's the main reason, just to come back and help the community. It was a good experience because I know some of them work here with us in our program but it was good to meet new people and see what they do around the community. Like if I was ever interested, I would know who to go to.

Corina continued to explain that through her tribal community connections she was able to obtain summer employment with her tribe and that experience gave her a new perspective on her purpose of attending college: "It seems like we have like a community that we want to help but everybody else is like I'm just going to do this for myself and help out people around the world, I guess but with me, it's just like I want to help my personal community because I know most of them." For Corina and other students who experienced similar interactions, TED officials were trying to offer opportunities for students to stay connected, to give them a purpose to persist in college, and to give them a reminder that other tribal members know they are attending college. Corina's experience embodies positive perceptions that can result from building relationships between funders and recipients of financial aid, but it is important to note that Type N&M tribes were more likely to facilitate formal opportunities similar to Corina's description.

Degree Choice. For some students, their perceptions of tribal financial aid and the messages received from tribal officials were linked to decisions related to degree choice. Michelle, a senior who grew up in her tribal community and received tribal funds from Type N&M tribe, offered a great insight on how her experiences with the TED and other tribal departments shaped her perceptions of her tribe and why she should attend college. She stated: "[Tribal leaders] always say oh we need doctors . . . we need nurses, we need physical therapists, and public health people and stuff like that. That's all I hear. So that's why I wanted to get a medical degree and because I was always told like that's where the money is . . . I started off as pre-physiology major." Michelle entered college with the intention of majoring in a science field. However, she explained how this degree choice was not ideal for her: "[my grades] went downhill. So it wasn't until three semesters ago that I changed my major to Gender and Women Studies that [my grades] actually started going back up again." As Michelle described her college experiences, she expressed a strong desire to go back to her community, and the messages she received in high school heavily influenced her to choose a degree path that appeared to have the best opportunity to make a good salary and to contribute to tribal capacity-building.

These types of messages were further substantiated through tribal financial aid documents, as some tribes have earmarked funds to support students in the STEM fields. Michelle's story is not unique when comparing her to her peers. Other students share similar experiences and it appears that a portion of students have to reassess and balance their desire to contribute back to their communities, while others are able to stay committed to their initial degree choice throughout their college tenure.

Ability to Contribute. As described in Michelle's experiences, the messages about helping her tribal community through STEM-focused fields was ideal and helped her decide to go to college. However, there was a subset of students who had no interest in obtaining a degree in the fields the tribe overtly promoted, and they described feeling displaced about their role as a college-educated tribal member. Shawn, a first-generation college student who grew up in his tribal community and received tribal funds from a Type (N&M) TED, offered his perspective about how his degree in English does not fit the model idea of giving back and how scholarship money is targeted toward students interested in specific fields.

> I think that's expected and I think that's what most of the students here are doing or expecting to do. And they're trying so hard to fit into the [idea of giving back]. It's almost like this pipeline that is set up by tribal nations to be like you have to do this, you have to become a lawyer so you become our lawyer. You become a doctor so you can work in our hospitals. You have to become an engineer so you can work on our roads. You have to [do] human services so you can become a secretary for our tribal nation. And those are like the only things you can do to be able to be a tribal nation builder to promote community or to be helping out your community . . . I think that's what's expected, you know, because we're 20, 21, 22. It's not like we're supposed to have our life figured out by that point. And they always look at me like I'm really weird because they're like, no, you're supposed to be going back. It's like, well, what are you going to do with an English degree, are you going to be teacher? . . . But then, I'm like no, that's nowhere near my plans. Well, I think [my plans are] more of like an indirect way because I look at it the same way that all the other Native authors are doing it and actually telling stories and just telling their lives and writing down all the stereotypes and really getting it out there and really getting out like globally.

Shawn continues by discussing how funding from the tribes further pushes students to pursue certain degrees.

> I think being more inclusive of all majors and sort of alleviating some of that pressure of you have to do these things in order to be successful . . . And [the

> tribe] promote those things through scholarships and you look at all the scholarships, most of them are for only science majors or math majors. And that's it. There's not any for fine arts majors. Humanities majors. To me they don't see those things as being successful degrees. Things that can contribute to a community.

For Shawn, the tendency for tribes to promote a Native Nation-Building culture has made him question his future role in the tribal nation and has confirmed that at this moment he does not see how his degree choice can allow him to give directly back to his tribe. Much like Shawn, Perry, a senior who grew up away from his tribal community and received tribal funds from a Type (M) TED, also states how his biochemistry degree choice and desire to work in a scientific lab has no place within his tribal community: "I know for a fact [the tribe doesn't] have anything like laboratory science based but I'm sure if you were like in medical school they would probably have something like that . . . you can go [back] when you had something like marketing or like accounting or something like that because, you know, it's always a need for that kind of stuff . . . I'm sure that they have more opportunities for those fields." Through Perry's and Shawn's testimonies, there is evidence that students are receiving messages promoting Tribal Nation-Building and tribal sovereignty. However, if those messages are not clearly aligned with a student's own reasons for attending college, the student begins to describe a complex process that requires them to understand their role in sustaining/developing tribal sovereignty.

Corina's, Michelle's, Shawn's, and Samuel's experiences contribute to our understanding of how TEDs and the funding they provide intersect with college-going. Currently, there exists only one study exploring the intersection of tribal education departments (TEDs) and higher education. Marling (2012) solely presents TED employee perceptions of their services and does not explore the student perspective of tribal funding and paying for college. This inquiry fills a knowledge gap and presents strong evidence that being an enrolled member of a tribe matters in paying for college and other college-going experiences. It also provides a foundation to understanding how tribal education departments (TEDs) and tribal community intersect with students' lived experiences.

Applying Knowledge Learned

Understanding and Respecting Tribal Sovereignty

Tribal financial aid provides more than access to college by alleviating financial barriers. This form of aid closely couples student experiences and perceptions to TEDs and tribal nation leaders' college-going messages of "giving back." Previous literature has found that Native students, and other students of color, state that they have a desire to give back to their community during and after college (Fryberg & Markus, 2007; Stephens, Fryberg, Markus, Johnson, & Covarrubias, 2012). This study affirms the notion of reciprocity, but it also demonstrates the important role tribal nations play in developing these perceptions. The point of differentiation for Native students from other students is the concept of Native Nation-Building. Tribal nations have a vested interest in encouraging their tribal members to return to their communities after college to capacity-build. Tribes operate to preserve tribal sovereignty and it is clear that Native students are internalizing these messages to inform college-going decisions.

Through this inquiry, students demonstrate varied perceptions of tribes encouraging Native Nation-Building. Some connect with the message and use it as a way to propel their experiences, while others expressed uncertainty on how and why they should fill the role of giving back to their tribe. Tribal policy and sovereignty is intersecting with student college experiences. When developing and examining higher education policy, the conversation commonly revolves around the federal, state, and local levels. There is rarely any mention of tribal constituents in policy-making, despite the fact that 39 states either have federally or state recognized tribe(s) within their state lines (NCSL, 2015). There are some states and higher education institutions that have initiatives to improve the communication with tribal nations, but rhetoric of the majority silences the role of tribal nations.

It is evident through this study that student tribal enrollment intersects with college-going and in order for institutions to better support Native students, more outreach needs to occur between institutions and tribal nations when higher education policy is developed. Beyond student engagement and support, tribal nations can help institutions meet their goals of higher education, such as increased community engagement and engaging in ethically sound research. More dialogue between institutions and tribal nations needs to occur regardless of how small or large tribal representation may be on campus. Even if a tribe is not physically located in the state of the institution, Native students who arrive on campus deserve the right to know that their institutions acknowledge the role of tribal nations and their tribal status while attending college. Francis-Begay (2013) suggests, "All postsecondary institutions should consider developing some type of tribal consultation policy to guide universities in working with tribes, bearing in mind that the most important element of policy development pertaining to tribes is developing the policy *with* the tribes, not *for* the tribes." Higher education institutions have a great opportunity to be inclusive of all student voices and experiences by extending invitations to tribal nations on policy-making. This not only improves Native student experience, it sets a higher standard of inclusivity and diversity on college campuses across the United States.

Student Perceptions of Native Nation-Building

It is important that tribal officials consider all significant outcomes that result from the expectation of a student returning to help their tribal community after college. Some student degree choices were influenced by their desire to return to their tribal community, but found the reason of giving back was not enough to continue with that degree due to personal lack of interest or being academically underprepared. The motivation to give back to tribal communities is a strength for our students, but students need support to process the best approach to meeting both their collective and individual needs. Currently, Native students are left to their own means to navigate this complex process. TEDs and university student services and academic units need to provide a space for students to explore how tribal sovereignty enters their purview of college-going. To continue to let students navigate this process on their own is a disservice and continues to marginalize tribes and their communities.

Future Research Recommendations

For years Native higher education advocates have argued the Native American identifier is more than a racial/ethnic identity and should be expanded to become a political status (Brayboy et al., 2012). This study confirms this assertion and highlights several areas where additional research is warranted. Future research projects need to investigate career outcomes of Native students by understanding if intent to return translates to actual contribution back to tribes. I also suggest that this study be replicated in other parts of the United States due to tribes in different regions having different tribal relations with universities and types of financial aid. Last, I encourage tribal nations to conduct their own inquiry on student outcomes and experiences. Such inquiries could provide valuable insight on Native college-going from a tribal perspective. If tribes are smaller or have fewer resources to dedicate to research, then I suggest conducting a collaborative inquiry across tribes. Through a collective effort, tribes can then communicate their findings to institutions of higher education. These findings can demonstrate how much tribal financial aid is filtered into colleges and universities and then what are the student outcomes at those institutions. This will begin to hold institutions accountable for the tribal financial aid money they accept and for the students that enroll in their colleges. By presenting empirical evidence to institutions, tribes can then fully advocate for their tribal citizens.

Reclamation and Conclusion

From a dominant Western viewpoint, financial aid is seen as a means to alleviating college costs to improve college access. From an Indigenous perspective and through the use of Native Nation-Building, Native student experiences begin to inherently include tribal sovereignty in the realm of financial aid research. By asserting an Indigenous research process in the higher education setting, the relationship between the researcher, the student, and their community becomes strengthened. The hope is that Native students will no longer be viewed, among their peers, as the subgroup with the most problematic college-going experience. Rather, future inquiries can begin to frame Native students as savvy participants of a complex college-going process, where the challenge is to find a balance between developing positive personal life trajectories and being contributors to the tribal communities they are connected to.

NOTE

1. Throughout this chapter, Native American will be used interchangeably with Native and Indigenous.

REFERENCES

Aud, S., Fox, M., & KewalRamani, A. (2010). *Status and Trends in the Education of Racial and Ethnic Groups* (NCES 2010–015). U.S. Department of Education, National Center for Education Statistics. Washington, DC: U.S. Government Printing Office.

Austin, R. D. (2005). American Indian nation parents and leaders. In M. J. Tippeconnic Fox, S. C. Lowe, & G. S. McClellan (Eds.), *Serving Native American Students* (New Directions for Student Services, No. 109, pp. 41–48). San Francisco, CA: Jossey-Bass.

Brayboy, B. M. J., Fann, A. J., Castagno, A. E., & Solyom, J. A. (2012). Postsecondary education for American Indian and Alaskan Natives: Higher education for nation building and self-determination. *ASHE Higher Education Report, 37*(5).

Carney, C. M. (1999). *Native American Higher Education in the United States.* Piscataway, NJ: Transaction Publishers.

Champagne, D. (2003). Education for nation-building. *Cultural Survival Quarterly, 24*(7), 35.

Corbin, J., & Strauss, A. (2008). *Basics of Qualitative Research*, 3rd Ed. Thousand Oaks, CA: Sage Publications.

Cornell, S., & Kalt, J. P. (1998). Sovereignty and nation-building: The development challenge in Indian Country today. *American Indian Culture and Research Journal, 22*(3), 187–214.

Cornell, S., & Kalt, J. P. (2010). *American Indian Self-Determination: The Political Economy of a Policy that Works.* Working paper. Harvard Kennedy School. Retrieved from www.hks.harvard.edu

Creswell, J. W. (2009). *Research Design: Qualitative, Quantitative, and Mixed Methods Approaches*, 3rd Ed. Thousand Oaks, CA: Sage Publications.

Deloria, Jr., V., & Wildcat, D. R. (2001). *Power and Place: Indian Education in America.* Golden, CO: Fulcrum Publishing.

DesJardins, S. L., & McCall, B. P. (2010). Simulating the effects of financial aid packages on college student stopout reenrollment spells, and graduation chances. *The Review of Higher Education, 33*(4), 513–541.

Francis-Begay, K. (2013). The role of the special advisor to the president on Native American affairs. In H. J. Shotton, S. C. Lowe, & S. J. Waterman (Eds.), *Beyond the Asterisks: Understanding Native Students in Higher Education* (pp. 81–93). Sterling, VA: Stylus.

Fryberg, S. A., & Markus, H. R. (2007). Cultural models of education in American Indian, Asian American, and European American contexts. *Social Psychology of Education, 10*, 213–246.

Gonzalez, R. G. (2008). From creation to cultural resistance and expansion: Research on American Indian higher education. In J.C. Smart (Ed.), *Higher Education: Handbook of Theory and Research*, Vol. 23 (pp. 299–327). Netherlands: Springer.

Guillory, R. M., & Wolverton, M. (2008). It's about family: Native American student persistence in higher education. *The Journal of Higher Education*, *79*(1), 58–85.

Kovach, M. (2009). *Indigenous Methodologies: Characteristics, Conversations and Contexts.* Toronto: University of Toronto Press.

Marling, D. (2012). *Higher education and native nation building: Using a human capital framework to explore the role of postsecondary education in tribal economic development* (Order No. 3538119). Available from ProQuest Dissertations & Theses Full Text. (1335509742). Retrieved from http://ezproxy.library.arizona.edu/login?url=http://search.proquest.com/docview/1335509742?accountid=8360

Maxwell, J. A. (2005). *Qualitative Research Design: An Interactive Approach.* Thousand Oaks, CA: Sage Publications.

Mendez, J. P., Mendoza, P., & Malcolm, Z. (2011). Impact of financial aid on Native American students. *Journal of Diversity in Higher Education*, *4*(1), 12–25.

National Conference of State Legislatures. (2015). *Federal and state recognized tribes.* Retrieved from http://www.ncsl.org/research/state-tribal-institute/list-of-federal-and-state-recognized-tribes.aspx

National Congress of American Indian Policy Research Center and MSU Center for Native Health Partnerships. (2012). *'Walk softly and listen carefully': Building research relationships with tribal communities.* Washington, DC, and Bozeman, MT: Authors.

Nelson, C. A. (2015). *American Indian college students as native nation builders: Tribal financial aid as a lens for understanding college-going paradoxes* (Order No. 3703169). Available from ProQuest Dissertations & Theses Global. (1690497941). Retrieved from http://search.proquest.com/docview/1690497941?accountid=14613

Perna, L. W. (2008). High school students' perceptions of local, national, and institutional scholarships. *Journal of Student Financial Aid*, *37*(2), 4–16.

Perna, L. W. (2010). Toward a more complete understanding of the role of financial aid in promoting college enrollment: The importance of context. In J. C. Smart (Ed.), *Higher Education: Handbook of Theory and Research* 25, 129–179. Memphis, TN: Springer Science.

Reyhner, J., & Eder, J. (2004). *American Indian Education: A History.* Norman, OK: University of Oklahoma Press.

Seidman, I. (2006). *Interviewing as Qualitative Research: A Guide for Researchers in Education and the Social Sciences.* New York, NY: Teachers College Press.

Smith, L. T. (2007). *Decolonizing Methodologies: Research and Indigenous Peoples.* New York, NY: Zed Books.

Stephens, N. M., Fryberg, S. A., Markus, H. R., Johnson, C. S., & Covarrubias, R. (2012). Unseen disadvantage: How American universities' focus on independence undermines the academic performance of first-generation college students. *Journal of Personality and Social Psychology*, *102*(6), 1178.

Swanson, J. L., & Tokar, D. M. (1991). College students' perceptions of barriers to career development. *Journal of Vocational Behavior*, *38*, 92–106.

Szasz, M. C. (2003). *Education and the American Indian: The Road to Self-Determination Since 1928.* Albuquerque, NM: University of New Mexico Press.

Tierney, W. G., Salle, M. W., & Venegas, K. M. (2007). Access and financial aid: How American Indian students pay for college. *Journal of College Admissions*, *197*, 14–23.

Wilson, S. (2001). Self-as-relationship in Indigenous Research. *Canadian Journal of Native Education*, *25*(2), 91–92.

CHAPTER 11

Toward Equity and Equality

TRANSFORMING UNIVERSITIES INTO INDIGENOUS PLACES OF LEARNING

Kaiwipunikauikawēkiu Lipe (Native Hawaiian)

Welina Mānoa ua kamaʻāina
He ʻāina i ka ihu la o nā moku
A moku mai ka pawa, ʻo ke ao aʻela
Ala aʻe kāua, ua ao ʻeā

A he ao mālama ko uhai aloha
He kilohana no Kānewai i ke pili
Hoʻi pili aloha me Ka-ua-waʻahila
Ia ua hoʻopulu i ke kula o Puahia

Pua ana ke kupa ala leia ke kama nei
Kama ʻia i kamaʻāina ke aloha
Aloha Mānoa i ka ua Tuahine
Halihali ʻia maila e ka ʻolu Kahaukani

Kani aʻela ia uka o Kahoʻiwai
Ia ʻāina kaulana i ka ulu lehua
Lehua-kea o ka uka la o Naniuapō
Pōwehi i ka wai peʻe palai o Waiakeakua

A ka pohu laʻi la aʻo Akaaka
I ka ua kokoʻula aʻo Kahala (Kahalaopuna)
Ua kau, ua holo, ua pae aku
Ua hoʻi ka uʻi o Mānoa, ua ahiahi[1]

(Basham & Lopes, 2002)

Aloha mai kāua e ka mea heluhelu![2] In 2015, the Association for the Study of Higher Education's (ASHE) annual conference theme was "Inequality and Higher Education" with a subtheme of "Indigenous Peoples." This pairing of themes stirred something inside of me that led to the presentation of the following chapter that focuses specifically on inequality and inequity in higher education in relation to Indigenous peoples.

Ancestral Connections to Land

I begin with the Hawaiian chant *Welina Mānoa Ua Kamaʻāina* as presented above for two reasons. First, it is a chant, composed by Professors Keawe Lopes and Leilani Basham, which describes Mānoa valley, the land where I work at the University of Hawaiʻi at Mānoa (UHM).[3] Therefore, presenting this chant is a way for me to introduce where I come from, where I spend most of my days, where most of my research is focused, and where I believe there is much promise and abundance for my Hawaiian people.[4]

Mānoa was once one of the most fertile and productive places for food cultivation on the island of Oʻahu (Kameʻeleihiwa, 2016). For one, Mānoa has great sources of fresh water and rich soil. Second, recognizing these gifts of natural resources, Native Hawaiians carefully and expertly managed and tended to the land, the water, and the abundant natural resources of the area to grow food and feed the multitudes. The staple food cultivated in Mānoa was kalo, not only a food crop but also ancestor of the Hawaiian people in our cosmogonic genealogies (Kameʻeleihiwa, 1992; Liliʻuokalani, 1897).

Today, Mānoa is no longer a primary location of kalo or food production. It is heavily populated with homes, small businesses, and the University of Hawaiʻi at Mānoa. As such, although Mānoa does not primarily feed people with her kalo anymore, the land of Mānoa continues to provide the natural resources of land and water, which sustains our state's research-intensive, largest public-serving university. The second reason I opened with the chant *Welina Mānoa Ua Kamaʻāina* (Basham & Lopes, 2002) is because it calls out to all of us to recognize what Mānoa truly is: Ancestral Native Hawaiian land. This is a critical point because if we are going to address inequality and inequity in higher education, we have to begin with at least this one truth: Every university in the United States of America and Hawaiʻi is situated on Indigenous land (Justice, 2004; Kameʻeleihiwa in Lipe, 2012). As such, each of our universities, and each of us who work at those universities, reaps resources from the Indigenous homelands upon which our institutions sit; land that was likely seized from those Indigenous peoples in less than legal ways (Dunbar-Ortiz, 2014).

Meanwhile, nearly all of our institutions of "higher education" have somehow managed to forget, erase, ignore, dishonor, and disrespect this truth. Further, most of our universities engage in little to no reciprocation with the Indigenous lands that sustain us and with the Indigenous peoples who have maintained those lands, who are genealogically connected to those lands, whose health and well-being depend on access to those lands, and whose ancestors are buried in those lands (Cajete, 2015; Dunbar-Ortiz, 2014; Kameʻeleihiwa, 1992, 2016; Lipe, 2013). The lack of recognition and reciprocation by universities across America and Hawaiʻi to the foundations of our institutions—the foundations of Indigenous lands, people, and knowledge systems—creates grave inequalities. Moreover, the foundation of inequity and inequality with respect to Indigenous peoples upon which our universities are built also creates inequities and inequalities for other ethnic groups because the culture of erasure and silencing has become normalized.

I do not believe in desperation, however. I was taught by my mentors, "ʻAʻohe loaʻa i ka noho wale. Nothing is gained by idleness" (Pukui, 1983, p. 21). My ancestors taught me to resist the status quo, rectify inequity and inequality, and find a better way for our children and grandchildren. Hence, the natural question for me becomes: How do we bring more equity and equality into higher education, beginning with reciprocation to the Indigenous lands, peoples, and knowledge systems of each of our areas?

Transformation into Indigenous Places of Learning

I would like to suggest that one way to engage in this work towards equity, equality, and reciprocation is to transform (Eckel, Hill, & Green, 1998; Engeström, 2001)[5] our universities into Indigenous places of learning: universities where Indigenous peoples of the place are recruited as students, staff, faculty, and administrators, and where they are invited and made to feel safe to bring their Indigenous histories, knowledge systems, languages, worldviews, and practices and where those gifts become foundations for curricula across the disciplines and throughout policies and practices. I am not suggesting that universities erase all other ways of knowing and being, however. Instead, I am suggesting that the Indigenous lands, peoples, and knowledge systems of the area be included, honored, and recognized as value added (Benham, personal communication) to the diversity and richness of our universities and to the well-being of our land and communities.

I fully recognize the enormity of my suggestion because the current reality of most institutions is vastly different. Every day I live through the slow and often painful process in which we are trying to transform my university into one that honors and includes Hawaiʻi and her first people.[6] Not long ago, as I sat in doctoral courses, my inclusion of Hawaiian knowledge or worldviews received blank stares and disregard. Most people at my university have never been able to say my name correctly. Today, even with "PhD" at the end of my name, white male administrators ask me to get them a cup of coffee in meetings. Right now

I am ashamed to say that my university and the state of Hawaiʻi are engaged in several projects that destroy and disrespect our natural resources, including but not limited to the attempt to build telescopes atop our sacred mountains Mauna Kea and Haleakalā. These are just limited examples of one Indigenous group who lives with the disregard of our land and culture by the university in our homeland.

In my short lifetime of 33 years, I have also been privileged to witness and participate in some great changes and transformations at my university. I have been raised and mentored by fearless educators who have taught me to work toward equity and equality through education. What I have learned from them is that our institutions will never change if we do not dream big and take critical steps toward those dreams.

I invite you to join me. Let us collectively raise our consciousness and transform our universities. Let us help our universities remember and embrace the long line of genealogies from which our institutions come, beginning with the commonality that all are built upon the foundations of Indigenous lands and peoples. When we help to wake our institutions from their current amnesia, starting with Indigenous roots, it will become a platform from which the stories and realities of many communities will begin to be included, moving our universities toward more equity and equality. As a step toward this awakening, I offer my story at my university with the hope that helpful lessons and approaches can be gleaned for other peoples, places, and contexts.

Beginning with Moʻolelo

I have been exploring and making sense of the moʻolelo—the interconnected stories and experiences—of my university for some time now. I continue to reflect on my experiences as a child of the university,[7] as both an undergraduate and graduate student there, and as a staff and faculty member at UH Mānoa. I have also studied and tracked the evolution of various policies, mandates, and reports created by and also about UHM with regard to it aiming to become a Hawaiian place of learning.[8] In addition, I have been mentored by and also have engaged in in-depth interviews with select Native Hawaiian female educational leaders who have been leading the hard work of transforming UHM and other related educational spaces back into Hawaiian places of learning. These are the sources from which I draw to share some moʻolelo.

Schein's Three Levels of Organizational Culture

All of the sources listed above have provided insight for me into UHM's journey toward becoming a Hawaiian place of learning. One of the helpful frameworks that has allowed me to frame my analysis and learning has been Schein's (2010) three levels of organizational culture, including artifacts, espoused values, and underlying assumptions. I use these levels to identify transformations that have occurred and also to help plan future efforts.

UHM's Artifacts—Increasing over Time. Artifacts are the easiest parts of the campus culture to identify because artifacts are the enacted events, programs, and practices of the institution (Schein, 2010). Although Schein (2010) does not include people in his list of what counts as an artifact, my research has pointed toward people being an impactful artifact on campus. For example, when students see more Hawaiian professors and more Hawaiian course offerings, they feel more like they belong in higher education (Lipe, 2014). Hence, I include people as artifacts of the organizational culture.

Those who have institutional memory can quickly comment on the increase of Native Hawaiian artifacts at UHM over time. For example, my mom, who was a student at UHM in the 1970s, recalls just a handful of Native Hawaiian students, even less Native Hawaiian faculty, and nearly no courses that were related to Hawaiian language or culture. My mom felt so out of place because of the lack of Hawaiian artifacts that she quit after her freshman year (Kame'eleihiwa, 2016). Institutional data support these claims: As late as 1977, the Native Hawaiian population comprised a mere 1.6% of the total student body at UH Mānoa ("Historical Enrollment," n.d.). Professor Haunani Kay Trask (1992), prominent Native Hawaiian political scholar, educational leader, and community activist, describes the UHM campus in the latter 1900s: "By mid-century, the University of Hawai'i seemed like just another college campus. American colonialism had been so thoroughly successful, no one questioned why the University of Hawai'i was not, truly, 'of Hawai'i' but was, rather, 'of America'" (p. 3). Trask's analysis largely directs our attention to the lack of any artifacts at UHM that helped to remind, recognize, and honor that UHM is in Hawai'i, homeland of the Native Hawaiian people.

Over time, however, Native Hawaiian artifacts on campus have grown. Balutski and Wright (2012) have documented much of the data on this progress. For example, whereas Hawaiian students once comprised only 1.6% of the total student body at UHM in 1977 (Historical Enrollment, n.d.), today they comprise nearly 15% (Balutski & Wright, 2012). Now there are dozens of courses focused on Hawaiian language and Hawaiian studies ("Spring 2014 Course Availability," 2014). Further, there is now a School of Hawaiian Knowledge, Centers for Hawaiian Language and Studies, Native Hawaiian Student Services, and Native Hawaiian support programs in disciplines across the campus including but not limited to Engineering, Medical School, Nursing, and Law (Native Hawaiian Advancement Task Force, 2012). In addition, Kūali'i Council—a UHM council comprised of Hawaiians and organized by Hawaiians—has been established and approved as the Native Hawaiian advisory body to the chancellor of Mānoa ("Organization Chart I," 2013). Though these advancements in Native Hawaiian artifacts are impressive compared to UHM's earliest years, Native Hawaiians are still underrepresented in student body, faculty, and administration across the campus (Native Hawaiian Advancement Task Force, 2012).

While there is still much work to do to attain parity, equity, and equality[9] at UHM for Native Hawaiians as we move toward a Native Hawaiian place of learning, the increase in artifacts is notable. Moreover, the advancements at UHM are quite unique. Very few research-one, predominantly non-Indigenous institutions[10] across the United States have programs in which there are Indigenous faculty leading Indigenous programs within larger academic units, such as is the case with Native Hawaiians at UHM. Most similar campuses, if they have any Indigenous programs at all, usually isolate Indigenous artifacts to the area of Native American student services and/or focused in an Indigenous Studies program ("Academics at Fort Lewis," 2012; Brown, 2005; "History and Native American Studies," n.d.; "Undergraduate Majors," n.d.). The question becomes, then, how has UHM been able to make such strides in its Native Hawaiian artifacts on campus? I suggest that we look to key espoused values documented in policies and mandates as well as transformative underlying assumptions modeled by Native Hawaiians.

Espoused Values—Establishing Accountability. Espoused values are the norms and values found in the language of documents, policies, mission statements, and also within conversations between members of the university community (Schein, 2010). There is a set of guiding documents that articulate very powerful and unique espoused values that are part of UHM's genealogy. These documents include the United Nations Declaration on the Rights of Indigenous Peoples (UNDRIP) ("United Nations Declaration," 2008), United States Public Law 103–150 (U.S. Congress, 1993), UH Board of Regents Policy (UH Board of Regents, 2012), UHM Strategic Plan ("Achieving Our Destiny," 2011), UH and UHM organizational charts, and several UH and UHM Task Force reports. The use of such documents can be helpful in educating stakeholders, raising consciousness, and holding the institution accountable.[11]

All of the policies, documents, and reports calling for a Hawaiian place of learning are examples of espoused values and artifacts (Schein, 2010) and can help in the transformation of campus culture (Kezar, 2012). In addition, within each of these documents there are specific recommendations that target further espoused values and artifacts, such as creating Native Hawaiian spaces on campus and providing tuition waivers to Native Hawaiian students (Native Hawaiian Advancement Task Force, 2012). Implementation of these artifacts can be difficult, however. According to Boyd (1993), "educators are inclined to minimize the personal costs of change by only partial or 'symbolic' implementation of innovations" (p. 513). Furthermore, Kezar (2012) reminds us, "people tend to operate unconsciously off, and rely most on their underlying assumptions" (p. 153). Therefore, genuine implementation of these policies and guiding documents has and will continue to be difficult without also addressing individual assumptions through a process of dialogue and deep reflection (Wheatley, 2009; Witham & Bensimon, 2012) and opportunity to offer, experience, and live into alternative value systems, and in the case of Hawai'i, Hawaiian values.

Transforming Underlying Assumptions—Where the Hard Work Begins. Underlying assumptions are the core beliefs that guide individual behavior (Schein, 2010). Based on the literature and my research and experience, if we are going to transform our institutions into Indigenous places of learning where Indigenous peoples, places, and knowledge systems are included, honored, and made to feel safe, we must focus on transforming the underlying assumptions of the individuals who comprise and collectively create the cultures of our universities. This is difficult work, however. As Kezar (2012) notes, underlying assumptions are "the most intangible and hidden aspects of culture" (p. 152). We often do not take the time to challenge and uncover our own values and also consider new and alternative ones. Further, the majority of universities across America and Hawai'i are predominantly non-Indigenous. Thus, the onus on Indigenous peoples in the academy is great. In Hawaiian, however, there is a proverb: "'A'ohe hana nui ke alu 'ia. No task is too big when done by all together" (Pukui, 1983, p. 18). I see this proverb as an invitation for all of us—Hawaiian and non-Hawaiian, Indigenous and non-Indigenous—to find our role in exploring and considering new and additional values, most specifically Indigenous ones. For the context in Hawai'i, I offer the Hō'ālani Framework (Lipe, 2014).

The Hō'ālani Framework—Ancestral Concepts, Contemporary Contexts

The Hō'ālani Framework (Lipe, 2014) was developed by reflecting on my own experiences as a Hawaiian woman growing up in my language and culture, from ancestral mo'olelo passed down from generation to generation, and also from my research in and about the university along with the lessons gleaned from select Native Hawaiian female transformative educational leaders. I consider the framework as a pedagogical tool, a guide to a pathway for any individual to engage in the world through a Hawaiian framework (see figure 11.1). In the case of UHM, I see the Hō'ālani Framework as a pathway for individuals at UHM to engage in their work from a uniquely Hawaiian set of underlying assumptions (Schein, 2010), which, then, would naturally help folks to recognize the

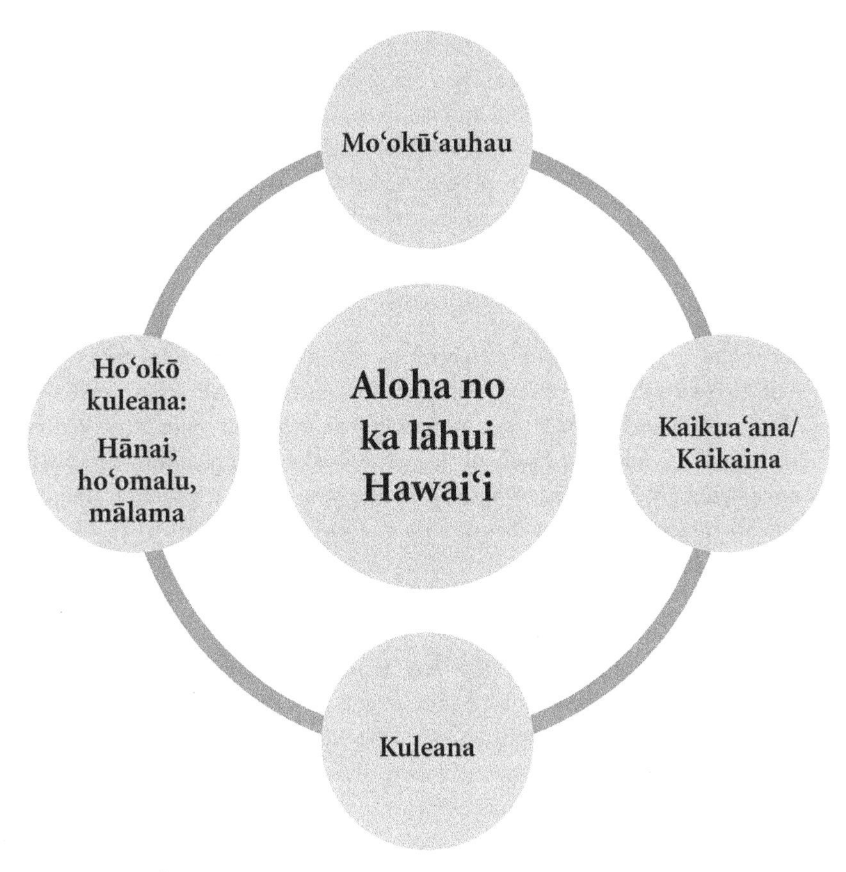

Figure 11.1. Hōʻālani Framework

importance of including and honoring Hawaiian land, people, and knowledge systems.

Papa and Wākea: A Foundational Hawaiian Moʻolelo

In order to best describe the principles of the Hōʻālani Framework (Lipe, 2014), I turn to the Hawaiian moʻolelo of Papa, Wākea, and Hāloa.[12] Kameʻeleihiwa (1992) re-tells this moʻolelo in her introduction of a Hawaiian model by which to understand Hawaiian society. Drawing on her retelling, I summarize it below:

> Papa is the Earth Mother and Wākea is the Sky Father. They parent many of the Hawaiian Islands together. In addition, they produce a human child, Hoʻohōkūkalani. Later, Wākea and Hoʻohōkūkalani unite[13] and she becomes pregnant. Her child is born prematurely and does not survive. They name him Hāloa-naka and bury him in the ground. From this burial site grows the first kalo, or taro plant, which becomes the staple food of the Hawaiian

people. Wākea and Hoʻohōkūkalani unite again, and their second child is born a healthy boy, whom they name Hāloa in honor of his elder sibling. Hāloa is the first high chief of Hawaiʻi and is the common ancestor of all Hawaiian people. Through careful and expert observation and management of the land and water by the Hawaiian people, loʻi kalo or taro fields are engineered throughout the islands and Hawaiians thrive because of their healthy staple food and ancestor.

Moʻokūʻauhau.[14] The first thing we learn from the moʻolelo above is the importance of moʻokūʻauhau, or the genealogical successions, connections, and stories (Pukui & Elbert, 1986). The telling and re-telling of Papa and Wākea generation after generation points to the necessity of understanding our various moʻokūʻauhau. Most importantly, it is the knowing and understanding of the moʻokūʻauhau that helps us to know how we are connected to all parts of our world through space and time.

Kaikuaʻana and Kaikaina.[15] In the Hawaiian worldview, when we know our genealogical connections, a relational order is established; namely, the kaikuaʻana/kaikaina relationship. Kaikuaʻana is translated into English as the "older sibling or cousin of the same sex; sibling or cousin of the same sex of the senior line" (Pukui & Elbert, 1986, p. 116). Similarly, kaikaina is translated into English as the "younger sibling or cousin of the same sex, as younger brother or male cousin of a male . . . sibling or cousin of the same sex of the junior line" (Pukui & Elbert, 1986, p. 116). The terms also refer to the senior and junior genealogical lines, respectively. The basic premise of kaikuaʻana and kaikaina, therefore, is that there is always a person or element that is interdependent on the next. Nothing is alone or without connection to the next; everything is intergenerational.

Kuleana.[16] Defining the relationship between kaikuaʻana and kaikaina is kuleana. English terms provided for kuleana by Pukui and Elbert (1986) include "right, privilege, concern, responsibility" (p. 179). In the moʻolelo of Hāloa, kuleana is captured well in the relationship of the land and the kalo—those elements being the kaikuaʻana—with the people, the kaikaina in that context. As the kaikuaʻana of the Hawaiian people, the land and kalo have the kuleana to provide for and feed the people. In return, the people, as the kaikaina, have the privilege of taking care of the land and cultivate it well so the kalo can continue to grow and nourish us (Kameʻeleihiwa, 1992). In other words, kuleana is about nurturing and sustaining the life of each of the entities in specific ways depending on our given roles.

———

Ka Hoʻokō Kuleana.[17] The last aspect of this framework is hoʻokō kuleana, or fulfillment of the kuleana. Without action, the kuleana is not fulfilled. Kameʻeleihiwa highlights hānai, hoʻomalu, and mālama (1992). In English, terms for hānai include "feeding, fostering, raising as a child, and providing for" (Pukui & Elbert, 1986, p. 56). Hoʻomalu is translated, "To bring under the care and protection of, to protect" (Pukui & Elbert, 1986, p. 234). This is what the elder sibling, such as the land or kalo, does for the younger line: it feeds, clothes, and protects us, the people. Mālama, in English, is to "tend to, take care of, and maintain" (p. 232). This is the kuleana of the junior line; to take care of the elder line as a younger child would tend to his grandparent or a kalo farmer tends to his loʻi.[18] When kaikuaʻana and kaikaina recongize their roles and fulfill their kuleana, there is pono or goodness, balance, and order (Kameʻeleihiwa, 1992).

Employing the Hōʻālani Framework

The inequalities and injustices that are part of UHM's track record with respect to Native Hawaiian people and land have been illuminated and called out with the upswing of consciousness that many have experienced when reconnecting to the guiding principles included in the Hōʻālani Framework. This is especially true as folks have recognized the lack of kuleana fulfillment and reciprocation by the university to Hawaiʻi and her first people. Further, many Native Hawaiians at UHM, especially those female leaders I studied with, have reconnected their kuleana to their land and people through the study of Hawaiian history, language, culture, and practices. Learning and re-engaging with these various genealogies, which delineate their roles and guide the fulfillment of their kuleana, is all tied back to their deep-rooted relationship, commitment, and ultimate aloha for their lāhui Hawaiʻi—their Hawaiian people and environment. This is the center of the Hōʻālani Framework. They have used this aloha—their love, commitment, and respect—as fuel to become fearless transformational leaders, working toward transforming UHM and other related spaces into Hawaiian places of learning.

The opportunity I see as emerging from the lessons of the women I studied with and the development of the Hōʻālani Framework is a pedagogical tool for teaching and learning. In particular, the framework can guide us, from a Hawaiian worldview, to become aware of the aloha we are nurtured with on a daily basis by Hawaiʻi's land, environment, and first peoples. Further, it provides a road map to engage in reciprocation to restore balance, equity, and equality to those important relationships to ensure that vitality of our island home for generations to come.

With all this said, we cannot forget that years of colonialism and hegemony have led us in Hawai'i to be fearful in one way or another because we have been stripped of the knowledge that connects us to our kuleana and that connects us to Hawai'i herself. Therefore, when we re-empower people to recognize their kuleana by recognizing their genealogies, they can then shed that fear, because no longer can they not find their place and their worth, Hawaiian or non-Hawaiian in the realm of caring for Hawai'i; no longer can they not find their role. It becomes empowering because we can be proud of the kuleana we fulfill in our given roles, because we have found a way to care and positively impact our interdependent kaikua'ana and kaikaina in a myriad of genealogies. That connectedness and interdependence will allow us to become fearless and thus lead to aloha for ourselves and aloha for the people and spaces around us. By doing so, folks will innately want to include and honor Hawaiian land, people, and knowledge systems, especially in our work in higher education.

Finally, each of the rays depicted in the Hō'ālani Framework represent the concrete pathways, strategies, and approaches that we can utilize to transform people and spaces. In my research with the Native Hawaiian female educational leaders, I learned that the strategies they use with others are the same as those that have allowed them to learn and live into the main principles of the Hō'ālani Framework and reinforce their aloha for their Hawaiian people and world. Thus, the rays point inward because the pathways keep strong and bright the radiance of aloha each of the women commit to their communities. The rays also point outward because the strategies similarly help to transform other people and places into zones of reciprocation and aloha (Lipe, 2014).[19]

Final Thoughts

I began this chapter by highlighting one truth: All institutions of higher education in America and Hawai'i are on Indigenous lands (Justice, 2004; Kame'eleihiwa in Lipe, 2012). However, most universities do not take that into account and do not engage in any type of reciprocation to the Indigenous lands or peoples upon which the institutions are situated. This lack of inclusion and awareness by universities has created serious inequalities for Indigenous peoples. Moreover, the foundation of inequality and inequity with respect to Indigenous peoples upon which our universities are built also creates inequalities for other ethnic groups because the culture of erasure and silencing has become normalized. In order to help steer our universities in a new direction away from such erasure and exclusion, I suggest transforming our institutions into Indigenous places of learning: Universities where Indigenous peoples of the place are recruited as students, staff, faculty, and administrators and where they are invited and made to feel safe to bring their Indigenous histories, knowledge systems, languages, worldviews, and practices and where those gifts become foundations for curricula across the disciplines and throughout policies and practices. Consequently, this type of inclusion can build a campus culture (Jayakumar & Museus, 2012) in which the experiences, realities, and worldviews of many will be uplifted. However, if we do not begin with those of Indigenous peoples, the foundation will never be set right.

In order to provide an example of work toward an Indigenous place of learning, I provided the example of my university, the University of Hawai'i at Mānoa, and its journey toward becoming a Hawaiian place of learning. Schein's (2010) three levels of culture can be useful, including artifacts, espoused values, and underlying assumptions. The UHM examples I gave point to the importance of each level and some ideas for how other institutions can think about including and implementing different aspects into their universities.

Perhaps the most important point I have attempted to make in this chapter deals with the Hō'ālani Framework (Lipe, 2014) as a means to transforming underlying assumptions of individuals to engage in more inclusive and Hawaiian worldviews. This is particularly important as I consider pathways toward equity and equality not only at my institution but also as I hope to partner with others to do the same at their universities. Thus, the value of the Hō'ālani Framework is at least threefold as we collectively move forward on this work together.[20]

First, an Indigenous researcher and scholar articulated the framework. Universities cannot attempt to move in the direction of Indigenous places of learning without including and being led by Indigenous peoples. In our scholarship and research we bring our genealogies of experience, values, and worldviews that are holistic and inclusive, which will surely help academia move toward equity and equality that is so necessary. We have historically been left out of the critical area of organizational change and transformation research, yet have been the ones at the heart of some of the most groundbreaking and innovative praxis (Freire, 1993). It is time for us to join this important conversation in the literature and to be invited and valued by our allies in this important work.

Second, the framework was informed by Indigenous ancestral knowledge. It is not enough for Indigenous bodies to be in academia if our ancestral knowledge in our research and scholarship is not present. To more fully understand and connect with Indigenous worldviews, Indigenous ancestral knowledge must be included because it is the essential foundation of who we are and makes our voices unique and necessary. Further, Indigenous peoples are responsible for that knowledge, thus we must be the leaders of teaching and gleaning lessons from that knowledge for contemporary contexts. This is a critical point of diversifying (Lipe, 2013) both research and praxis (Freire, 1993) because until recently, Indigenous ancestral knowledge has been nearly non-existent in research and the academy yet holds immense amounts of wisdom and use for today and the future.

Third, the framework was also informed by the contemporary experiences of many Indigenous individuals and their 21st-century life stories. The transformational work that is necessary is collective work and needs to include multiple Indigenous voices because we are not homogenous peoples. Further, our ancestral memories and contemporary experiences are both similar and also unique. As we reclaim space in our homelands, in our academies, and in higher education research, we do so by honoring and gleaning lessons from our many stories and our many realities. Then, we build off of one another and we lift each other up as move forward (Kenolio, personal communication).

I highlight these three points of including Indigenous peoples, their ancestral knowledge, as well as their contemporary experiences to illuminate this final point: Indigenous ancestral knowledge coupled with Indigenous contemporary experiences and contexts is powerful. The lessons to be gleaned can be helpful for all, both Indigenous and non-Indigenous peoples. Mostly, Indigenous worldviews are holistic and inclusive because our ancestral stories connect us to our entire natural world. Thus, engaging in these worldviews in higher education will expand the way we are able to recognize, include, and honor many stories, many experiences, and many realities as we move toward equity and equality for our communities. Mahalo.

NOTES

1. The composers of this chant do not translate it into English, therefore I do not provide an English translation.
2. Greetings, dear reader!
3. UHM is the flagship campus of the ten-campus Univeristy of Hawai'i system. For more information, visit www.hawaii.edu.
4. When I refer to "Hawaiian people," I am referring to those who descend from the Indigenous inhabitants of the Hawaiian Islands prior to 1778 when Captain Cook arrived.
5. For the term "transformation," I draw from two definitions in particular. First, Eckel, Hill, and Green (1998) define transformational change as that which "alters the culture of the institution by changing select underlying assumptions and institutional behaviors, processes, and products; is deep and pervasive affecting the whole institution; is intentional; and occurs over time" (p. 3). Furthermore, I draw from Engeström's (2001) discussion on transformation in which an activity or institution can be "reconceptualized to embrace a radically wider horizon of possibilities than in the previous mode" (p. 137).
6. Over the past 30 years there have been many initiatives to push UHM to become more Hawaiian and more Hawaiian-serving. Some will be discussed in this chapter. One of the informative links is http://www.manoa.hawaii.edu/chancellor/NHATF/index.html
7. My mother is a professor at my university. She is also a single mother, so I spent a lot of time with her at work when I was not in school.
8. I specifically use the term "Hawaiian place of learning" because this is the term used in UH Mānoa's strategic plan with a goal to "Promote a Hawaiian Place of Learning" ("Achieving Our Destiny," 2011, p. 6).
9. I use the term "parity" because it is a term Native Hawaiians are using at UHM to argue for parity between the percentage of Native Hawaiian students, faculty, and administration with the percentage of Native Hawaiians in the general population (25%). I use the term "equity" to refer to fairness toward everyone having access to the same opportunities. Finally,

after equity is established, I use the term "equality" to refer to sameness in which everyone can attain and have the same things ("Equality vs. Equity," 2015).

10. I use the term "predominantly non-Hawaiian university" for UH Mānoa because Native Hawaiians are less than 4% of faculty, 1% of administration (Native Hawaiian Advancement Task Force, 2012), 15.8 % of undergraduates, and 12.5% of graduate students (Balutski & Wright, 2012). Hence, I use the term "predominantly non-Indigenous institutions" to similarly describe universities that are majority non-Indigenous.

11. A description and analysis of these documents can be found in my dissertation.

12. I am specifically referring to the Hawai'i island version of this mo'olelo, which follows the Ulu line rather than the O'ahu island story that follows the Nanaulu line (Fornander, 1969). The reason for my selection of the Hawai'i island version is because that is the version I grew up learning and knowing.

13. Only gods/goddesses and ali'i nui (high chiefs) could engage in the practice of nī'aupi'o (Kame'eleihiwa, 1992). Kame'eleihiwa (1992) describes nī'aupi'o mating as an incestuous relationship. If children are born from this union, they are akua children, meaning they are divine (Malo, 1951).

14. Mo'okū'auhau is the top circle in the Hō'ālani Framework image.

15. Kaikua'ana/Kaikaina is the circle to the right of 'Mo'okū'auhau.'

16. Kuleana is the bottom circle of the Hō'ālani Framework image.

17. Ka ho'okō kuleana, represented by the terms hānai, ho'omalu, and mālama, is represented as the left-most circle in the Hō'ālani Framework image.

18. Lo'i: "Irrigated terrace, especially for taro" (Pukui & Elbert, 1986, p. 209).

19. For a complete list of the strategies (the rays) that the women in my study employed, visit Appendix H of my dissertation (Lipe, 2014).

20. I am by no means trying to claim that the Hō'ālani Framework is or should be the only such guide. I want to encourage many similar Indigenous frameworks to emerge and be utilized. I highlight the value I see in the Hō'ālani Framework as a way to direct our attention to how such research and frameworks can be useful in other places with other peoples.

REFERENCES

Academics at Fort Lewis College. (2012). Retrieved from http://www.fortlewis.edu/Home/Academics.aspx

Achieving Our Destiny: The University of Hawai'i at Manoa 2011–2015 Strategic Plan. (2011). Retrieved from http://manoa.hawaii.edu/vision/pdf/achieving-our-destiny.pdf

Balutski, N., & Wright, K. (2012). *2012 Native Hawaiian student profile.* Unpublished manuscript, Native Hawaiian Student Services, Hawai'inuiākea School of Hawaiian Knowledge, University of Hawai'i at Mānoa, Honolulu, Hawai'i.

Basham, L., & Lopes, K. (2002). *Welina Mānoa ua kama'āina.* Unpublished manuscript, University of Hawai'i at Mānoa, Honolulu, Hawai'i.

Benham, M. K. P. Personal communication, ongoing.

Boyd, W. L. (1993). Policy analysis, educational policy, and management: Through a glass darkly? In Jane Hannaway and Martin Carnoy (Eds.), *Decentralization and School Improvement: Can We Fulfill the Promise?* (pp. 501–522). San Francisco, CA: Jossey-Bass.

Brown, Donna L. (2005). American Indian student services at UND. *New Directions for Student Services, Serving Native American Students, 109,* 87–94. doi: 10.1002/ss.157

Cajete, G. A. (2015). *Indigenous Community—Rekindling the Teachings of the Seventh Fire.* St. Paul, MN: Living Justice Press.

Dunbar-Ortiz, R. (2014). *An Indigenous Peoples' History of the United States.* Boston, MA: Beacon Press.

Eckel, P., Hill, B., & Green, M. (1998). *En Route to Transformation.* Washington, DC: American Council on Education.

Engeström, Y. (2001). Expansive learning at work: Toward an activity-theoretical reconceptualization. *Journal of Education and Work, 14*(1), 133–156.

Equality vs. Equity. (2015). Retrieved from http://www.sewallfoundation.org/uploads/pdf/Social%20Equity.pdf

Freire, P. (1993). *Pedagogy of the Oppressed*. New York, NY: Continuum International.

Hawaiian Studies Task Force. (1986). *Ka'u: University of Hawai'i Hawaiian Studies task force report*. Unpublished manuscript, University of Hawai'i at Mānoa, Honolulu, Hawai'i.

Historical Enrollment 1955–1995. (n.d.). Retrieved from https://www.hawaii.edu/iro/maps.php?category=Enrollment

History and Native American Studies. (n.d.). Retrieved from http://www.ecok.edu/colleges/liberalarts_socialsciences/history_native/index.htm

Jayakumar, U. M., & Museus, S. (2012). Mapping the intersection of campus cultures and equitable outcomes among racially diverse student populations. In S. Museus & U. M. Jayakumar (Eds.), *Creating Campus Cultures: Fostering Success Among Racially Diverse Student Populations* (pp. 1–27). New York, NY: Routledge.

Justice, D. H. (2004). Seeing (and reading) red: Indian outlaws in the ivory tower. In D. A. Mihesuah & A.C. Wilson (Eds.), *Indigenizing the Academy: Transforming Scholarship and Empowering Communities* (pp. 100–123). Lincoln, NE: University of Nebraska Press.

Kame'eleihiwa, L. K. (2016). "How do we transform the University of Hawai'i at Mānoa into a Hawaiian place of learning? Generational Perspectives—Part 1." In B. Ledward, R. Keahiolalo-Karasuda, & S. Kana'iaupuni (Eds.), *Hūlili: Multidisciplinary Research on Hawaiian Well-being, 10*. Honolulu, HI: Kamehameha Publishing.

Kame'eleihiwa, L. (2016). Kaulana O'ahu me he 'āina momona. In A. H. Kimura & K. Suryanata (Eds), *Food and Power in Hawai'i: Visions of Food Democracy*. Honolulu, HI: University of Hawai'i Press.

Kame'eleihiwa, L. (1992). *Native Land and Foreign Desires*. Honolulu, HI: Bishop Museum Press.

Kenolio, L. Personal communication, ongoing.

Kezar, A. (2012). Shared leadership for creating campus cultures that support students of color. In Samuel D. Museus & Uma M. Jayakumar (Eds.), *Creating Campus Cultures: Fostering Success Among Racially Diverse Student Populations* (pp. 150–167). New York, NY: Routledge.

Lili'uokalani. (1897). *Hawai'i's Story by Hawai'i's Queen*. Boston, MA: Lee and Shepard. http://digital.library.upenn.edu/women/liliuokalani/hawaii/hawaii.html

Lipe, D. (2013). *Diversifying science: Recognizing indigenous knowledge systems as scientific worldviews* (Doctoral dissertation). University of Hawai'i at Mānoa.

Lipe, K. (2012). Kēia 'āina: The center of our work. In Jonathan Osorio (Ed.), *I ulu i ka 'āina: Land* (pp. 99–109). Honolulu, HI: University of Hawai'i Press.

Lipe, K. (2014). *Aloha as fearlessness: Lessons from the mo'olelo of eight Native Hawaiian female educational leaders on transforming the University of Hawai'i at Mānoa into a Hawaiian place of learning* (Doctoral dissertation). University of Hawai'i at Mānoa.

Native Hawaiian Advancement Task Force. (2012). *Ke au hou*. Unpublished manuscript. University of Hawai'i at Manoa.

Native Hawaiian Task Force. (2011). *Hawai'i papa o ke ao*. Unpublished manuscript. University of Hawai'i System, Honolulu, Hawai'i.

Organization Chart I—Office of the Chancellor UH Manoa. (2013). Retrieved from http://manoa.hawaii.edu/ovcafo/OrgChart2013/2013_MCO_Stamped.pdf

Pukui, M. K. (1983). *'Olelo no'eau*. Honolulu, HI: Bishop Museum Press.

Pukui, M. K., & Elbert, S. H. (1986). *Hawaiian Dictionary*. Honolulu, HI: University of Hawai'i Press.

Schein, E. (2010). *Organizational Culture and Leadership* (4th ed.). San Francisco, CA: Jossey-Bass.

Spring 2014 course availability. (2014). Retrieved from https://www.sis.hawaii.edu/uhdad/avail.classes?i=MAN&t=201430

Trask, H. K. (1992). *Welcoming address for the Hawaiian Studies building groundbreaking—October 27, 1992*. Unpublished manuscript, Center for Hawaiian Studies, University of Hawai'i at Mānoa, Honolulu, Hawai'i.

UH Board of Regents Policies and Bylaws. (2012). Retrieved from http://www.hawaii.edu/offices/bor/policy/borpch4.pdf

Undergraduate Majors. (n.d.). Retrieved from http://www.nsuok.edu/Academics/Degrees Majors/UndergraduateMajors.aspx

United Nations Declaration on the Rights of Indigenous Peoples. (2008). Retrieved from http://www.un.org/esa/socdev/unpfii/documents/DRIPS_en.pdf

U.S. Congress. (1993). United States Public Law 103–150: 103d Congress joint resolution. Retrieved from http://www.hawaii-nation.org/publawall.html

Vizenor, Gerald. (2008). *Survivance: Narratives of Native Presence*. Lincoln, NE: University of Nebraska Press. Retrieved from http://lib.myilibrary.com.eres.library.manoa.hawaii.edu?ID=195840

Wheatley, M. J. (2009). *Turning to One Another: Simple Conversations to Restore Hope to the Future*. San Francisco, CA: Berrett-Koehler Publishers.

Witham, K. A., & Bensimon, E. M. (2012). Creating a culture of inquiry around equity and student success. In Samuel D. Museus & Uma M. Jayakumar (Eds.), *Creating Campus Cultures: Fostering Success Among Racially Diverse Student Populations* (pp. 46–57). New York, NY: Routledge.

CHAPTER 12

Indigeneity in the Methods

INDIGENOUS FEMINIST THEORY IN CONTENT ANALYSIS

Stephanie Waterman (Onondaga, Turtle Clan)

Kateri Tekakawitha, Mohawk, was canonized by the Vatican in 2012, based largely on the Jesuit written record of her conversion. Kateri's (pronounced Gaw dah lee) interpretation of her conversion was not recorded. She, and her home Mohawk community near what is now Auriesville, New York, had suffered great loss due to removal(s), war, and smallpox. She herself was stricken with smallpox and had lost most of her family due to the disease. We can only imagine her emotional and physical suffering, and considering the devastation of disease and community and its impact on everyday life, it may be completely inconceivable to us in the present day.

Kateri's move to Kahnawake alone was likely enough for Jesuits to assume she sought Christian conversion. People, generally, are urged to make a good first impression; her very presence, her seeming voluntary move to a Jesuit community, was the lens through which her subsequent life was evaluated by non-Natives.

Palmer (2014) contends that the Jesuit narrative deracinates and erases Kateri's traditional narrative. The Jesuit narrative had a purpose; it was a tool for conversion to Christianity from spiritual practices they interpreted as "degrading, pagan, and unholy" (p. 268). Palmer interprets how Kateri would understand Christianity through Haudenosaunee principles including Condolence. Condolence, how the Haudenosaunee deal with loss, is foundational. The process, or philosophy, of Condolence, heals the community in addition to the family experiencing the loss. In the midst of near-devastation, Kateri traveled to Kahnawake for sanctuary, where she engaged in seclusion, prayer, "extreme piety, self-mortification, and self-denial" (p. 286). Her Jesuit mentors would have brought her food, likely prayed with her, and provided comfort. Kateri prepared and slept on a mattress of thistles that the Jesuits interpreted through Christianity. Yet, Palmer (2014) explains that in the Haudenosaunee Creation story, the twins born to Sky Woman, thistles and down were used "to mark the children's fastness and also to serve as a warning" that the children were in seclusion (p. 286). In other words, Kateri's use of thistles was more complex than a "mimicry of medieval Christian piety" (p. 286). Her use of thistles is an example of Kateri's cultural knowledge and an indication of her spiritual journey. "At the Jesuit mission [Kahnawake] she found a refuge in which to explore and to transform the meaning of her losses and those of her community into something of value for her and her people" (Palmer, 2014, p. 287). The Haudenosaunee understanding of that transformation has been largely ignored; instead, the Jesuit interpretation provided the world with a one-dimensional, de-culturalized, de-racinated convert. Kateri was much more complex.

In this chapter, I discuss a study of Native American Student Affairs (NASA) webpages through my lens as an Indigenous researcher. Webpages are external documents produced to provide information for prospective and current students, and their families. These webpages provide an external representation of an Indigenous unit with a larger non-Native college and university (NNCU) (Shotton, Lowe, & Waterman, 2013) founded on settler colonial principles. My research is exploratory: What messages do these webpages convey? Kateri's story opens this chapter, as her story is an example of interpretative lenses that mask bias and promote misunderstanding. Through an Indigenous feminist lens I offer a methodology of the document analysis of these webpages and present them as re-claimed Indigenous spaces.

Methods

Through an Internet search, 55 First Nations student support units in Canada and 90 Native American student support units in the United States have been identified. Using National Association for Student Personnel Administrators (NASPA) Regions strictly as an organizer, this chapter discusses the content analysis of the home webpages of five U.S. units found in NASPA Region I. Data are limited to the opening pages of five institutions because this chapter is about methodology more than findings.

Webpages are the first impression NASA units put forward on the World Wide Web. Like the first sentence or opening paragraph of an article or novel, the opening webpage should grab the reader. Qualitative document analysis, focusing on images and text, is the appropriate methodology (Bogdan & Biklen, 2007) for this study. Content analysis methodology articles regarding the World Wide Web (Altheide & Schneider, 2013; McMillan, 2000; Weare & Lin, 2000, for example) refer to Klaus Krippendorff. Generally, procedures for content analysis involve five stages: (1) Documents, (2) Protocol Development and Data

Collection, (3) Data Coding and Organization, (4) Data Analysis, and (5) Report (Altheide, 1996; Krippendorf, 2015).

Webpages were located by a web search using keywords such as "Native American student affairs," "Native American student services," "Indigenous student services," and "American Indian student services" or "student affairs." The five pages were alike in that they represent the same type of student affairs office located within a NNCU website, thus allowing for contrast and comparison analysis. The unit of analysis is the NASA opening webpage. In their discussion of the document analysis process, Altheide and Schneider (2013) write that "meaning and emphasis are key categories" in document analysis (p. 50). They share an illustration in their explanation to guide analysis: A large circle that represents FORMAT surrounds a square that represents the FRAME, surrounding a triangle that represents the THEME. Inside the triangle is the word DISCOURSE with arrows from the border of the circle, or format, leading into discourse. The format is just that: the format that delivers the content, for example a newspaper article, television newscast, or sitcom. Frames create an interpretive border of the discourse. Althiede and Schneider (2013) use examples such as framing news articles through "fear" or "underdog themes" (p. 16).

The format in this study is the opening NASA webpage, downloaded from universities in the United States. They share, broadly, the academic environment and audience. They do not convey entertainment or government messages. The frame is "the focus, a parameter or boundary, for discussing a particular event" (Altheide & Schneider, 2013, p. 53). The frame is the content of the Native American Student Affairs unit that conveys educational information for Indigenous students. I expected that the discourse would feature Indigeneity including Indigenous language. All five NASA webpages were downloaded and saved to PDF on the same date for analysis. The webpage PDFs were saved to folders organized by NASPA region and coding began by highlighting common themes and outlying information.

While Weare and Lin (2000) cite Krippendorff (1980) regarding quantitative and objective analysis in content analysis, Krippendorff writes:

> Although counts of evident incidences of such phenomena can give the impression of objectivity, they make sense only in the context of accepting certain social norms, such as the value of giving equal voice to both sides of a controversy, neutrality of reporting, or affirmative representations. Implying such norms hides the context that analysts need to specify. Unless analysts spell out whose norms are applied, whose attitudes are being inferred, who is exposed to which mass media, and most important, where the supposed phenomena could be observed, their findings cannot be validated. (2013, p. 34)

In other words, underlying norms or worldviews influence the construction of the documents under analysis. The positionality of the individuals who construct a unit's webpage as well as the larger institutional context, including location, are all factors in construction and the interpretation by a webpage's audience. I next explain why context is so important and my conceptual framework.

Indigenous Feminism or Native American Feminist Theory

In this section, I elaborate on Indigenous feminism by explaining the terminology in use and why Indigenous feminist theory is useful in reclaiming our space in research. First, I explain my use of terms. Arvin, Tuck, and Morrill (2013) emphasize the term "Native Feminist Theorists" (p. 11) to acknowledge and include the work of feminists who do not identify as Native, yet who have contributed to Indigenous feminism. The term also engages and includes marginalized and racialized scholars and a wider audience of women who associate feminism with whiteness and thus do not identify with feminism. Many Indigenous scholars who do not identify as feminists work from and critically engage in gender in their work for the benefit of their communities.

Indigenous feminist theory includes the work of Native feminist theories across imposed international and disciplinary borders. As Ross (2009) writes, there are many definitions of feminism including Chicana feminism and black feminism. Feminist scholars are often situated in the field of gender and women studies which, unless your institution is Berea College (bell hooks) or the University of Maryland (Patricia Hill Collins), then these departments are typically associated with Whitestream feminism. By implication, Indigenous feminist theory includes scholars working in First Nations, Native American, and American Indian Studies, and scholars from Australia and New Zealand. Ross (2009) problematizes the varying definitions of feminism, crediting Ramirez (2007) with the term transnational feminism as inclusive of Indigenous women who are urban or off-territory, and those without official enrollment status (Ross, 2009, p. 48). That we have populations who live off-territory and/or are disenfranchised is the result of colonialism. International borders were imposed on long-established Indigenous communities with long, complex histories. By using the term Indigenous feminist theory, the emphasis is on indigeneity and inclusivity beyond borders.

Indigenous feminism is important to my work as an Indigenous scholar as an emphasis on the re-, as in re-claiming our story, the re-introduction of histories and stories, the re-mapping that "we as Native people hold the power to *rethink* the way we engage with territory, with our relationships to one another, and with other Native nations and settler nations" [emphasis mine] (Goeman, 2013, pp. 38–39). Freida Jacques, an Onondaga clan mother, emphasizes the responsibility that comes with knowledge. In Western dominant thought knowledge is often considered power, not a responsibility. Indigenous feminism is about responsibility and relationship to our communities; it is about the benefit and empowerment of our community, not foremost the equality of the sexes. The concept of equality is a dominant way of thinking based on ways of being that were not balanced or equal and a topic for another time. While colonialism has left heteropatriarchal and sexist systems that influence our lives as Indigenous people, our common goal is a re-centering of Indigeneity, survival, and sovereignty. Restoring our Indigenous traditions could better the lives of women and hence strengthen our communities, nations, and sovereignty. That is the core of Indigenous feminism.

As an Indigenous researcher, restoration, rebalance, "(re)mapping" (Goeman, 2013), relationships, responsibility, restory, and restoring are underlying concepts through which a research question is developed, data gathered and analyzed, and then a report is written. All researchers have a worldview through which they approach research, whether they try to bracket (Jones, Torres, & Arminio, 2014) or claim objectivity. No scholar, image, piece of data, or text can escape context. Kateri's story interpreted through the Jesuit record was largely done without context. Palmer (2014) restored Kateri's "conversion" through a Haudenosaunee interpretation.

On surface value, through a dominant lens, Kateri's conversion was celebrated by the Jesuits. We know she experienced great loss (relationships), removed herself from her homeland, and through oral tradition shared today, stories question (restore) the extent of her conversion. I have heard these stories that contest her conversion. Without context, her life was used as a tool for domination. Next I share preliminary findings and discuss the possibilities of employing Indigenous feminist theory as a conceptual framework in research. First, a short history of the institutions in this study.

Context

The institutions in this study are Dartmouth College, Harvard University, the University of Maine (UMaine), the University of Massachusetts-Amherst (UMass-Amherst), and Yale University. Dartmouth, Harvard, and Yale are private as well as Ivy League institutions. Because Dartmouth and Harvard struggled financially early in their establishment, they have a troubled history with regard to their missions that are linked to Indigenous education and misleading fund-raising. The UMaine and UMass-Amherst are large public institutions founded later than the private Ivy institutions. There is more public institutional history available for some institutions than others. Institutional demographics are included for institutions that provided that information.

Dartmouth College

Dartmouth is located on Abenaki territory in the rural hills of Hanover, New Hampshire, a state with no federally recognized tribes or territories. Founded in 1769 by Eleazar Wheelock, a Puritan preacher with an interest in converting the Indigenous population, Dartmouth is one of the oldest institutions of higher education in the United States. Wheelock's mission in starting a college was to prepare Indigenous missionaries who would return to their communities to convert their people. With his protégé, Samson Occom, Mohegan, Wheelock was able to fund-raise based on that mission. However, Wheelock changed his mind and instead sought a college for whites who would then "do the mission work among the Indians" (Carney, 1999, p. 34). Continued access to missionary funds from England and Scotland were necessary for the success of the college. Hence, the final charter emphasized "the education and instruction of youth of the Indian tribes in this land . . . and also of English youth and any others" (Carney, 1999, p. 34) despite the lack of Indigenous students. Only 25 Indigenous students attended by 1800. By 1973, 187 students had enrolled, with 25 of them graduating (Carney, 1999). While these students were enrolled at Dartmouth they were in the "Indian college" and not with the white students.

In 1970, the 13th president of the college, John G. Kemeny, "recommitted Dartmouth to its founding purpose" and "established a Native American Program" (NAP) and increased Native student recruitment (www.dartmouth.edu/~nap/about/). Since then Dartmouth has enrolled more than 700 students. NAP has a Native American House, a living/learning unit, with programming, a fellow, and works with the Native American Studies program. Dartmouth's NAP is the only endowed program of its kind in the United States. According to Dartmouth's main website, they are classified as a very higher research activity (Carnegie Classifications), and enroll more than 6,000 undergraduate and graduate students. Thirty-five percent of their undergraduate population identify as students of color.

Harvard University

Harvard University, located in Cambridge, Massachusetts, on Wamponoag lands, was chartered in 1636. The original charter was changed to include "the education of English and Indian youth" in 1650 (Carney, 1999, p. 25) in order to fund-raise, as the education and conversion of the Indigenous population was popular at the time in England and Scotland. An Indian College was built to house the Indigenous students; however, built in 1656, the first Indigenous student arrived in 1660 and while it stood only four students lived there. It was eventually destroyed. From 1660 to 1712, only six students attended. In 1970, the Harvard University Graduate School of Education received funding to train educators and the American Indian Program was established within that school. In 1990, the AIP became the Harvard University Native American Program (HUNAP), an interfaculty initiative. While HUNAP supports students, recruitment, outreach, and scholarship, Harvard does not have a Native Studies program and has a highest research activity Carnegie classification. Harvard reports demographic data by degrees awarded, not enrollment. Out of 7,595 degrees and certificates awarded in 2014–15, nine awardees were identified American Indian/Alaska Native (Harvard University, Office of Institutional Research, 2016). Massachusetts is home to two federally recognized tribes.

University of Maine

The University of Maine (UMaine) is located on Wabanaki lands, in Orono, Maine, north of Bangor. Maine is home to four U.S. federally recognized tribes. Originally established in 1862 as the Maine College of Agriculture and the Mechanic Arts, a Morrill Act institution, the name was changed to the University of Maine in 1867. UMaine is a Carnegie 2015 Community Engagement Classification and a higher research activity institution and prides itself on providing service to Maine. UMaine enrolls approximately 9,300 undergraduate and 1,600 graduate students, mostly from Maine, but also matriculates students from across the United States and other countries. The website provides no history regarding the founding of their Native student support office, the Wabanaki Center.

University of Massachusetts-Amherst

The University of Massachusetts-Amherst, located on Pocumtuc territory, in rural northern Massachusetts, is also a land grant institution founded in 1863. From institutional data (University of Massachusetts Amherst/Office of Institutional Research, 2015) in 2015, out of 22,748 undergraduates, 27 identified as Native American. In 1996 that number was 68. Their Carnegie classifications are highest research activity and community engagement institution. According to the UMass-Amherst website they offer a Native American Indian Studies Certificate Program. That website was last updated in 2010; however, there appears to be recent academic activity, such as their Massachusetts mapping project (see Native American Trails, 2016). No history of their Native American Student Support Services program was found. However, in a later search the Josephine White Eagle Cultural Center (JWECC) was found under their Center for Multicultural Advancement and Student Success website (UMass Amherst CMASS JWECC, 2016). That page does not include a history of the center but appears to offer programming such as films and a pow wow, and a space for a sense of community.

Yale University

Yale University is located on Quinnipiac land in New Haven, Connecticut, a large-sized city, approximately 80 miles northeast of New York City. Yale is a private institution with a highest research activity Carnegie Classification. Yale enrolled 5,400 undergraduates and 5,800 graduate and professional students in the fall of 2016 (Yale Facts, 2015). Of that number, 2% identify as Native American (Yale Facts, 2016). Its Charter was granted in 1701, becoming Yale College in 1718. The first Native graduate was in 1910; however, for decades Native enrollment was "sparse" (Yale College Native American Cultural Center, 2016). The Association of Native Americans at Yale was founded by John Bathke, Diné, in 1989. The Native American Cultural Center (NACC) was established in 1993. Originally one room, the Center expanded to three rooms, then five in a "house shared with the Asian American Cultural Center" (History NACC) to their own building that opened in 2013. The Yale Group for the Study of Native America is a "working group" for academics (YGSNA, 2016).

Discussion of Findings

At first glance, images and text convey an Indigenous context located within the webpages of institutions from NNCU context. This discussion will first utilize Altheide and Schneider's (2013) format, frame, theme, and discourse content analysis guiding process, and then complicate those findings through Indigenous feminist theory. Figure 12.1 is a graphic representation of these data using Altheide and Schneider's content analysis process.

Webpages are familiar formats, especially to those of us in higher education, as they are a communication medium used by our institutions. We know what to expect from this format: there is typically a banner across the top, images and/or photos, detailed and/or bulleted information, links, sometimes maps, and contact information. As an audience we have an expectation of how to navigate the webpages. Financial institutions, K-12 schools, and other organizations use webpages for communication. The NASA webpages are linked to this format and framed in this study by the NASA unit that targets a Native American student audience. The NASA unit informs the academic and student support content. Content about anything not intimately linked would not be found on the unit's webpage. The discourse within the page is information about the NASA unit and links to other websites that have a relationship to the NASA unit or is important to their community.

The discourse within the pages share a welcome theme. Each website includes a banner in school colors with an institutional logo or school name and navigation links. Under the banner three out of the five NASA webpages have the word "welcome" in large font. Dartmouth's Native American Program displays "Welcome" in large text above their mission statement. Directly under UM's "Welcome to Wabanaki Center" is a statement of thanks to visitors to their website followed by a mission statement. Yale also includes their mission directly under a rotating photo of students and events.

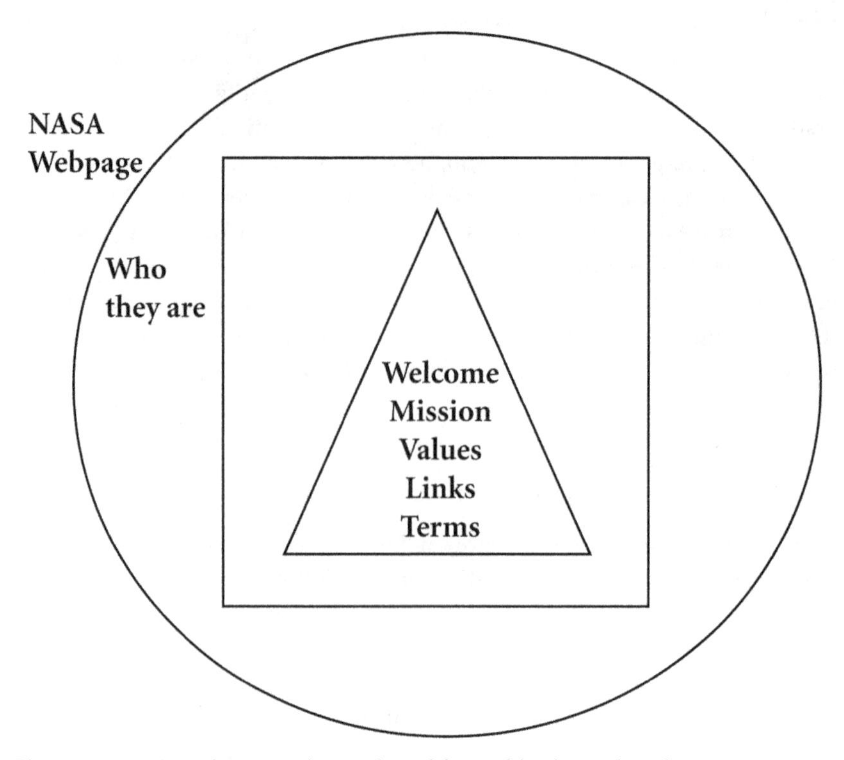

Figure 12.1. NASA webpage analysis. Adapted from Altheide & Schneider, 2013

While the HUNAP's webpage does not use the word "welcome," the program is vibrant with many activities, news, and photos to share. When the webpage was downloaded there was a large rotating banner featuring the "Economic Vibrancy in 21st Century Communities" conference, there were references and links to three other events, a blog link, student update, a link to their Facebook page, and in the third right column their Twitter feed. While the word "welcome" was not used, HUNAP appears to be a place that is inviting, a place where Indigenous students and scholars might feel welcome due to the many activities and people at Harvard and associated with HUNAP.

Images and links also convey a welcoming message. Dartmouth, HUNAP, and NACC include photos of Indigenous people, and/or artwork. At the time the Dartmouth webpage was downloaded, a large photo under the Dartmouth banner was a piece of ledger art. HUNAP has a distinctive Indigenous styled logo and that can be found farther down on its page. NACC also has an Indigenous styled logo that can be found in the right column and as a watermark behind the webpage's text. The Wabanaki Center did not have any Indigenous focused photos or images; however, the center is named after the local Indigenous people and the links in the right-hand column are: Wabanaki Center Home, The Alumni

Mentoring Program—AMP!, Contact Us, Mission and Vision, Prospective Students, Waiver Program, Eligibility, Room and Board Grant, and FAQs. These links imply a community, one that mentors and supports students with funds. A difficult task for students, any student, is finding community (Shotton, Oosahwee, & Cintrón, 2010; Minthorn & Shotton, 2015). These webpages are designed to help students find an Indigenous community.

Through the initial search the UMass Amherst's Native American Support Services Program webpage appears to have been developed in 2000 and not kept up to date, as evidenced by some dead-end links. There was an Indigenous styled logo on the left top, the text "Native American Student Support Program" in red font, a gray line, and then eight links in red font to such resources as Program Objectives and Staff. The UMass logo and contact information appeared at the bottom of the page. When I was looking for contact information regarding another matter, I stumbled upon the UMass-Amherst Josephine White Eagle Cultural Center (JWECC) under the Center for Multicultural Advancement and Student Success website. This webpage does not include Indigenous images or text, but in the lower left-hand corner there is a photo of students of color, one of whom may be Indigenous as she is wearing beaded earrings. Under the center's name is their mission statement that indicates their commitment to supporting "Native and Indigenous students through collaborations and programming that bring visibility and respect of Native and Indigenous peoples" (UMass-Amherst CMASS JWECC, 2016). This website states that they offer weekly study nights, films, discussions, a symposium, and pow-wow. This page conveys a welcoming image although it was buried within other pages. The JWECC page is included in this analysis.

Overall, the missions and goals of the units support student success and student growth. HUNAP's mission is not on the first page, but is found through an "About" link located on the banner. On the NASA webpages "Native American" is found 14 times, the word "Native" 27 times, and "Indigenous" twice. UMass JWECC never uses the term "Native American," only "Native" and "Indigenous." Native American is the accepted term for Indigenous people in the Eastern United States. Other important terms are "community" or "communities" which is found five times, and "support, support services" and "leaders/leadership" which are each found twice. NACC has an "affiliated faculty" link on their webpage. The other pages convey scholarship by including links to scholarly activity (conferences), and terms such as "scholars," "intellectual," and "teaching, research, and publication." The Wabanaki Center identifies "advancing Wabanaki Studies" in its mission statement. The content and discourse reflect a commitment to Indigenous student success, academically and socially, and a place for community and for connection to the Indigenous community. Only the Wabanaki Center uses Indigenous language in its webpage and is consistent with UMaine's emphasis on service to Maine. The other webpages are more pan-Native in their student population attracting students from across Turtle Island.

The webpages are a statement, a claim, about who they are within the dominant NNCU. The images, such as the ledger art which is uniquely Indigenous, on Dartmouth's webpage, and other symbols and photos project an Indigenous content, an Indigenous space. Other webpages on the institutions' webpages do not have Indigenous images unless featuring special events such as an art exhibition, film series, or museum exhibition. The mission statements reflect who NASA supports, their connection to community, and Indigenous intellectuals, and resources. Addresses and contact information and links to outside Indigenous sources are also found here.

Webpages as Reclaimed Spaces

Indigenous values informed the content, as evidenced by respectful representation of images and text. The pages convey strength, achievement, relationships, and community which reflect common Indigenous values. The webpage discourse rejects the damage-centered framing often associated with Indigenous issues (Tuck, 2009), instead reclaiming a message of success and engagement ethically. The pages appear to have been designed by personnel with an understanding of Indigenous communities, students, and student affairs which informs the content and its integrity.

Not only is this Indigenous space, it is contemporary space. Even though ledger art is linked to the 19th century, Dartmouth's Hood Museum hosted a "Contemporary Native American Ledger Art: Drawing on Tradition" exhibition. The conference featured in the banner on Harvard's downloaded webpage was titled "Economic Vibrancy in 21st Century Native Communities." Another conference featured in their rotating banner was the "Native Peoples, Native Politics" conference held in partnership with the Radcliffe Institute for Advanced Study in April 2016. The NACC features a photo of Yale's president with three current Indigenous students wearing ribbon shirts. Several pages had links or photos from their recent pow-wow. Reflecting current activity, these pages reclaim contemporary Indigenous identity; a vibrant and intellectually charged group, not relics of the past, a vanished people, or solely poverty-stricken.

One could argue that any student affairs page would offer photos, links, support programs, department news, and programming activities. However, given the near invisibility Indigenous students have in higher education, 1% or less of the national student body (Kena, Hussar, McFarland, et al., 2016; Shotton, Lowe, & Waterman, 2013), these pages reflect the Indigeneity of the NASA unit, their personnel, and of the Indigenous academic and local community. They include information that Indigenous students and scholars need to know, for example, the Wabanaki tuition waiver. They signal a space to be Indigenous within the potentially thousands of webpages an institution hosts.

Limitations and Future Research

This analysis is based on only five NASA unit opening pages. Some NASA webpages have an additional 20 or more links. Those were not included in this analysis. There are 12 First Nations student affairs units in Canada in Region I that were not included in this analysis. Future research will include the Canadian institutions as well as webpage links. Telephone interviews to clarify webpage content are planned. For example, who developed the webpage, were there any institutional guidelines or restrictions, and what does "success" mean to the unit?

Conclusion

Traditional methods of data collection, content analysis, and coding produced themes and areas for future research. Indigenous feminist theory enhanced the analysis to complicate the content as a form of restoration, as a way to interpret the content and NASA activities through a lens of sovereignty. Feminist theory, broadly, is underutilized in higher education research and "can offer different interpretations of social interactions, and potentially, provide possibilities for change in both higher education as well as in other settings" (Ropers-Huilman & Winters, 2011, p. 668). With increased calls for diversity, for just policies for sexual assault, for responding to Black Lives Matter and other social movements, for example, feminist theory and Indigenous feminist theory offer ways to complicate higher education research, responses, and practice. I have discussed in this chapter using Kateri as an example of a how a dominant lens can intentionally misinterpret the actions of an individual to influence others. Kateri's life was very complicated, yet through the written record, the Jesuits removed her Indigeneity. As Palmer (2014) restored the telling of Haudenosaunee principles in Kateri's life, Indigenous feminist theory is a tool for researchers to restore, to rethink, to add balance, and to express our sovereignty in research.

References

Altheide, D. L. (1996). *Qualitative media analysis*. SAGE University Paper. 38, Thousand Oaks, CA: Sage.

Altheide, D. L., & Schneider, C. J. (2013). *Qualitative Media Analysis* (2nd Ed.). Los Angeles, CA: Sage.

Arvin, M., Tuck, E., & Morrill, A. (2013). Decolonizing feminism: Challenging connections between settler colonialism and heteropatriarchy. *Feminist Formations*, 25(1), 8–34.

Bogdan, R. C., & Biklen, S. K. (2007). *Qualitative Research for Education: An Introduction to Theories and Methods*. Boston, MA: Pearson/Allyn and Bacon.

Carney, C. L. (1999). *Native American Higher Education in the United States*. New Brunswick, NJ: Transaction.

Carnegie Classification (2016). Institution Lookup. https://carnegieclassification.iu/edu/lookup.lookup.php

Goeman, M. (2013). *Mark My Words: Native Women Mapping Our Nations.* Minneapolis, MN: University of Minnesota Press.

Harvard University Office of Institutional Research (2016). Degrees awarded: Demographics 2014–15. http://oir.harvard.edu/fact-book/degrees-awarded-demographics

Jones, S. R., Torres, V., & Arminio, J. (2014). *Negotiating the Complexities of Qualitative Research in Higher Education: Fundamental Elements and Issues* (2nd Ed.). New York, NY: Routledge.

Kena, G., Hussar, W., McFarland, J., de Brey, C., Musu-Gillette, L., Wang, X., Zhang, J., Rathbun, A., Wilkinson-Flicker, S., Diliberti, M., Barmer, A., Bullock Mann, F., & Dunlop Velez, E. (2016). *Condition of Education 2016* (NCES 2016–144). Washington, DC: U.S. Department of Education, National Center for Education Statistics. Retrieved from http://nces.ed.gov/pubsearch

Krippendorff, K. (2013). *Content Analysis: An Introduction to Its Methodology* (3rd Ed.). Los Angeles, CA: Sage.

McMillan, S. J. (2000). The microscope and the moving target: The challenge of applying content analysis to the world wide web. *Journalism & Mass Communication Quarterly, 77*(1), 80–98.

Minthorn, R., & Shotton, H. (2015). Native American Students in Higher Education. In P. Sasso & J. DeVitis (Eds.), *Today's College Students: A Reader* (Adolescent cultures, school and society, Vol. 57). New York, NY: Peter Lang.

Native American trails: Putting tribal lands on the map. (2016). https://www.umass.edu/gateway/feature/native-american-trails

Palmer, V. B. (2014). The devil in the details: Controverting an American Indian conversion narrative. In A. Simpson & A. Smith, (Eds.), *Theorizing Native Studies* (pp. 266–296). Durham, NC: Duke University Press.

Ramirez, R. K. (2007). *Native hubs: Culture, Community, and Belonging in Silicon Valley and Beyond.* Durham, NC: Duke University Press.

Ropers-Huilman, R., & Winters, K. (2011). Feminist research in higher education. *Journal of Higher Education, 82*(6), 667–690. doi:10.1353/jhe.2011.0035

Ross, L. (2009). From the "F" word to Indigenous/feminisms. *Wicazo Sa Review*, 24(2), 39–52.

Shotton, H. J., Lowe, S. C., & Waterman, S. J. (2013). *Beyond the Asterisk: Understanding Native Students in Higher Education.* Sterling, VA: Stylus.

Shotton, H., Oosahwee, S., & Cintrón, R. (2010). Island of sanctuary: The role of an American Indian cultural center. In L. Patton (Ed.), *Culture Centers in Higher Education: Perspectives on Identity, Theory and Practice* (pp. 49–62). Sterling, VA: Stylus.

Tuck, E. (2009). Suspending damage: A letter to communities. *Harvard Educational Review, 79*(3), 409–427.

University of Massachusetts Amherst/Office of Institutional Research. (2015). Race/ethnicity of undergraduate students (U.S. Citizens) Fall 1996 to Fall 2015. (October 2, 2015). Retrieved from http://umass.edu/oir/sites/default/files/publications/factsheets/race_ethnicity/FS-rac_01.pdf

UMass Amherst CMASS JWECC (2016). University of Massachusetts Center for Multicultural Advancement and Student Success Josephine White Eagle Cultural Center (JWECC). Retrieved from https://www.umass.edu/cmass/get-involved/multicultural/jwecc

Weare, C., & Lin, W. (2000). Content analysis of the world wide web: Opportunities and challenges. *Social Science Computer Review, 18*(3), 272–292.

Yale College Native American Cultural Center, (2016). History. http:// http://nacc.yalecollege.yale.edu/history

Yale Facts (2015). Yale Facts. Retrieved from http://yale.edu/about-yale/yale-facts

Yale Group for the Study of Native America (2016). http:// http://ygsna.sites.yale.edu/

CHAPTER 13

Iḷisaġvik College

ALASKA'S ONLY TRIBAL COLLEGE

Pearl Kiyawn Brower (Iñupiaq Eskimo/Chippewa/Armenian)

Indigenous leadership is a concept that has been present within Indigenous communities since time immemorial. However, because Indigenous communities have been subjugated to colonial policy for hundreds of years, the concept of Indigenous leadership has not been celebrated as it once was. This chapter will provide insight and information from the perspective of Indigenous leadership in a higher education context from Alaska's only Tribal College, Iḷisaġvik College, in reference to what Indigenous leadership is, how it is exhibited within higher education, and what we can do to support our next generation of Indigenous leaders.

Iḷisaġvik College, which in the Iñupiaq language means, "a place to learn," was officially recognized as a stand-alone higher education program during the 1995–1996 school year. Prior to that, the institution had taken on many forms of higher education to support the needs of the residents of the North Slope—the most northern region in the state of Alaska, home to the Iñupiaq Eskimo people.

The long-standing support for formal education was a priority for the first mayor of the North Slope Borough, Eben Hopson, Sr., who is known on the North Slope for saying, "Education is the key to success." Mayor Hopson knew that in order for the Iñupiaq people to succeed in the ever-globalizing world, they would need to be able to function, to thrive, in a society that recognized the importance of the Iñupiaq cultural heritage, as well as to function in a westernized system. With that in mind, Mayor Hopson pushed for a K-12 school system that was locally controlled and then incorporated culture into the curriculum, along with a higher education program that supported workforce development on the North Slope for its residents.

In Ray Barnhardt's article, "Higher Education in the Fourth World," he states, "Very early in the deliberation, the people of the North Slope Borough identified education as a critical concern—in fact gaining control of their schools from the federal Bureau of Indian Affairs was one of the incentives for establishing the Borough in the first place. Control over education was viewed as essential if Iñupiat people were to have access to the kind of education they felt they needed to share their own destiny" (1991, p. 1).

Higher Education on the North Slope: The Beginning

From the 1980s to present day, formalized education within a context of a western world has been a driving economic force on the North Slope. The roots of Iḷisaġvik College date back to 1986, when the North Slope Borough reinstituted locally controlled higher education programs in the region through the creation of the North Slope Higher Education Center, a cooperative effort between the North Slope Borough and the University of Alaska Fairbanks (Iḷisaġvik College, Three Year Self Study, 2013, p. 5).

Prior to 1980, the Iñupiat University of the Arctic was established with the goal of "an Iñupiat University based on Iñupiat educational perspectives, philosophies, principles and practices" (Barnhardt, 1991, p. 2). The concept stemmed from the need to staff schools and offices with local professionals. "The University offered a range of continuing education classes and vocational courses" (Condon, 1989, p. 2). One of the leaders of the University of the Arctic Program on the North Slope was Bill Vaudrin. Vaudrin supported education in rural communities. He touted a philosophy that those in rural communities would have an opportunity to be community, regional, and statewide leaders; therefore, educational systems should be designed at the local level, with local decision making being the driver (Vaudrin, 1975).

Due to the nature of organizations, and the tumultuous times on the North Slope, the program had little success and was closed down. That did not stop Mayor Hopson, or the passion that was invoked in the people of the North Slope, from seeking a program that was culturally based and would support the people of the North Slope into the future. The next step was to implement the North Slope Higher Education Center.

In January 1986, Mayor George Ahmaogak, Sr., passed North Slope Borough Ordinance 85–23 establishing the North Slope Higher Education Center (NSHEC). The University of Alaska provided the credentials to sponsor the institution and certify credits (Condon, 1989). The goal of the institution was to be responsive to the needs of the North Slope and to work toward stand-alone accreditation. With a more developed program, there was a lot of hope riding on the foundation of this institution.

Iñupiaq self-determination was key as the higher education outlook morphed throughout the next decade. Through programs such as the North Slope Arctic Sivunmun Iḷisaġvik College, the Mayor's Workforce Development Program, the

University of the Arctic, and other iterations of higher education in the early 1990s, it became evident that the North Slope and the state of Alaska needed a rural higher education program that supported both academic and workforce development programming. Dr. Shirley Holloway, supported by Executive Vice President Benjamin P. Nageak, was hired to create a workforce development program that would become a recognized community college. In 1995, Dr. Edna Ahgeak MacLean was hired as the President of Iḷisaġvik College—a local Iñupiaq from Barrow, who had recently obtained her Ph.D. from Stanford University.

Research on Indigenous leadership in higher education is limited. Though scholars (Minthorn & Chavez, 2015) have begun to address this topic in recent years, the scholarship remains inadequate for the importance of the topic. Indigenous leadership in higher education is a subject that has not been researched much in the past. This chapter was written as a part of the author's dissertation to understand what differences exist between higher education leaders who are Indigenous and those who are not. It was important to this research to focus on a particular tribally centered higher education institution. Iḷisaġvik College was a perfect choice for this study. Knowing an organization's past helps to focus on considering what the future can bring. The following sections will review Iḷisaġvik College's history and will provide documented research on what Indigenous leadership in higher education means to leaders of Iḷisaġvik College.

Early in 1996, the state and federal governments officially recognized Iḷisaġvik College as a higher education institution. At that point it was important for Iḷisaġvik to begin taking the steps to become an accredited institution. That process took quite a few years due to the nature of the accrediting system. In June 1998, Iḷisaġvik was granted candidacy by the Northwest Commission on Colleges and Universities (NWCCU). In 2003, the college achieved initial accreditation. With that goal accomplished, an application to become Alaska's first tribal college was submitted to the federal government. In 2005, Iḷisaġvik College became Alaska's first tribal college (E. MacLean, personal communication, December 7, 2015). In 2008, the college's accreditation was reaffirmed, and currently the organization is working on its next affirmation cycle. Iḷisaġvik College is unique within the state of Alaska. Not only is it the only tribal college in a state that is home to more than 200 recognized tribes, but it also serves as the only independent community college, as it is not associated with the state's university system. Located at the "Top of the World," Barrow, Alaska, the most northern community in the United States, the college primarily serves a student base from the North Slope Borough, the northernmost county in the state. The North Slope encompasses eight distinct communities ranging in population from approximately 200 residents in the smallest community of Atqasuk, to approximately 4,000 people in the hub community of Barrow. The population in the outlying "villages," as they are known, remains primarily Iñupiaq. More than 90% of the population in the villages is Iñupiaq. In Barrow that percentage is much less, with Iñupiaq people comprising approximately 60% of the population. The area of the North Slope Borough is approximately 94,000 square miles, which is the size of the state of Oklahoma. With a resident population of around 7,000 people, many have taken advantage of what Iḷisaġvik College has to offer. Iḷisaġvik College's mission statement and core themes are as follows, and can also be found on Iḷisaġvik's website at www.ilisagvik.edu.

Ilisaġvium Sivunniutigivlugu Savaaksraŋa

Iḷisaġvik College iḷisalluataġviqaqtitchiruq, savaaqallasiñiaġniġmun suli suna sivuniġivlugu iḷisaksraumman iḷisaġviqaqhutiŋ sivunmun suli suaŋŋaktaallavlugu Iñupiat iñuuniaġusiat, Iñupiuraaġnikun, piqpagiraŋich suli piraġausiŋich. Sivuniġigaa iḷisalluataŋalugi suli iḷitchiḷḷuataŋalugi iḷisaqtitiŋ itquvlugi savaaqaġumiñaqsiḷugich pigiraksraġiraŋiññik North Slope-mi Savaaqaqtitchisuuruat.

The Iḷisaġvik College Mission

Iḷisaġvik College provides quality post-secondary academic, vocational and technical education in a learning environment that perpetuates and strengthens Iñupiat culture, language, values and traditions. It is dedicated to serving its students and developing a well-educated and trained workforce who meet the human resource needs of North Slope employers and the state of Alaska.

Core Themes

As an expression of this mission, Iḷisaġvik College pursues the following core themes:

Academic Education—that education embodied in the Associate of Arts, the Associate of Science and the Associate of Applied Science degrees from which students either enter the workforce or transfer to four-year institutions.

Applied Knowledge and Skills to Develop the Local Workforce—that education and training embodied in Certificates, Workforce Development programs, and partnerships with business and industry which either prepare participants to enter the workforce or to gain additional skills to enhance their abilities in the workforce.

Access and Support—those activities which either prepare students to enter college level programs or enable students to undertake college programs by providing classes to villages and providing the financial and learning resources to enable them to be successful in their endeavors.

Iñupiaq Culture and Values—Instruction and activities which incorporate principles of traditional education, including the promotion of Iñupiaq culture and values and which provides opportunities for participation in cultural events important to the essence of being an Iñupiaq. (Iḷisaġvik College, *Three Year Self Study*, 2013)

The traditional Iñupiaq values of the organization, which can also be found at www.ilisagvik.edu, are outlined in table 13.1. As is evident in both the mission statement and the core themes, weaving Iñupiaq culture into all aspects of the college is a primary goal of Iḷisaġvik and its employees. It is evident given the statistics of Indigenous student success that programs that are based within a cultural context, are perceived by students to be more comfortable and welcoming.

Iḷisaġvik College is an Indigenous-centered institution that has been led by local Indigenous people since its inception. These leaders were interviewed to ascertain how they believed their Indigenous background helped them in leading a higher educational institution to be both accredited within a Western higher education context as well as to maintain perpetuation of Iñupiaq culture, language, values, and traditions. The following section will discuss research methodologies for these interviews.

Research Methodologies

According to Linda Tuhiwai Smith, "A research methodology is a theory and analysis of how research does or should proceed" (2012, p. 144). Smith notes that the methodological debates are "ones concerned with the broader politics and

TABLE 13.1
TRADITIONAL IÑUPIAQ VALUES

Aviktuaqatigiigñiq	*Sharing*
Iñupiuraallaniq	*Knowledge of Language*
Paammaaġigñiq	*Cooperation*
Iḷagiigñiq	*Family and Kinship*
Quvianġuniq	*Humor*
Aŋuniallaniq	*Hunting Traditions*
Nagliktuutiqaġniq	*Compassion*
Qiñuiññiq	*Humility*
Paaqłaktautaiññiq	*Avoidance of Conflict*
Ukpiqqutiqaġniq	*Spirituality*
Qiksiksrautiqaġniq Iñuuniaġvigmun	*Respect for Nature*
Piqpakkutiqaġniq suli Qiksiksrautiqaġniq Utuqqanaanun Allanullu	*Love and Respect for Our Elders and One Another*

strategic goals of Indigenous research. It is at this level that researchers have to clarify and justify their intentions" (p. 144). The research presented in this chapter focuses on researching Indigenous leadership in higher education.

Brayboy et al. (2013) note that it is important for Indigenous people to take on the role of the researcher in communities. It is only the Indigenous researcher who will have the ability to identify and overcome the issues that Indigenous people have faced for so long. Indigenous people understand these issues because they are the ones who have been studied in the past. No longer is it okay for "Indigenous knowledge to be understood as being in binary opposition to 'scientific,' 'western,' 'Eurocentric,' or 'modern' knowledge" (p. 428).

"Research was talked about [in Indigenous communities] both in terms of its absolute worthlessness to us, the Indigenous world, and its absolute usefulness to those who wielded it as an instrument" (p. 429). This must change. Indigenous researchers must create the opportunity to make research useful and worthwhile to Indigenous communities. The gathered information must be used to support community development. The information gathered will then result in supporting healthy, vibrant communities.

When reflecting upon the changes that need to take place in Indigenous communities, and working toward supporting that change, consider Eve Tuck's (2009) "Suspending damage: A letter to communities" in which she writes, "The trouble comes from the historical exploitation and mistreatment of people and material. It also comes from feelings of being over-researched yet, ironically, made invisible" (pp. 411–412).

It is important to recognize the concerns Indigenous people have with regard to research. Through the methodology and methods presented in Indigenous settings, the aim will be to erase these concerns within Indigenous settings forever. Whitinui, Glover, and Hikuroa (2013) note that an important aspect of this is the "demystification" of academics and research. In addition, "These questions, and others like them, allow us to critically reflect on our own research practice so that the resulting research is well-placed to be transformative for participants, for ourselves as researchers, and for our society as a whole" (Ormond, Cram, & Carter, 2006, p. 177).

Methods for Conducting Research

"Researchers are knowledge brokers, people who have the power to construct legitimating arguments for or against ideas, theories, or practices. They are collectors of information and producers of meaning which can be used for, or against Indigenous interests" (Ormond et al., 2006, p. 177). There are various approaches to this study with outcomes that address and encourage Indigenous interests. It is important for a project such as this that research methods be far-reaching because of the need to hear the right voices throughout the process. As

Smith (2012) notes, "Methods become the means and procedures through which the central problems of the research are addressed" (p. 144).

It is important to note that this research follows Melanie Cheung's statement, "If we consider tika and tikanga, they are about doing the right things in the right way with the right people at the right time for the right reasons" (Whitinui et al., 2013, p. 78). The research presented in this chapter will take on all of the responsibilities that Cheung enumerates. Research has to come from the community that is being researched. It must be useful to us as Indigenous people. Our people have always been knowledge brokers, but today, it is important for some of us to be credentialed so that we can speak and be recognized within the Western setting of academics. All of these reasons are about doing right—right things, the right way, right people, right time, right reasons.

Leadership Development at Iḷisaġvik College

Leadership from a community, within a community, is incredibly important, especially within an Indigenous context. Barnhardt notes, "The chances of such an initiative being sustained over the long term are greatly enhanced if the leadership originates from the local community and is able to effectively represent the interests of the community in the day-to-day milieu of the institutions' development and operation" (1991, p. 18).

The next section will review a case study of three of Iḷisaġvik College's local, Indigenous leaders, from the beginning of the establishment of the college, to the current term of the President of the institution.

Iḷisaġvik College Leadership: A Case Study

Iḷisaġvik College has been led by Indigenous leaders since its inception, first with Benjamin P. Nageak, as Iḷisaġvik's Executive Vice President, then by Dr. Edna MacLean, from 1995 to 2005; Beverly Grinage from 2005 to 2010; Dr. Brooke Gondara, 2010–2011; and Pearl Brower, 2011 to the present. All but Dr. Gondara have been local Iñupiaq leaders. Representative Nageak, Dr. MacLean, and President Brower are committed to education on the North Slope and to giving back to the community that raised them.

In an effort to understand their thoughts on Indigenous leadership, their vision of education on the North Slope, their successes and challenges while leading Iḷisaġvik College, and their thoughts on Indigenous leadership development, Benjamin P. Nageak, Dr. Edna MacLean, and Pearl Brower were interviewed. For the purpose of this research, I was both a researcher and participant. As one of the Presidents of Iḷisaġvik College it was important for me to provide information. I used a reflective narrative method for my portion of the research, answering the questions that were posed to my colleagues.

Participant Background

Representative Benjamin Piniqluk "Bennie" Nageak. Bennie Nageak is a lifelong Alaskan who was born in Kaktovik, Alaska. He is currently an Alaska State Representative for the Arctic region, House District 40, and started serving his second House term January 2015. Representative Nageak served in the U.S. Army from 1970 to 1972 and returned home to begin a long career in public service. He served as North Slope Borough Assemblyman (1995–1996) and Mayor (1996–1999).

His statewide involvement includes Vice-Chair of the State of Alaska Board of Game, Commissioner of the State of Alaska Local Boundary Commission, Chairman of the Subsistence Resource Commission for Gates of the Arctic Park and Preserve, and a founding member of the Alaska Gasline Port Authority, 1998–1999.

He is a former board member for the Ukpeaġvik Iñupiat Corporation (UIC), a regional Native corporation. His past leadership roles also include President of RurAL CAP, Chairman of the Eskimo Walrus Commission, Chairman of the Indigenous Peoples Council on Marine Mammals, Chairman of the Rural Alaska Resource Association, President of Indigenous Survival International, and Ruling Elder in the Utqiaġvik Presbyterian Church.

In the state House, Representative Nageak is currently one of the Co-Chairs for the House Resources Committee. He is also a member of the Community & Regional Affairs, Transportation and Energy Committee and sits on the Finance Subcommittees of Community & Regional Affairs, Natural Resources, Public Safety, and Fish & Game. He is a member of the Majority Caucus as well as the rural "Bush" Caucus in the state House. He was appointed by House leadership to the Suicide Prevention Council and the Alaska Native Language and Preservation Advisory Council. He is also a former House-appointed commissioner for the Alaska Arctic Policy Commission.

Representative Nageak lives in Barrow with his wife Bonnie. He is the father of Robert, Eva, and Perry (deceased), and grandfather to Angeline Isabella and Madilyn Karmella Nageak.

Dr. Edna Ahgeak Maclean. Edna Ahgeak MacLean, Ph.D., an Iñupiaq from Barrow, Alaska, and President Emeritus of Iḷisaġvik College, is a member of the Iñupiat History, Language, and Culture Commission. She served as President of the northernmost college in the United States, Iḷisaġvik College in Barrow, Alaska from 1995 to 2005.

Before serving as Special Assistant for Rural Education for the Commissioner of Education in Alaska from 1987 to 1990, Dr. MacLean developed and taught the Iñupiaq language B.A. degree program courses at the University of Alaska Fairbanks from 1976 to 1987. Edna received her B.A. from the University of California-Berkeley, her Master's degree from the University of Washington, and her Ph.D. in education from Stanford University. Dr. MacLean was inducted into the Stanford University Alumni Hall of Fame in 2003. She was named the Alaska Federation of Natives Citizen of the Year in 2005, and in 2006 she received the State of Alaska Distinguished Service to the Humanities Award. Edna received a Contributions to Literacy in Alaska (CLIA) award in 2015 for the publication of the *Inupiatun Uqaluit Taniktun Sivuninit/Iñupiaq to English Dictionary* from the Alaska Center for the Book, the State of Alaska's liaison to the U.S. Library of Congress Center for the Book in Washington, DC. She recently received a lifetime achievement award from the Ukpeaġvik Iñupiat Corporation for her dictionary work.

Edna is extremely proud of her two sons, Stephen Ahgeak MacLean and Andrew Okpeaha MacLean and feels especially blessed to have two wonderful granddaughters, Gwendolyn Sirrouna MacLean and Ilụsiña Lucia Marcous MacLean.

Dr. Pearl Kiyawn Nageak Brower. Pearl Brower earned a B.A. in Anthropology and B.A. in Alaska Native Studies from University of Alaska Fairbanks in 2004. She also earned a Master's in Alaska Native and Rural Development from University of Alaska Fairbanks in 2010. In 2016, she earned a Ph.D. in Indigenous Studies with an emphasis in Indigenous Leadership, from the University of Alaska Fairbanks. Dr. Brower is currently the President of Iḷisaġvik College, Alaska's only tribal college. She has been with the College for the past nine years, working in External Relations, Institutional Advancement, Student Services, and Marketing. She has served as President since 2012. Prior to working for the College, Dr. Brower managed an education and culture grant for the North Slope Borough and worked as the museum curator of the Iñupiat Heritage Center.

Dr. Brower grew up in both Barrow, Alaska, and northern California, practicing a subsistence lifestyle in both locations. She has a daughter, Isla Qannik, who is 4, and along with her husband, Jesse Darling, lives in Barrow, Alaska, where she loves to be close to her culture and community. Brower was named one of Alaska's Top 40 Under 40 in 2015. She is Board Member of the Friends of Tuzzy Library, and is a co-founder of Leadership:Barrow.

Analysis

Each of the three past Presidents of Iḷisaġvik College were asked a series of interview questions. The 14 questions focused on three themes. Theme one was structured around each individual's understanding of Indigenous leadership pre- and post-contact, as well as their thoughts on what characteristics Indigenous leaders have today. A second theme was the importance of nurturing a next generation of Indigenous leaders and how that is happening through Iḷisaġvik College. The last theme focused on each individual and their Indigenous leadership styles and how that affected them while leading at Iḷisaġvik. For a listing of all the interview questions, please see appendix 13.A.

Theme one relied upon the respondents discussing their thoughts of what Indigenous leadership meant to them and how it was exhibited in higher education today. Respondents discussed 14 different characteristics that, as the leaders of Iḷisaġvik College said, were important to Indigenous leaders in higher education. Some are as follows: honesty, integrity, resourcefulness, having the Indigenous perspective, and working across the state, as well as family support. The last two certainly cross boundaries, regardless of whether one is a president in Alaska, or elsewhere in the nation.

Comparing leaders in higher education—Indigenous and non-Indigenous—two presidents who were interviewed did not comment too deeply upon this. Dr. Edna MacLean noted that perhaps one of the differences is that when you are Indigenous to the community in which you serve, you will know more about the community and, therefore, might be a better fit for the leadership role. Pearl Brower, current President of Iḷisaġvik College, noted that an important difference is the aspect of being place-based. She provided an observation that reflected upon non-Indigenous leaders within education and their constant movement within the higher education system. "Within Indigenous leadership, relationship building is easier. They are not as loud and disruptive of the community and will know more of what the community needs/wants" (E. MacLean, personal communication, December 7, 2015).

Pearl Brower noted,

> Indigenous leaders tend to stay at their institutions—they are committed to their people and their land. Non-Indigenous leaders seem to move from one position to another, from one higher education institution to another. I can remember attending a President's Institute with the American Association of Community Colleges—and in discussions with new Presidents around the room—I was floored by how many of them knew each other from working at the same institutions at some point in their career. It baffled me as within a TCU context, some leaders have been leading since their college was created. (P. Brower, personal communication, November 16, 2015)

Theme two asked the respondents to discuss the importance of leadership development in the next generation of Indigenous youth, and how this task is being accomplished today. Past leaders at the College noted that most of the leadership development occurred through academic, vocational, and workforce development programs that were directly connected to education and training to prepare students to enter the workforce. In addition, it was noted that many of the programs today within the Indigenous leadership arena are still based within a Western framework.

Trying to understand how historically through oral traditions, leadership was supported and encouraged, the interviewer asked the respondents to discuss stories about leadership that were based on a nontraditional model of leadership. Much of the discussion centered around past leaders on the North Slope, including Mayor Eben Hopson, Sr. President Pearl Brower shared a story that had been told to her by her relations regarding her great-great uncles and their leadership in taking in a small baby to raise in hard times. Within a Western context, this might not seem to be leadership, but within an Indigenous perspective, this showed great leadership and courage. It is interesting to note that not many stories were shared that had a foundation in a tribal concept of Indigenous leadership. The argument could be made that in our acculturation, many of these stories have been lost.

Wanting to understand the respondents' thoughts on Indigenous leadership development and the importance of programs that supported this type of leadership development within an Indigenous context, all respondents noted a resounding yes to that question. Leaders said it is important to encourage the younger generation to become leaders—give them tools so that they can overcome obstacles and barriers and learn to lead. Everyone was optimistic about the future and noted that with so much knowledge available now, the opportunities for the next generation of leaders continue to grow. The encouragement from this question is important, as programs are developed to continue to support growing the next generation of Indigenous leaders.

Theme three focused more on the individual respondents and their own leadership style. Questions pertained to whether the leaders' Indigenous perspective had affected their leadership style while serving as President at Iḷisaġvik. Articulated leadership styles included words like cooperative, listening, educated, family centered, consensus-building, respect, and honesty. In addition, it was important that the leadership of the organization provided and continues to provide opportunity to residents—to benefit them for the future. Last, it was noted that being within an Indigenous setting allowed for flexibility to incorporate the Indigenous perspective. These are so important because connections are being made—leadership styles across tribal colleges reflect leadership characteristics, which support the ability to incorporate an Indigenous perspective into all aspects of the TCUs. "My leadership style is cooperative. Constantly learning. Asking questions, hearing different ideas from different types of people. Listening to what is going on . . . working together with a goal, plan in place" (B. Nageak, personal communication, November 16, 2015).

Dr. MacLean said, "I wanted to help in making sure that the young people on the North Slope had the opportunity to become employed, because I knew that in order to lead a hunting life, you now needed cash. In order to have cash you needed a job . . . But there was no real opportunity for those who wanted to stay in Barrow, to learn the trades, or get higher education" (E. MacLean, personal communication, December 7, 2015). Pearl Brower added, "My leadership style is that of consensus building, community building, informed decision making, respect, commitment, and honesty" (P. Brower, personal communication, November 16, 2015).

The interviewer wanted to understand how each individual became President and why they wanted to be a leader at the institution. As a part of that discussion, it was important to understand what each interviewee believed were their greatest accomplishments. Not surprisingly, but reaffirming in nature, the leaders placed great value on giving back to their community. That is why they chose to work for Iḷisaġvik College. Other significant accomplishments included college-wide endeavors such as accreditation, tribal college status, family-centered organization, and employee development and support. The accomplishments were not centered on individuals, but on groups of people, connection with a community. "The College being run by local people. We accomplished setting this up for the future—for local Iñupiaq leaders" (B. Nageak, personal communication, November 16, 2015).

As Indigenous leaders within the organization, they were asked why Iḷisaġvik is unique. Respondents noted that its uniqueness is delineated in its being created by a grassroots effort, its Indigenous perspective, its ability to be responsive to community need, culturally sensitive, and based on its Iñupiaq values. These are so important to an institution, but also to the sense of connection to community. These unique qualifiers of Iḷisaġvik College could very well be the key components to the foundation of an Indigenous leadership program based upon an Indigenous core. "I think it's unique because we have the policy makers, the trustees, who can make decisions right then and there and they come from the communities themselves" (E. MacLean, personal communication, December 7, 2015).

Implications and Further Research

The responses to the interview questions provided an important insight into the leadership from Iḷisaġvik College's perspective. What this case study emphasizes is that there is a gap that needs to be filled with regard to Indigenous leadership programs that are based within a cultural context. However, the study also illustrates that Indigenous people are ready for such a program to exist, which provides a great deal of excitement and optimism for the future. There is opportunity for further research in this area. Is an Indigenous leadership program based within an Indigenous framework possible? How could one be implemented at both the Tribal institutional level as well as "mainstream" higher educational institutions?

What would this mean for "mainstream" higher education institutions? Would it change these institutions?

Using Indigenous methodologies in researching Indigenous leadership in higher education was important because, first of all, as Indigenous people we communicate with one another differently when we can immerse ourselves within our cultural context. The individuals who were interviewed for this project were able to connect with me not only as a fellow President, but as an Iñupiaq person like they are. They derived comfort from these connections. These relationships are built upon a shared history and trust. When you omit these cultural connections, the information drawn from research is lacking.

The implications for using an Indigenous methodology within this context support reclaiming Indigenous research in two ways. First, it is incredibly important for Indigenous people to have a voice within an academic research context. For too long the Indigenous perspective was nonexistent, or was communicated through a non-Indigenous person, which in translation loses much of what it means to be Indigenous. Second, particularly with regard to Indigenous leadership in higher education, the academy needs to recognize that Indigenous knowledge is a vast and deep resource that needs to be a part of the higher education discussion, not only for Indigenous people, but for all people. Being able to contextualize this research, using Indigenous methodologies, allows for the support of this important endeavor.

Conclusion

As an Indigenous person, I have found it easy to compare Indigenous and non-Indigenous forms of leadership in this study. Having the capacity to see these differences because I live them every day as an Indigenous person allowed my approach for this research to be supportive within an Indigenous context. The questions that were asked were focused from an Indigenous perspective, which resulted in concrete data that are useful and pertinent in an Indigenous context.

Iḷisaġvik College, Alaska's Only Tribal College, has had a long history of supporting its students and creating opportunities for students to grow. A more educated population is a healthier one. Iḷisaġvik's motto is: More Education, More Options, More Out of Life. That is an important mantra. As institutions such as Iḷisaġvik College grow, programs need to grow as well. Is an Indigenous leadership program one such growth opportunity? The research from this study says, yes.

Appendix 13.A. Iḷisaġvik College Presidents and Vice Presidents Interview Questions

Note: For the purpose of this chapter, the questions that are analyzed include #6–14, as they are concentrated on the concept of leadership within a higher education spectrum, and at Iḷisaġvik College, in particular.

1. What is your cultural heritage/Indigenous identity?
2. Please provide me with a short biography of yourself, or identify where an already existing biography can be found.
3. What do you know about pre-contact (western) Indigenous leadership? What did leadership look like in Indigenous communities?
4. A leader takes on many roles within Indigenous communities. What are characteristics of Indigenous leaders today? What does Indigenous leadership "look" like?
5. Compare, in your own words, the two above—pre-contact and post-contact Indigenous leadership.
6. In your experience, what are some specific characteristics that Indigenous leaders in higher education exhibit?
7. Comparing leaders in higher education, what are some of the main differences between Indigenous leaders and non-Indigenous ones? Are there similarities as well?
8. In relation to preparing the next generation of Indigenous leaders, what is happening today in higher education supporting this endeavor? Did you implement any leadership programs at Iḷisaġvik while you were leading the organization?
9. Are there any stories within an Indigenous/Cultural framework regarding leadership you'd like to share? Perhaps any stories of Indigenous leaders that transcend the western concept of leadership?
10. As an Indigenous leader at Iḷisaġvik College, please tell us how your Indigenous perspective affected your leadership style within the organization. What was your leadership style? How is your style different than leaders who are not in a primarily Indigenous setting?
11. What drove you to want to be in a leadership role at Iḷisaġvik? What do you feel your greatest accomplishments were while at the head of the institution?
12. Iḷisaġvik College is a unique higher education institution within the state of Alaska. Please share your thoughts about how unique an institution it is, and how that uniqueness might be a result of being led by your predecessors and yourself as Indigenous people. One way to look at this would be to compare Iḷisaġvik to other higher educational institutions that are solely based within a western context.

13. Is it important to you to help mentor the next generation of Indigenous leaders? Why? Please feel free to give examples, recommendations, etc.
14. Please share any other comments you might have in regard to Iḷisaġvik College, Indigenous leadership (both in general and within higher education), and thoughts on the next generation of Indigenous leaders.

REFERENCES

Barnhardt, Ray. (1991). Higher education in the fourth world: Indigenous people take control. *Canadian Journal of Native Education, 18*(2).

Brayboy, B. M. K., Gough, H. R., Leonard, B., Roehl II, R. F., & Solyom, J. A. (2013). Reclaiming scholarship: Critical Indigenous research methodologies. In S. D. Lapan, M. T. Quartaroli, & F. J. Reimer (Eds.), *Qualitative Research: An Introduction to Methods and Designs* (pp. 423–450). San Francisco, CA: Jossey-Bass.

Condon, R. G. (1989). Higher education on Alaska's North Slope. *Cultural Survival Quarterly, 13*(1), 1–6. Retrieved from https://www.culturalsurvival.org/publications/cultural-survival-quarterly/united-states/higher-education-alaskas-north-slope

Iḷisaġvik College. (2013). *Three Year Self Study.* Barrow, AK: Iḷisaġvik College.

Minthorn, R. S., & Chavez, A. F. (2015). *Indigenous Leadership in Higher Education.* New York: Routledge.

Ormond, A., Cram, F., & Carter, L. (2006). Researching our relations: Reflections on ethics and marginalisation. *AlterNative: An International Journal for Indigenous People, 2*(1) 175–192.

Smith, L. T. (2012). *Decolonizing Methodologies: Research and Indigenous Peoples* (2nd Ed.). London: Zed Books.

Tuck, E. (2009). Suspending damage: A letter to communities. *Harvard Educational Review, 79*(3), 409–427.

Vaudrin, B. (1975). Iñupiat University of the Arctic Catalog, 1975–1976. Barrow, AK. *Iñupiat University of the Arctic.*

Whitinui, P., Glover, M., & Hikuroa, D. (2013). *Ara Mai he Tētēkura. Visioning Our Futures: New and Emerging Pathways of Māori Academic Leadership.* Dunedin: Otago University Press.

CONCLUSION

Repositioning the Norms of the Academy

RESEARCH AS WISDOM

Heather J. Shotton (Wichita/Kiowa/Cheyenne)

Robin Starr Zape-tah-hol-ah Minthorn (Kiowa/Apache/Umatilla/Nez Perce/Assiniboine)

> In June 2016, we came together with a group of authors from this book to begin the process of gathering our collective thoughts about what it means to reclaim Indigenous research in higher education. As we approached the conclusion of this journey, to reclaim our space in higher education research, we began in much the same way we did as we embarked on this journey, with good thoughts, intentions, and prayer. As we gathered with our fellow authors we stood together and acknowledged the work that had been done and those who had contributed to this collective effort. We stood together as extensions of our various tribes, people, homelands, communities, and families. Together we offered up prayers and gave thanks for this work, we acknowledged our ancestors and those who came before us, we expressed gratitude for those fierce Indigenous scholars who laid the foundation for this work and made a way for us, we asked for blessings on our youth and those who will come after us, and we asked that we do our work with good intentions and in a way that would benefit and be pleasing to our communities. It was with those collective thoughts, intentions, and wisdom that we entered into the final stages of this work.

In this concluding chapter, we thought it was of particular importance to have collective voices and responses to how we tie together and connect the takeaways and that we approach "research as wisdom." In the following sections we will address (1) What it means to reclaim Indigenous research in higher education, (2) Important takeaways the authors hope readers will gather, (3) Next steps for Indigenous research in higher education, and (4) Concluding thoughts from the authors themselves. We hope you will read through this chapter and share with others so that they may understand the value and importance of Indigenous research in higher education.

Before we begin our discussion, it is necessary to explain our process for honoring our collective voices in this final chapter. In reflecting on the values of Indigenous research methodologies, and our own values as Indigenous people, we felt that in the concluding chapter we had to move beyond the norm of providing our own interpretation of the connecting themes and recommendations for next steps. Rather, we felt it was more appropriate to ask our authors to join us in developing our concluding thoughts in an effort to respect all of our voices. We sent a call out to the contributing authors and invited them to a writing retreat following a conference at the Arizona State University (ASU) campus at which many of us would be in attendance. The ASU Center for Indian Education generously offered to provide space for our gathering and host our group. In total, six authors (including the editors) from this book participated in the writing retreat.

In this chapter's opening, we described how we began our writing retreat. We intentionally chose to begin our work in a way that honored our own traditional teachings and to enter our writing space with good thoughts and intentions. During the retreat, each author discussed our individual chapters and we provided overviews of the chapters of those authors who were not in attendance. Following the chapter overviews, we presented the authors with a series of questions and had a day-long discussion about what it means to reclaim Indigenous research in higher education and how we move Indigenous research in higher education forward. In an effort to capture all of the authors' voices, we also provided opportunities for those authors who could not attend the writing retreat to provide their thoughts and feedback on the same questions presented during the retreat. What follows is our collective response to our journey and efforts to reclaim Indigenous research in higher education.

What Does It Mean to Reclaim Indigenous Research in Higher Education?

This is the pivotal question that we hope each of the authors have helped answer through their chapters, including their own context as Indigenous scholars and the methodologies and topics of their research. In each of the chapters, authors have presented examples of the various ways they are utilizing and embodying Indigenous methodologies in their scholarship. They have demonstrated the fluid nature of Indigenous methodologies; some applying it through their own tribal lens, others privileging ancestral knowledge, and some utilizing it as a framework to guide their approach to Indigenous higher education research. Through their scholarship, each of the authors has worked to reclaim academic spaces and helped to answer the critical question of what it means to reclaim Indigenous research in higher education. We delve further into this question by providing our collective narratives.

As demonstrated throughout this book, reclaiming Indigenous research in higher education and applying Indigenous research methodologies is a fluid process. Wilson (2008) spoke to this and cautioned against being dogmatic in our thinking about Indigenous Research Paradigm. As we work to reclaim our spaces in higher education research through Indigenous Methodologies, we cannot be afraid to take our work in new directions. While we look to previous scholarship or established frameworks, there is not a singular approach to Indigenous Methodologies. As the authors in this book have demonstrated, Indigenous Methodologies provide us the space to approach our research from our own frameworks and to privilege our own Indigenous and tribal epistemologies.

Reclaiming Indigenous research in higher education also requires an acknowledgment that our work is not about us as scholars; rather, it is for our people. One common thread throughout the scholarship presented herein is the constant effort to produce scholarship that ultimately benefits our communities and to honor values of reciprocity; it is what is at the core of our work as Indigenous scholars. Our research is meant to support and encourage positive change in Indigenous communities. This is an intentional departure from the historical relation between research and Indigenous communities, where research resulted in harm and trauma. Within this context we are taking research back, and as scholars who have gained the necessary academic tools we are utilizing it to create sustainable, healthy communities. One of the authors described the process of reclaiming Indigenous research in higher education as what emerges when higher education meets grandma, "This work is hard, but this consciousness is a way to liberate our grandmothers and grandfathers."

Finally, reclaiming Indigenous research in higher education means not only reclaiming our space, but also reclaiming our voices and stories. Kaiwipunikauikawēkiu Lipe (see chapter 11 of this volume), beautifully described the process in this way:

> "Reclaiming" means, for me, taking our stories back and telling them in our own voices—our Indigenous peoples have always been thinking, writing, and doing higher education praxis and now we have a growing group of Indigenous scholars to tell our own stories in our own ways. It reminds me of the 'auwai metaphor we use in our community. 'Auwai are enhanced natural waterways which used the natural topography of the land to irrigate our crops. Not only did it help us to grow what we needed for sustenance, it also insured

> we properly managed our water resources to insure its sustainability. With colonialism, waters were diverted to grow foreign crops (like pineapple and sugar) and for development, so ‘auwai were left dry. Education is like these ‘auwai. So I think when we reclaim our education research, we're putting the waters back into our ‘auwai to grow and support our people while also surveying the landscape to see where else we may enhance these natural pathways.

An important aspect of the process of reclaiming this academic space is honoring our stories and the knowledge of our ancestors. As Indigenous scholars, we must continue our work to collectively strengthen our voices and tell our stories in our own ways.

Takeaways from This Book

As you have read through the chapters and descriptions of research from each of the contributors, we hope that you have been able to identify some takeaways and how you might reposition your own thoughts on research in higher education. Each of the authors identified takeaways they would like to see readers add to their own toolbox of approaches to research in higher education. Two overarching themes in takeaways emerged: (1) There is not one singular approach to Indigenous Methodologies, and (2) Indigenous research is necessary and vital to the health of our communities.

As we have previously stated, Indigenous Methodologies are fluid and constantly evolving. There is not a singular approach to Indigenous Methodologies or the ways in which we apply them. We are aligning our work with our own lived realities and Indigenous ways of knowing, so we must recognize that there are multiple ways to approach this work. Amanda Tachine and Charlotte Davidson both utilized rug weaving as an approach to Indigenous Methodologies; just like rugs, there are different approaches to applying Indigenous Methodologies in higher education research, but they're all distinct and beautiful in their own way. We are far from exhausting all of the approaches to Indigenous research in higher education and the application of Indigenous Methodologies as this work continues to emerge. As we journey to extend the work of scholars like Linda Tuhiwai Smith, Bryan McKinley Jones Brayboy, Shawn Wilson, and Margaret Kovach, we recognize that this work is never finished, but rather it is always becoming. It is our hope that other Indigenous scholars will find their own ways to move us forward.

As Indigenous scholars, we are deeply connected to Indigenous research in higher education. The work that we do is our life, it represents our families, tribes, and communities; we aren't just doing the work, we are living the work. We are utilizing our scholarship to heal from destructive encounters with education and to remove power structures in the academy that have excluded Indigenous people and knowledge for far too long. Indigenous research is imperative to healing our communities and fostering our overall well-being. Furthermore, Indigenous research and knowledge in higher education serves Indigenous and non-Indigenous populations alike. Our knowledge systems provide important insight and are fundamental to refashioning higher education in ways that are compassionate, innovative, integrative, inclusive, and that focus on the collective good.

Next Steps for Indigenous Research in Higher Education

One of the fundamental aspects of reclaiming Indigenous spaces in higher education research is to continually reflect on how we move this work forward. What are the next steps? How do we ensure a continued reclamation of space and voice in higher education research? Collectively we offer some suggestions for next steps for Indigenous research in higher education. For some these may be seen as a wish list, but more than anything these are expectations of how to transform the academy to be more inclusive of Indigenous voices in higher education research.

We have discussed at length the systems within academia that have served to oppress, marginalize, harm, and silence Indigenous knowledge and scholars. One of the goals of this book was to push back against the systems that have excluded Indigenous research and to create an academic space for Indigenous scholars in higher education. We must continue to push for systemic changes that honor and respect Indigenous knowledge and Indigenous Methodologies. Therefore, an important next step is to institutionalize Indigenous, cultural, and community protocols and create processes to formalize these protocols within institutions of higher education. A few institutions have taken steps to do this, but far too many have not. This also means pushing our non-Indigenous colleagues to be more inclusive of Indigenous Methodologies in scholarly spaces such as journals and academic conferences.

Another step involves making room for emerging Indigenous scholars. We must constantly work to create a community of scholars that fosters support and encouragement. Far too often in systems that represent oppressive structures, such as higher education, people unintentionally recreate harm based on their own experiences and trauma within those systems. It is important that as Indigenous scholars, and non-Indigenous scholars as well, we acknowledge our responsibility to future scholars and are creating spaces of support and encouragement. This requires faculty to be more receptive and encouraging of Indigenous Methodologies and to respect the different types of work emerging from our future Indigenous scholars.

Finally, it is imperative that we continue to honor our responsibility to our communities by ensuring that our scholarship is accessible, worthy, embodies values of respect and reciprocity. This will require continued conversations about how to honor and protect community-held knowledge. As Indigenous scholars we must strike a delicate balance between pushing for the inclusion of Indigenous knowledge, while also respecting that Indigenous knowledge does not belong to us and not all knowledge is meant for public consumption. This is an important conversation in honoring our responsibility to our communities. Another part of our responsibility is to think critically about how we produce scholarship that informs fundamental transformation in higher education structures. In doing this, we have to continually ask ourselves and our communities, "What work needs to be done?" There remains much work to be done, but we must always ensure that the work we are doing is responsive to the needs of our communities. Our scholarship must be worthy.

Recommendations for Higher Education Scholars

In this section, the authors provide recommendations for higher education scholars. These are recommendations that can be addressed or incorporated by future, emerging, and seasoned scholars. No matter our place in the academy, each of us has a role in making changes or deconstructing the norms that are embedded in the system and hierarchy of higher education institutions.

The first recommendation is to honor the voice of Indigenous scholars. We have repeatedly addressed the importance of Indigenous voice throughout this book and it's a central tenet to reclaiming our space in higher education. Honoring Indigenous voices requires first acknowledging the systematic silencing of Indigenous voices in higher education scholarship. As higher education scholars it is imperative that we interrogate how and in what spaces Indigenous scholars have been marginalized, excluded, and silenced. Then we must work to ensure that Indigenous voices are not only included, but also honored and respected as valuable to the transformation of higher education.

The second recommendation is to acknowledge the role of relationships in Indigenous research and for Indigenous scholars. Our discussions of the previous work on Indigenous Methodologies (Kovach, 2009) and Indigenous Research Paradigm (Wilson, 2008) have pointed to the centrality of relationships in Indigenous research. Higher education scholars must come to understand the role of relationships and the multiple ways that it functions in Indigenous research. Our relationships with our families, tribes, and communities are important aspects of our work as Indigenous scholars. Indigenous research is deeply connected to those relationships and our responsibility to honor those relationships first. This sometimes means that those relationships are more important than the task at hand. Our responsibility to relationships also extends beyond the present tense. As Indigenous people we acknowledge that our ancestors live within us and we have a responsibility to their teachings; our relationship to our ancestors is central to who we are and by extension to our work. We also recognize our responsibility to those who have yet to come—those relationships are equally as important. Acknowledging the role of relationships means understanding and acknowledging our connections to one another.

Finally, we ask that higher education scholars acknowledge the need to deconstruct the norms of the academy that serve to privilege some voices while silencing others. And in that acknowledgment we encourage you to actively push back against those systems and hierarchies to foster inclusivity in the academy. Utilize your privilege and power when possible to widen the circle and help to create more space for Indigenous research in higher education.

Concluding Thoughts from Indigenous Scholars

And finally, we would like to offer some concluding thoughts for readers from the authors and contributors. Each of them has existed within academic systems and hierarchies that often do not accept and honor Indigenous knowledge or scholars. For Indigenous scholars a great deal of time and energy is spent fighting for the acknowledgment and recognition of our beliefs, values, and ways of being. We ask you to read through these concluding thoughts from the authors and find ways that you may change or alter your own ways of approaching research in higher education and transform the academy to be a more welcoming space that honors and supports all ways of being.

- One truth is that all institutions of higher education are on Indigenous land, and institutions have to begin with acknowledging that.
- We have to figure out how to approach education with love/aloha.
- It's important for Indigenous people to do this work, incorporate ancestors' knowledge, and we have to incorporate contemporary Indigenous perspectives.
- There are non-Indigenous scholars doing this work as well; it is important that they have good teachers so that they know their place and their role in this work.
- Reclaim research by using your own story and showing personal connection to the research.
- It is important to position Indigenous identity from the political relationship that we have with education as a trust responsibility and the land on which institutions sit.
- Institutions often have partnerships and relationships with corporations; why can't they do that with tribes?
- The story of an embodied lens-making process is centered in hózhó.
- Methodologies are beings.

- The salience of coyote in creating this methodological space is important. There are people/beings that you encounter that make you think and challenge you; you must work to protect your work from harm.
- Research is very personal. From a Western perspective, research in general is static and you separate yourself. We're saying that it is okay to incorporate yourself into your research, to be yourself.
- Research as medicine. "I'm sharing my medicine."
- Research is weaving a story rug.
- When we're allowed to be ourselves in the process it allows for creativity. Indigenous methodologies allow for that creativity to flourish.
- Indigenous knowledges have value and relevance to transforming higher education.
- Lean on your Indigenous self-location and reframe your experience so that it can align with your own community ontology.

Ah-ho (thank you), for reading and opening your mind and heart to a different way of viewing scholarship in higher education. As Indigenous scholars we work to continue efforts to reclaim our space in higher education and replace the narrative that has been imposed on us with our own. We do this with the beauty and wisdom of our ancestors and for future generations of Indigenous scholars.

REFERENCES

Kovach, M. (2009). *Indigenous Methodologies: Characteristics, Conversations and Contexts.* Toronto: University of Toronto Press.

Wilson, S. (2008). *Research Is Ceremony: Indigenous Research Methods.* Winnipeg, MB: Fernwood Publishing.

Notes on Contributors

BRYAN MCKINLEY JONES BRAYBOY (Lumbee) is President's Professor and Borderlands Professor of Indigenous Education and Justice in the School of Social Transformation at Arizona State University. At ASU, he is Special Assistant to the President for American Indian Affairs, Director of the Center for Indian Education, Acting Director of the School of Social Transformation, and co-editor of the *Journal of American Indian Education.*

DR. PEARL KIYAWN BROWER, Iñupiaq Eskimo/Chippewa/Armenian, earned a B.A. in Anthropology and a B.A. in Alaska Native Studies from the University of Alaska-Fairbanks, 2004. She earned a Master's degree in Alaska Native and Rural Development from University of Alaska-Fairbanks in 2010, and a Ph.D. in Indigenous Studies, with an emphasis in Indigenous Leadership, from the University of Alaska-Fairbanks, in 2016. Dr. Brower serves as President of Iḷisaġvik College, Alaska's only Tribal College. She has been with the College since 2007 working in External Relations, Institutional Advancement, Student Services, and Marketing. She has served as President since 2012. Prior to working for the College, Dr. Brower managed an education and culture grant for the North Slope Borough for three years and worked as the Museum Curator of the Iñupiat Heritage Center. Brower grew up in both Barrow, Alaska and northern California, practicing a subsistence lifestyle in both areas. She has a daughter, Isla, who is 4 and, along with her husband, Jesse Darling, lives in Barrow, Alaska, where she loves to be close to her culture and community. Brower was named one of Alaska's Top 40 Under 40 in 2015. Brower is active in her community in Barrow, on the North Slope, and statewide. She is Board Member of the Friends of Tuzzy Library and is a co-founder of Leadership:Barrow. She serves on the Wells Fargo Community Advisory Board, the Alaska Airlines Community Advisory Board, serves as the Vocational/Tribal representative on the Alaska Postsecondary

Access and Completion Network, and is the Chair of the Tribal College Journal Advisory Board.

DR. CHARLOTTE DAVIDSON is Navajo and a member of the Three Affiliated Tribes (Mandan, Hidatsa, and Arikara). A proud alumna of Haskell Indian Nations University, where she graduated with a B.A. in American Indian Studies, Dr. Davidson earned her Master's and Doctorate degrees in Educational Policy Studies from the University of Illinois at Urbana-Champaign. Her practice and scholarship focus on questions and concerns linked to the participation of Indigenous people in higher education. Prior to becoming an independent scholar, Dr. Davidson was the Special Assistant to the President for Diversity and Native American Affairs at South Dakota State University, where she also served as the Director of the American Indian Education and Cultural Center and taught courses within the department of teaching, learning, and leadership and the American Indian Studies program. Beyond her scholarly interests, Dr. Davidson considers being a mother to her sons, William and Matthew, to be her most sacred project.

ADRIENNE KEENE (Cherokee Nation) is an Assistant Professor of American Studies and Ethnic Studies at Brown University. Her research areas include college access, transition, and persistence for American Indian, Alaska Native, and Native Hawaiian students, including the role of pre-college access programs in student success. Additionally, she examines representations of Native peoples in popular culture, Native cultural appropriation in fashion and design, and the ways that Indigenous peoples are using the Internet, social media, and new media to challenge misrepresentations and create new and innovative spaces for art and activism. She earned her B.A. from Stanford University in Native American Studies and Cultural Anthropology, and her doctorate from the Harvard Graduate School of Education in Culture, Communities, and Education. Her publications have appeared in *Harvard Educational Review*, *Journal Committed to Social Change on Race and Ethnicity*, and *Journal of Critical Thought and Praxis*.

DR. KAIWIPUNIKAUIKAWĒKIU LIPE is a Native Hawaiian granddaughter, daughter, mother, wife, hula dancer, and educator. Her dissertation, which won the dissertation of the year award for research in postsecondary education at the 2015 American Education Research Association annual conference, focused on the central question: How can the University of Hawaiʻi at Mānoa, a predominantly non-Hawaiian university, transform into a Hawaiian place of learning? She is currently the Native Hawaiian Affairs specialist at the University of Hawaiʻi at Mānoa. She lives in Heʻeia, Koʻolaupoko, Oʻahu with her family.

MATTHEW VAN ALSTINE MAKOMENAW, an enrolled member of the Grand Traverse Bay Band of Ottawa and Chippewa Indians tribes of Michigan, is the

College Pathways Administrator for the American Indian College Fund. Prior to his role as College Pathways Administrator he served as the Faculty Fellowships Program Officer at the college fund. He was responsible for recruiting applicants for faculty fellowship programs and managing all aspects of the fellowship selection process. Makomenaw comes to the College Fund from Montana State University, where he was an Assistant Professor of Native American Studies. Prior to his position in Montana, he served as the Director of the American Indian Resource Center at the University of Utah and as the Director of Native American Programs at Central Michigan University. Makomenaw has experience with providing college access and retention for American Indian students in higher education. He holds a doctorate degree in higher, adult, and lifelong education from Michigan State University, where he completed his dissertation on the success of tribal college students transferring to four-year predominantly white institutions. Makomenaw's research focuses on tribal college transfer students, Native American student college choice, and Native American student success factors.

Robin Starr Zape-tah-hol-ah Minthorn, Ph.D. (Kiowa/Apache/Umatilla/Nez Perce/Assiniboine), is an Assistant Professor at the University of New Mexico in Educational Leadership and Native American Studies and teaches courses surrounding Indigenous leadership, leadership and organizations in educational settings, and conflict resolution. Prior to becoming a faculty member at the University of New Mexico she served as Coordinator of Native American Affairs at Oklahoma State University, an adjunct faculty at Pawnee Nation College, preceding that, academic advisor at Comanche Nation College, Oklahoma's first tribal college. She is also a cofounder of Gamma Delta Pi, American Indian Sisterhood, RAIN (Retaining American Indians Now) as an undergraduate, and as a professional she cofounded ONASHE (Oklahoma Native American Students in Higher Education), a statewide Native American student leadership conference. Her research interests include areas around Indigenous leadership in higher education, intergenerational leadership perspectives in tribal communities, supporting Native American college students, campus climate for Native American college students, and Native student participation in study abroad. Robin recently served on a Board of Directors for the National Indian Education Association (NIEA), is currently the President of the National Indian Youth Council, Inc. (NIYC), and is a current member of the Board of Directors for the National Coalition for the Advancement of Natives in Higher Education (NCANHE). She is also a former NASPA IPKC (Indigenous Peoples Knowledge Community) Chair. Dr. Minthorn is also the coeditor of the recently released book, *Indigenous Leadership in Higher Education*, published by Routledge Educational Leadership Research Series.

Christine A. Nelson, Ph.D. (Laguna/Navajo), is an Assistant Professor at the University of Denver in the Morgridge College of Education–Department of

Higher Education. Professor Nelson received her doctorate in higher education from the University of Arizona's Center for the Study of Higher Education. She also holds a Master's degree in Higher Education from the University of Arizona and a Bachelor's degree in business from the University of Phoenix. With more than ten years of higher education experience, she has a cross-section of experiences ranging from educational pathways in STEM, to policy research, and student affairs. She has served as a summer research associate with the American Council on Education and is an alumna of the Jack Kent Cooke Dissertation Fellowship.

Professor Nelson utilizes a Native Nation-Building lens and critical theory to explore the purpose of higher education by addressing the collective and political factors influencing Indigenous college students and tribal communities. Her research challenges the socially accepted norm that college is an individual pursuit resulting in primarily individual benefits. Ultimately, as a first-generation college student, she works for underserved communities and their students, who deserve every chance to access, persist, and complete a higher education degree.

David Sanders is an enrolled member of the Oglala Sioux Tribe. He was born in Pine Ridge, South Dakota, and grew up in the small community of Oglala. He earned a Bachelor's degree in Mathematics, a secondary mathematics teacher's certificate, a Master's and a Ph.D., both in Curriculum and Instruction in Mathematics Education, all from the University of Colorado. He taught secondary mathematics at Chinle High School in Chinle, Arizona on the Navajo Nation and worked as the Director of the University of Colorado Upward Bound Program prior to accepting his current position as Research Director/Co-Director of the Office of Research and Sponsored Programs for the American Indian College Fund. His research includes AIAN student access/success, mathematics education situated in Indian Education pedagogy and self-determination and AIAN student outcomes.

Heather J. Shotton is a member of the Wichita & Affiliated Tribes, and is also of Kiowa and Cheyenne descent. She currently serves as an Associate Professor in Native American Studies at the University of Oklahoma. Dr. Shotton's research focuses on Indigenous students in higher education and Indigenous women, particularly in the areas of Indigenous women and leadership and Indigenous women scholars. She served as a co-editor for the book, *Beyond the Asterisk: Understanding Native Students in Higher Education*, which addresses strategies for serving Native college students. Dr. Shotton is the past president for the National Indian Education Association. She has spent her career working with Native students and is a strong advocate for Native education and serves Native students and communities on a national and local level.

Theresa Jean Stewart is from the San Luis Rey Band of Mission Indians and also of Gabrieliño-Tongva and Tohono O'odham descent. Theresa is a doctoral candidate in Higher Education and Organizational Change at the University of California, Los Angeles (UCLA) Graduate School of Education and Information Studies. She previously received a B.A. in American Indian Studies and M.Ed. in Student Affairs from UCLA. Her doctoral research focuses on Southern California tribal communities and explores tribal-institutional relationships and partnerships between public postsecondary institutions and tribes. Theresa also has experience examining the role of campus climate, diversity, in-college experiences, and involvement and their impact on the persistence and degree attainment of low-income, first-generation, and underrepresented racial groups.

Dr. Amanda R. Tachine is Navajo from Ganado, Arizona. She is Náneeshtʼézhí Táchiiʼnii (Zuni Red Running into Water clan) born for Tlʼizilani (Many Goats clan). Her maternal grandfather's clan is Tábaahí (Water's Edge) and her paternal grandfather's clan is Ashiihi (Salt). She is a postdoctoral scholar at Arizona State University's Center for Indian Education, where she advances ideas and strategies to increase Native college student success. Her dissertation, titled, "Monsters and Weapons: Navajo Students' Stories on Their Journeys to College," was awarded the 2016 American Educational Research Association Division J Dissertation of the Year as well as Honorable Mention recognition from the International Congress Qualitative Inquiry Dissertation Award. She was recognized by President Barack Obama with the White House Champions of Change: Young Women Empowering Communities award. She has published thought pieces in the Huffington Post, Al Jazeera, and The Hill through her role as a Public Voices Op-Ed Fellow.

Stephanie Waterman, Ph.D., Onondaga, Turtle Clan, is Associate Professor at the Ontario Institute for Studies in Education/University of Toronto, in Leadership, Higher & Adult Education, and coordinates the Student Development/Student Services in Higher Education program. Her research interests are Native American college experiences, First Nations/Native American Student Affairs units, the role staff play in student retention, Indigenous methodologies/ pedagogy, and critical race theories. She is a co-editor of *Beyond the Asterisk: Understanding Native Students in Higher Education* (Stylus) with Dr. Heather J. Shotton and Shelly C. Lowe, published in 2013. She has been published in the *Journal of American Indian Education*, the *Journal of Student Affairs Research and Practice*, the *Journal About Women in Higher Education*, and *The Urban Review*.

Sweeney Windchief, Ed.D., is a member of the Fort Peck Tribes (Assiniboine) in Montana and serves as an Assistant Professor of Adult and Higher Education at Montana State University. His research interests fall under the umbrella of Indigenous intellectualism and its intersection with higher education. Sweeney is currently a Co-PI on an NSF sponsored AGEP-T Grant entitled Pacific Northwest Collaborative Opportunities for Success in Mentoring of Students

(PNW-COSMOS). Among others, his teaching privileges include Critical Race Theory, Indigenous Methodologies in Research, Law and Policy in Higher Education, and Institutional Research. His outreach and community engagement activities include the American Indian and Minority Achievement Council (AIMA) for the Montana Office of the Commissioner on Higher Education, and MSU's American Indian Student Center Executive Committee. He has been published in the *Journal of American Indian Education, The Diaspora, Indigenous, and Minority Education*, and the *Howard Journal of Communications*. He coaches at a local wrestling club in Bozeman and he and his wife Sara have two sons who help keep things in perspective.

ERIN KAHUNAWAIKAʻALA WRIGHT is Kanaka ʻŌiwi Hawaiʻi (Native Hawaiian) from Kalihi, Oʻahu, raised on the land that has fostered her mother's family for the last five generations. She has genealogical ties to Oʻahu, Hawaiʻi Island, and Southern China. Currently, she serves as an Assistant Professor of Educational Administration in the College of Education at the University of Hawaiʻi at Mānoa. Previously, Kahunawai served as Director of Native Hawaiian Student Services at the University of Hawaiʻi at Mānoa in Hawaiʻinuiākea School of Hawaiian Knowledge, an award-winning program designed to support all Native Hawaiians interested in pursuing higher education in ways that are culturally grounded and lāhui-minded. Kahunawai's scholarly work focuses on Native Hawaiian and Pacific Islander identities in higher education and the ways these identities inform educational environments and kuleana lāhui (native nation-building). She prioritizes collaborative research and writing and has utilized and disseminated her research in a variety of ways, including successful grant proposals, book chapters, technical reports, journal articles, and local and national professional presentations. Among her most recent publications are two books, *A Nation Rising: Hawaiian Movements for Life, Land, and Sovereignty* (co-edited with Noelani Goodyear-Kaʻōpua and Ikaika Hussey, 2014) and *Kanaka ʻŌiwi Methodologies: Moʻolelo and Metaphor* (co-edited with Kapā Oliveira, 2016).

NATALIE ROSE YOUNGBULL is enrolled in the Cheyenne and Arapaho Tribes and descended from the Ft. Peck Assiniboine & Sioux tribes. She grew up in El Reno, Oklahoma. Natalie was awarded the Gates Millennium Scholarship upon her high school graduation. She earned her Bachelor's degree in Psychology from the University of Oklahoma. She continued her education at the University of Arizona (UofA), earning her Master's degree in Higher Education and Ph.D. in the Educational Policy Studies and Practice, with an emphasis in Higher Education, from the UofA. The findings of her dissertation research are published in this book chapter and in a chapter in the forthcoming book, *Clearing the Path: Qualitative Studies of the Experiences of First Generation College Students* with Dr. Robin Starr Minthorn. Natalie has also published her work on service learning and mentorship among American Indian college students in *the education* online journal with Dr. Christine Nelson. Being a product of college prep programs, she contributed a chapter in the forthcoming book *Beyond College Access: Indigenizing Programs for Student Success* based on her experiences and knowledge of these types of programs for American Indian students. Previously, she served as the Director of Student Services at Comanche Nation College, the first tribal college in Oklahoma. Recently, Natalie started a new position with the American Indian College Fund as the Faculty Development Program Officer in the Office of Research and Sponsored Programs, where she administers fellowships to assist Tribal College/University faculty in the completion of their Master's and Doctorate degrees. Previously, she worked as Director of Student Services at Comanche Nation College and Retention Coordinator in the Native American Student Affairs (NASA) center at the UofA. Youngbull's board service includes Student Board Member of the National Indian Education Association (2010–2012) and board member of the Indigenous Peoples Knowledge Community (IPKC) of NASPA. She is a Gates Millennium Scholar alumna and mentor.

Index

CPSIA information can be obtained
at www.ICGtesting.com
Printed in the USA
LVHW091133180321
681791LV00001B/1